LABOUR IN THE GLOBAL SOUTH

CHALLENGES AND ALTERNATIVES FOR WORKERS

LABOUR IN THE GLOBAL SOUTH

CHALLENGES AND ALTERNATIVES FOR WORKERS

edited by Sarah Mosoetsa and Michelle Williams

INTERNATIONAL LABOUR OFFICE • GENEVA

Mosoetsa, Sarah; Williams, Michelle

Labour in the global South: Challenges and alternatives for workers / edited by Sarah Mosoetsa and Michelle Williams; International Labour Office – Geneva: ILO, 2012

232 p.

ISBN 978-92-2-126238-1 (print)
ISBN 978-92-2-126239-8 (web pdf)

International Labour Office

labour relations / trade union / labour movement / developing countries / Argentina / Bangladesh / Brazil / India / South Africa R / Uruguay

13.06.1

ILO Cataloguing in Publication Data

ILO publications and electronic products can be obtained through major booksellers or ILO local offices in many countries, or direct from ILO Publications, International Labour Office, CH-1211 Geneva 22, Switzerland. Catalogues or lists of new publications are available free of charge from the above address, or by email: pubvente@ilo.org

Visit our website: www.ilo.org/publns

Front cover image: *El Vendedor de Alcatras* by Diego Rivera © Banco de México Diego Rivera & Frida Kahlo Museums Trust, México D.F. / 2012, ProLitteris, Zurich.

Typeset by Magheross Graphics, France & Ireland *www.magheross.com*

Printed in Switzerland   GEN

PREFACE

In the decades following the Second World War, the mature industrial relations systems of the advanced economies served as an example and even as a model for labour movements in the South. Informal employment in the South was largely seen as a problem of insufficiently regulated markets and high labour surpluses in developing countries, one which would disappear through the process of industrialization.

Trade unions in industrialized countries, with their long and proud history, were in many cases regarded and often saw themselves as representatives of a trade union practice that could also inspire and guide the labour movements of the industrializing South. Their potential to serve as role models has proved to be an illusion on several counts. In the age of globalization and financialization, the traditional industrial relations system has been undermined, and trade unions in the North are losing ground. Social dialogue, corporatism and collective bargaining are, in a growing number of instances, changing from institutions that ensure fair sharing of productivity gains to instruments that accommodate the demands of capital and governments to lower wages and erode working conditions in the name of competitiveness. Labour market reform, the downsizing of welfare state provisions and the return of mass unemployment created precarious employment for millions of workers, and the wage share in nearly all industrialized countries has been declining for decades. The current crisis has reinforced and intensified the pressures on the traditional models of trade unionism, social dialogue and collective bargaining, particularly in Europe.

In sum, instead of "good" labour market systems of the North acting as models for development in the South, features of unregulated and informal labour markets associated with the South have increasingly been adopted in industrialized countries.

At the same time, it is increasingly evident in the developing and industrializing countries that informality is not merely a transitional phenomenon. A relatively small formal sector is linked through outsourcing and sophisticated supply chains with large numbers of workers in different forms of precarious and informal employment. Trade union movements face the harsh reality that this is not some backward model of industrial production, but rather cutting-edge twenty-first-century capitalism used by the most advanced multinational companies to maximize their profits.

Given these structural changes and new challenges, trade unions in all countries are discussing and exploring new forms of organizing and mobilizing, new means of international cooperation, and new alliances with other civil society organizations. Trade unions in the South have been pioneering many of these new strategies. SEWA in India shows that even the most vulnerable workers – women in the informal economy – can organize successfully. The Brazilian trade unions were an important partner in the launch of the World Social Forum, and the political achievement of the Lula Government would be unimaginable without the role of organized labour. COSATU is running one of the strongest campaigns against labour brokers and is a crucial pillar of democracy in South Africa. In Uruguay, the trade unions were instrumental in achieving nearly universal collective bargaining coverage and extending social protection to many vulnerable informal workers. And significantly, the new International Domestic Workers' Network has many of its key affiliates and leaders in countries of the South.

Industrial workplaces have also shifted to new destinations, which has had the inevitable effect of reshaping the international labour movement. The Global Labour University (GLU) itself is part of this shift in international trade union and labour research cooperation. GLU works as a global knowledge and research network to overcome the traditional concept of the North–South knowledge transfer. Working in close cooperation with the national and international trade union movements, GLU offers masters' programmes at universities in Brazil, Germany, India and South Africa, through which it provides the opportunity to look at the world and the labour movement from different perspectives, and it creates a forum in which to debate responses to the changing world of industrial relations.

Labour in the global South is an example of these debates. In their introductory chapter, editors Sarah Mosoetsa and Michelle Williams put today's challenges for organized labour in the context of the seismic changes in the global distribution and organization of work. Globalization has largely extended the possibilities for multinational companies to evade national regulations. However, the editors point out that this new world of corporate globalization is not so new for the global South, precisely because Keynesian capitalism, including the powerful institutional role for organized labour and a comprehensive welfare state, never made it to the South.

In a competitive race to provide ever more generous investment climates, even governments historically close to labour have shifted the balance of power further in favour of capital through a whole range of deregulatory policies. The current volume discusses the very different experiences of trade unions with governments they had mobilized to vote for. It shows that winning elections is not enough, and that real change also requires a movement that has the strength and public authority to keep those elected accountable to their voters as well as to help them to withstand the lobbying pressure of the countervailing forces. This, as some of the authors highlight, will not be possible without trade unions that reach out and mobilize beyond their traditional strongholds. Facing a crisis that is not only economic and social but also ecological rules out the possibility of another century of global economic growth during which the South is supposed to catch up to the North by growing even faster than the North does. Labour needs new strategies to mobilize and organize and to build new alliances, but it also needs development concepts that question capitalism's insatiable appetite for growth, without denying the necessity of income growth for the billions of people living in abject poverty.

By selecting diverging and potentially controversial views on these issues, this book contributes the much-needed southern perspective to this essential debate, as well as to the global discourse.

Bheki Ntshalintshali
Deputy Secretary-General
Congress of South African Trade Unions

CONTENTS

LIST OF TABLES

LIST OF FIGURES

NOTES ON CONTRIBUTORS

Ruy Braga is a professor in the Department of Sociology at the University of São Paulo, Brazil (USP). He was Director of USP's Center for the Study of Citizenship Rights (Cenedic) from 2006 to 2010 and is the Correspondence Secretary of the magazine *Outubro* (periodical of the Brazilian Institute of Socialist Studies) and Deputy Editor of the magazine *Societies Without Borders* (organ of the association Sociologists Without Borders). He was Vice-Chair of USP's Department of Sociology from 2005 to 2009 and is President of the Human Resources General Commission of USP's Faculty of Philosophy, Literature and Human Sciences.

Akua Britwum is Senior Research Fellow at the Institute for Development Studies, University of Cape Coast, Ghana, where she has been teaching and carrying out research in gender and labour studies since 1996.

Jacklyn Cock is a professor emeritus in the Department of Sociology, and an honorary research associate of the Society, Work and Development Institute, at the University of the Witwatersrand, South Africa.

Bruno Dobrusin is an adviser to the International Relations Secretariat of the Argentine Workers' Confederation and a PhD candidate at the University of Buenos Aires. He has an MA in Globalization and Labour from the Tata Institute of Social Sciences, Mumbai, a member institution of the Global Labour University.

Karen Douglas is a Senior Industrial Officer of the Health and Community Services Union, Victoria, Australia, and a graduate of the Masters in Labour Policies and Globalization programme of the Global Labour University.

Luciana Hachmann is undertaking her PhD at the International Center for Development and Decent Work at Kassel University, Germany. She is a graduate of the Masters in Labour Policies and Globalization programme of the Global Labour University.

Tom Langford is a professor in the Sociology Department at the University of Calgary, Canada. He can be reached at langford@ucalgary.ca. His collaborative work with Zia Rahman includes "The limitations of global social movement unionism as an emancipatory labour strategy in majority world countries", which was published in the Canadian journal *Socialist Studies* in 2010.

Sue Ledwith is Leverhulme Emeritus Scholar in International Labour and Trade Union Studies at Ruskin College, United Kingdom, www.ruskin.ac.uk, and can be contacted by email at sledwith@ruskin.ac.uk.

Babalwa Magoqwana is a PhD candidate in sociology at Rhodes University, South Africa. Her thesis focuses on call centre labour processes within local government in South Africa.

Sandra Matatu is a PhD candidate in sociology at Rhodes University, South Africa. Her thesis focuses on e-government and workplace restructuring in South African municipalities.

Sarah Mosoetsa is Senior Lecturer in Sociology at the University of Witwatersrand, South Africa, where she is a member of the Global Labour University executive committee. Her publications include *Eating from one pot: The dynamics of survival in poor South African households* (Wits University Press, 2011).

Zia Rahman is an Associate Professor in Sociology at the University of Dhaka, Bangladesh. He can be reached at zia_soc71@yahoo.com. His collaborative work with Tom Langford includes "The limitations of global social movement unionism as an emancipatory labour strategy in majority world countries", which was published in the Canadian journal *Socialist Studies* in 2010.

Sarbeswara Sahoo is an Assistant Professor in Economics at Mahatma Gandhi Labour Institute, Gujarat, India, and can be reached by email at mgliahmedabad@gmail.com.

Christoph Scherrer is Professor for Globalization and Politics and Executive Director of the International Center for Development and Decent Work at the University of Kassel, Germany.

Jana Silverman is the Programme Director of the AFL-CIO Solidarity Center for Brazil and Paraguay. In addition, she is a PhD candidate in labour and social economics at the State University of Campinas in Brazil and holds a Master's degree in international affairs, specializing in human rights, from Columbia University. She has published and presented extensively in academic forums in English, Spanish and Portuguese on union strategies and labour relations in the Southern Cone countries in the post-authoritarian period.

Michelle Williams is Associate Professor of Sociology at the University of Witwatersrand, South Africa, where she is chairperson of the Global Labour University programme. Her publications include *The roots of participatory democracy: Democratic communists in South Africa and Kerala, India* (Palgrave, 2008) and *South Africa and India: Shaping the global South* (co-edited with Isabel Hofmeyr; Wits University Press, 2011).

ACKNOWLEDGEMENTS

Books are always collective projects; edited volumes especially so. We would like to thank the following organizations: the International Labour Organization, the Friedrich-Ebert Stiftung and the Department of Sociology, University of the Witwatersrand. Many people have contributed to this volume either directly or indirectly, and while we cannot thank them all individually, a few deserve special mention: Pulane Ditlhake, Frank Hoffer, Claire Hobden, Musa Malabela, Vishwas Satgar, Edward Webster, Jacklyn Cock, Devan Pillay, Chris Edgar, Alison Irvine, our copy editor Gillian Somerscales and three reviewers who reviewed the manuscript in a "double blind" process. We would also like to thank all the contributors, who worked to very strict deadlines in order to keep up with an extremely stringent publication schedule.

LIST OF ABBREVIATIONS

AAFLI	Asian American Free Labor Institute
ACD	automatic call distributor
ADOS	Asociación de Obras Sociales (Argentina)
AFL-CIO	American Federation of Labor–Congress of Industrial Organizations
AITUC	All India Trade Union Congress
ANC	African National Congress
ANTA	Self-administered Workers' Association (Argentina)
AO	automatic operator
APCOL	All Pakistan Confederation of Labour
ATE	State Workers Association (Argentina)
BAG	Bargaining Agenda for Gender
BEE	Black Economic Empowerment
BGMEA	Bangladesh Garment Manufacturers and Exporters Association
BGWUC	Bangladesh Garment Workers Unity Council
BIGU	Bangladesh Independent Garment-Workers Union
BNCL	Bengal National Chamber of Labour
BNDES	Brazilian Development Bank
BNP	Bangladesh Nationalist Party
CAN	Climate Justice Network
CDES	Economic and Social Development Council (Brazil)
CDM	Clean Development Mechanism
CGT	General Labour Confederation (Argentina)
CIFE	Chief Inspector of Factories and Establishment (Bangladesh)
CJN	Climate Justice Now
CJNSA	Climate Justice Now South Africa

CLC	Canadian Labour Congress
COB	customer-oriented bureaucracies
COP	Conference of the Parties
COSATU	Congress of South African Trade Unions
CS	*consejos de salarios* (Uruguay)
CTA	Workers' Confederation of Argentina
CTAs	tele-activity centres (Brazil)
CUT	Central Única dos Trabalhadores (Brazil)
CWU	Communication Workers Union (South Africa)
DGB	Deutscher Gewerkschaftsbund
DIEESE	Inter-Union Department of Statistics and Socioeconomic Studies (Brazil)
DL	Directorate of Labour (Bangladesh)
EPFL	East Pakistan Federation of Labour
EPZ	export processing zone
ETUC	European Trade Union Confederation
FA	Frente Amplio (Uruguay)
FASINPAT	*Fábrica sin patrones* (Argentina)
FDI	foreign direct investment
FEDUSA	Federation of Unions of South Africa
FORU	Uruguayan Regional Workers' Federation
GATS	General Agreement on Trade in Services
GDP	gross domestic product
GEAR	Growth, Employment and Redistribution
GHG(s)	greenhouse gas(es)
GLU	Global Labour University
HR	human resources
ICFTU	International Confederation of Free Trade Unions
IFL	Indian Federation of Labour
ILO	International Labour Organization
IMF	International Monetary Fund
INTUC	Indian National Trade Union Congress
IRP	Integrated Resource Plan (South Africa)
ITUC	International Trade Union Confederation
IUF	International Union of Food, Agricultural, Hotel, Restaurant, Catering, Tobacco and Allied Workers' Associations
IVR	interactive voice response
LGBT	Lesbians, gays, bisexuals, transvestites, transsexuals and transgendered people
LRK	Little Rann of Kutch
MEF	Ministry of Economy and Finances (Uruguay)

MPN	Movimiento Popular Neuquino (Argentina)
MTSS	Ministry of Labour and Social Security (Uruguay)
NACTU	National Council of Trade Unions (South Africa)
NGO	non-governmental organization
NGP	New Growth Path (South Africa)
NLC	Nigerian Labour Congress
NMM	Nelson Mandela Bay Metropolitan Municipality
NPM	New Public Management
NUM	National Union of Mineworkers (South Africa)
NUMSA	National Union of Metalworkers of South Africa
OECD	Organisation for Economic Co-operation and Development
PIT-CNT	Uruguayan labour confederation
PSDB	Partido da Social Democracia Brasiliera (Social Democratic Party of Brazil)
PT	Partido dos Trabalhadores (Workers' Party, Brazil)
RDP	Reconstruction and Development Programme
REDD	Reducing Emissions from Deforestation and Degradation
RG	research group
RMG	ready-made garments
SACP	South African Communist Party
SALGA	South African Local Government Association
SAMWU	South African Municipal Workers Union
SATAWU	South African Transport and Allied Workers Unions
SC	Solidarity Center (Bangladesh)
SEWA	Self Employed Women's Association (India)
SKOP	Sramik Karmachari Okkyo Parishad (Bangladesh)
SOECN	Sindicato de Obreros y Empleados Ceramistas de Neuquén (Argentina)
SPD	Sozialdemokratische Partei Deutschlands
SUTRASPRIN	Sindicato de Salud Privada del Neuquén (Argentina)
TRIPS	Trade-Related Aspects of Intellectual Property Rights
UACs	utilities, agencies and corporatized entities
UCR	Unión Cívica Radical
UNEP	United Nations Environment Programme
UNFCCC	United Nations Framework Convention on Climate Change
WFTU	World Federation of Trade Unions
WTO	World Trade Organization
WWF	World Wildlife Fund

CHALLENGES AND ALTERNATIVES FOR WORKERS IN THE GLOBAL SOUTH

1

Sarah Mosoetsa and Michelle Williams

In recent years, news broadcasts across the world have been awash with stories of governments in advanced capitalist countries such as Britain, France, Germany and the United States, saving corporations and banks in a desperate attempt to rescue the global economic system. These events signal the emergence of a new global crisis of capitalism triggered by the actions of an unscrupulous financial sector. This new crisis is global in character, originating in and most directly affecting the global North, and is compounded by the widespread crisis of the State. At the root of the economic crisis is a greedy financial sector, motivated by the ideals of the free market and self-regulation, whose disregard for its own fiscal and credit rules led to a credit collapse. Despite their culpability in creating the crisis, banks, transnational corporations and domestic firms have been bailed out by governments in coordinated efforts to save local and global economies from ruin, proving anew that states and capital can work together to save each other, especially in times of instability. Our question is: at whose expense?

The recent crisis must be seen within the context of the past 30 years of neoliberal globalization, with its increasingly pernicious effects on growing numbers of people: "The number of people unemployed and the number of unstable, insecure jobs has actually increased – from 141 million to 190 million (1993 to 2007) and from 1,338 million to 1,485 million (1997 to 2007) respectively" (War on Want, 2009, p. 4). This crisis has exacerbated trends that have been under way for some time, with effects felt across the globe. While responses to the crisis in the global North have focused inward on national economies and companies, they also affect the global South. Promises to support development in the global South have been forgotten, with foreign development aid declining at an alarming rate. Corporate bailouts are accompanied by "austerity" measures that are being forced on populations, threatening such meagre safety nets as are still in place to protect the poor and the working class. The focus in mainstream debate has been on simultaneous intervention of the State in saving negligent corporations and in disciplining populations, purportedly in pursuit of the public good. As Bowles (2011) reminds us, neoliberal globalization is a political project aimed at increasing the power of capital in relation to the State and labour.

While the importance of state action in regulating and facilitating markets has gained a new salience across the globe, less attention has been given in the popular media to the effects of the crisis on organized and unorganized workers. For example, the loss of over one million jobs in 2010–11 in South Africa alone hardly registered on the news radar of even local broadcasters. And yet the repercussions of this crisis in global capitalism for the developing and post-colonial world are immediate, albeit indirect.

For these countries of the global South, crisis has been a familiar state of affairs for at least three decades. In the 1980s and 1990s it came in the wake of the Structural Adjustment Programmes orchestrated by the world financial institutions, the International Monetary Fund (IMF), the World Bank and the World Trade Organization (WTO), which took over from the General Agreement on Tariffs and Trade in 1995. Structural adjustment really meant financial and trade liberalization, and its imposition ushered in crisis after crisis across countries in the developing world. The effects were retrenchments, unemployment, poverty and rising inequalities.

These events have come as no surprise for many who have noted rising inequalities between and within states, over-consumption and high levels of household debt, and over-extraction in the natural environment. Neoliberal globalization has created growing insecurity and deteriorating conditions for workers across the globe, often pitting workers against each other (Bieler and Lindberg, 2011). Yet the warning signs have been ignored. The world chose to focus on giant US technology and IT companies such as Apple as examples of the success of global capitalism, paying little attention to labour conditions in these companies. As soaring profits were registered by transnational corporations, increasingly precarious conditions for labour were seen as the necessary price to be paid for such spectacular "success" in profits and growth. We thus see alongside extraordinary wealth an increase in informalization of production through, for example, outsourced workers, export processing zones (EPZs) and the growth in the informal economy. The effects have been global, with "global inequality [rising] steadily from .43 in 1980 to .67 in 2005" (Bieler and Lindberg, 2011, p. 3).

As predicted by scholars such as Karl Polanyi in *The great transformation*, such times require a return from the market to society to resolve the crisis brought about by the contradictions of marketization and the commodification of labour, land and money. Polanyi argued that capitalism came at a high cost for industrial workers and democratic political institutions: "[T]he idea of a self-adjusting market implied a stark utopia. Such an institution could not exist for any length of time without annihilating the human and natural substance of society; it would have physically destroyed man and transformed his surrounding into a wilderness" (Polanyi, 1944, p. 3). A counter-movement, he argued, would rise against such forces of marketization and commodification. Since the 1990s we have seen increasing numbers of global protests, starting with Seattle in 1999 and continuing through Genoa (2001) and the emergence in the latter year of the World Social Forum to the recent Occupy Wall Street movement and the Arab Spring. Indeed, recent world events could be described as further examples of such movements in the demands for political and economic democracy witnessed in Argentina, Bolivia, Egypt, Greece, South Africa and the Syrian Arab Republic. The question arises: what is the role of labour in the counter-movements for change?

Within this context, it is evident that global economic and political insecurity pose enormous challenges, both new and old, for labour in the global South. It is therefore not surprising that there has been renewed academic interest in exactly these questions and many projects focusing on the challenges faced by labour (see e.g. Harrod and O'Brien, 2002; Munck, 2002; Clawson, 2003; Phelan, 2006; Bronfenbrenner, 2007; Bieler, Lindberg and Pillay, 2008; Chun, 2009; Taylor, 2009). Across the disciplinary spectrum from economics to sociology, politics, history and development, and reaching beyond the academy to include labour activists, researchers and practitioners, there has been a turn towards seeking new ways of understanding labour's challenges, identifying creative responses, and suggesting possible future implications of these new realities (Webster, Lambert and Bezuidenhout, 2008; Bieler and Lindberg, 2011). We have seen different types of labour responses to the political challenges faced today: initiatives such as corporate codes of conduct, international framework agreements, global unions and international labour standards have all been proposed in an attempt to reclaim labour's lost power (Webster, 2011). In some countries, such as Argentina and Bolivia, social movements have become rivals to traditional labour movements, while in others, such as Brazil, India, the Republic of Korea and South Africa, labour has forged alliances with political movements both in and out of government. Sometimes the alliances emerge after political parties come to power, but more often they are formed before that point. In yet other instances, such as Bangladesh and India's Self Employed Women's Association (SEWA), labour movements have remained non-aligned and independent.

It is against this backdrop that the Global Labour University (GLU) hosted the interdisciplinary conference on "The Politics of Labour and Development", which brought together over 150 labour scholars and activists from over 25 countries.[1] The conference was held at the University of the Witwatersrand in Johannesburg, South Africa, in September 2011. Themes highlighted included challenges faced by labour, workplace issues, new forms of power and leverage, policy engagements, labour alliances with political parties and social movements, and alternative forms of production, consumption and distribution. The location in South Africa gave the proceedings a natural bias towards South Africa, but one of the notable features of the conference was the overwhelming number of labour scholars and activists from countries in the global South.

The essays brought together in this volume arise out of this conference. Like the conference itself, the volume has a natural bias towards South Africa, with three chapters dealing with issues of labour in that country; but it also explores more widely labour's attempts to shift the balance of power away from capital and unelected bureaucracies and in favour of labour and broader society. In other words, we look at the ways in which labour has tried to reconfigure the multiple relations of power and oppression, including their economic, political and cultural aspects, that reproduce and sustain subordinate classes. One of the strengths of this volume is that it includes chapters by both labour scholars and practitioners, and thus contributes important case studies from the global South to the field of global labour studies. The focus on the global South may prompt reservations in some readers. We chose this focus quite deliberately as the sister volume, *Trade unions and the global crisis: Labour's visions, strategies and responses* (Serrano, Xhafa and Fichter, 2011), largely focused on OECD countries. This volume, therefore, presents an opportunity to examine research on the global South and largely by scholars from the global South.

The term "global South" might itself be unfamiliar to some readers as, while commonly used among scholars, it is less commonly understood outside academia. Its genealogy is rooted in the vocabulary of the Brandt Commission in the 1980s, which used the term "South" to refer to a North–South, rich–poor duality. With the collapse of the Soviet Union, the old terminology of Eastern bloc and Western bloc, and the concomitant idea of three worlds – First World, Second World and Third World – lost meaning as the Second World, the countries of the former Eastern bloc, were now being absorbed into the categories of First and Third Worlds, developed and developing countries. As Hofmeyr and Williams explain: "In this context, the term 'Global South' came to stand in as a proxy for the term 'Third World'" (Hofmeyr and Williams, 2011, p. 17). But the concept denotes more than the residual hierarchical category of the "Third World". The idea of the global South is meant to identify countries in similar economic and geopolitical positions in the global capitalist system and to highlight their shared strategic objectives and interests. Reference to the "global South" rather than simply the "South" highlights the political, rather than merely geographical, coordinates that unite the countries. Thus, countries in the global South may be located in the geographical north, south, west or east, but they share basic geopolitical and strategic interests. In the next section of this introduction we summarize the challenges for and responses by labour, both of which are covered in the chapters that follow. We then outline the structure of the volume. The first set of chapters, Part I, look specifically at different challenges faced by labour in the global South. The second set of chapters (Part II) explore the various linkages between politics and labour. The chapters in Part III focus more specifically on responses that labour has initiated.

Challenges for and responses by labour in the twenty-first century

We begin by discussing the challenges for labour arising from the dual crises of the economy and ecology. Neoliberal globalization, which includes the financial crisis that erupted in 2008 and evolved into a full-blown economic crisis by 2010, has had far-reaching effects on economies around the world and has a variety of dimensions that must all be understood in order to appreciate its effects on labour. One of these is the change in ownership patterns over the past 30 years as international capital investors – who are not directly involved in running companies – have come to dominate corporate life (Bieler and Lindberg, 2011, pp. 3–5). Thus, states and companies are increasingly influenced by the global economy rather than by local and national conditions. This new international ownership structure weakens local and national trade unions as decisions about the company are often made in distant places (Hyman, 2011). One of the outcomes of this new ownership pattern is to give transnational corporations a great deal more structural power than labour, as unions' regulatory capacity has been systematically undermined. Alongside this new ownership structure, outsourcing has led to decentralization of production and fragmented industrial systems, with smaller companies often unwilling to recognize collective bargaining structures (Hyman, 2011, p. 17). As a result, unions are struggling to secure increases in wages and social benefits, leading in turn to the loss of membership and status (Hyman, 2011, p. 16). Moreover, with the penetration of the market has come not a retreat of the State, but rather a shift in the State's priorities. States no longer prioritize being responsive and accountable to their populations, but rather increasingly look to protect and advance the interests of corporations and economies at the expense of society. Thus their involvement has often come at the expense of labour. For example, the Republic of Korea recently passed a draconian law effectively making labour responsible to the company for profits lost during a strike.

Neoliberal globalization has, moreover, not only intensified exploitation at the workplace and extended exploitation to the sphere of social reproduction, in such matters as health care and education; it has extended its own reach to the furthest corners of the global South. The conditions for labour in the global South differ from those prevailing in the global North, as labour in the global South was never incorporated into the Keynesian welfare state system in which trade unions had influence over decision-making (Bieler and Lindberg, 2011, p. 7). Instead of fostering welfare state conditions, neoliberal globalization forced the global South to open up to imports and foreign direct investment (FDI), which undermined national development (Saad-Filho, 2005). By the late 1990s, developing countries were being battered by draconian accords such as the Trade-Related Aspects of Intellectual Property Rights (TRIPS) Agreement and the General Agreement on Trade in Services (GATS), and forced to dismantle tariff barriers. As a result of trade liberalization during the 1980s and 1990s, Africa and Latin America experienced "large-scale job losses, increasing unemployment and declining wages" (Bieler and Lindberg, 2011, p. 8). One of the most important outcomes of neoliberal globalization has been job losses across many sectors and the concomitant loss of economic leverage by trade unions. Put simply, job losses translate into fewer union members, which weaken unions' positions with regard to capital. Ultimately, for workers in the global South, the continuous drive to lower costs and intensify exploitation has led to a crisis of legitimacy (Silver, 2003, p. 81).

There have also been long-term structural changes that have posed serious challenges to labour. In the nineteenth and twentieth centuries, manufacturing was responsible for the lion's share of labour-absorbing economic growth. By the late twentieth century, however, manufacturing was shrinking both in terms of its share in the economy and in its capacity to sustain the working class and create increases in well-being (Amsden, 2001; Evans, 2008, pp. 8–10). Manufacturing's leading role in job creation has diminished as advanced technology has increasingly replaced labour, causing the sector to shed jobs at an alarming rate. As manufacturing has lost its centrality, the strategic significance of the service sector has mushroomed. To take one example, in South Africa services have taken a leading role in the economy: the service sector grew from 51.1 per cent of GDP in 1983 to 63.7 per cent by 2002, while the high labour absorbing sectors of mining and manufacturing dropped from 44.5 per cent of GDP in 1983 to 32.2 per cent of GDP in 2002 (World Bank, 2004). Thus, services have become the engine of growth and the sector creating most jobs. The service sector is especially conducive to the use of informal labour and the employment of casual workers, a situation that capital has exploited to its advantage. As Standing (2011) has shown, the process of neoliberal globalization has changed the nature of work and ultimately weakened the standard employment relationship. Employment is no longer characterized by full-time, secure contracts that maintain social reproduction. With these changes, trade unions' traditional forms of power – workplace bargaining and regulatory capacity – have also been eroded.

These changes in the structure of the economy have had profound implications for labour. Labour in the traditional manufacturing sectors has had to find new forms of power and leverage in an effort to combat job losses and the diminishing significance of the sector in the economy and in response to the changing nature of work. At the same time, the new importance of the service sector, in which trade unions were formerly less interested in organizing, has forced labour to think about new approaches to organizing and new tactics for mobilizing. Perhaps one of the most serious challenges facing labour is how to organize the so-called "precariat", from the unemployed to casual workers, domestic workers, migrant workers and informal workers. According to Standing (2011), this new precariat is part of a new global class structure. Clearly, the various forms of labour have a crucial role to play in countering the destructive logic of capitalism and championing Polanyi's movement of society in response to the perils of the market.

Compounding the economic crisis is an ecological crisis that many analysts say is quickly reaching the point of no return. Global temperatures are rising; storms are becoming more violent and more frequent; some regions are suffering from extreme flooding while others are subject to record-breaking droughts; clean water is becoming a scarce resource in many areas (see Chapter 2 by Cock in this volume; Bellamy-Foster, 2011).

Together, the economic and ecological crises have seen the dispossession of the commons (including local resources as well as public goods such as health and education), the informalization of labour, and increases in unemployment and social inequality at the national and global levels. As well as damaging impacts on the human environment, with the rapid spread of urban areas without adequate access to housing, water or electricity, and increases in pollutants that threaten livelihoods and endanger public health, they have exacerbated processes in the natural environment that threaten the very earth itself, including declining biodiversity and climate change. At the same time, the extension of state and market control over daily life is narrowing electoral choices and increasing restrictions on protest. These two intertwined crises of the economy and nature are having profound impacts on subordinate classes around the world, especially in the global South. The challenge for labour is how to forge new solidarities in response to these trends.

Solidarity is always constructed. Trade union solidarity has traditionally been based on the mutual interests of workers. In today's conditions, however, there is a need for broader forms of solidarity, requiring unions to look beyond their narrow interests to issues of neoliberal development (Hyman, 2011). Perhaps what is required is a return to the solidarities of social movement unionism prevalent in many places in the global South in the 1980s and 1990s. Certainly, to face today's challenges, new solidarities need to be constructed that prioritize universal rather than particular interests. Hyman suggests (2011, p. 26) that trade unions have to move beyond common interests to solidarity built on interdependence (that is, mutuality despite difference). Linked to the need for new forms of solidarity is the need to explore new forms of power. Historically, trade unions primarily used their structural and associational forms of power in pursuing workers' interests. In social welfare states, unions also had political power within their repertoire. In today's conditions, however, these forms of power are proving less efficacious than they once were, requiring labour to look for new sources of power. Chun (2009) has shown the importance of symbolic power in struggles by marginalized labour. Symbolic power builds legitimacy around the workers' demands by invoking moral and discursive stories that frame the struggles in such a way as to resonate with the public (Chun, 2009, pp. 13–15). Thus symbolic power is forged through classification struggles over legitimacy (p. 18). While labour laws can facilitate this process, tapping into moral legitimacy is of paramount importance.

It is clear from this summary that labour faces many challenges arising from both economic and ecological crises, but also that there are hopeful openings for resistance in forging broader forms of solidarity and exploring new forms of power. The chapters that follow, outlined in the next sections of this introduction, all deal with these issues to varying degrees.

Countering exploitation and marginalization

The first set of chapters (Part I) deal with the challenges posed by the intensification of exploitation and marginalization. Jacklyn Cock; Akua Britwum, Karen Douglas and Sue Ledwith; Babalwa Magoqwana and Sandra Matatu; and Zia Rahman and Tom Langford all address various forms of intensified exploitation and marginalization. Cock explicitly looks at new areas of exploitation emerging out of "green capitalism", in which the "efficiency of the market [is brought] to bear on nature" (p. 20), and the concomitant creation of "green jobs". Cock shows that the idea of "green jobs" has been formulated erroneously, pitting jobs against nature, with little attention to the job losses that would result in the transition to a low-carbon economy. As a result, organized labour has been ambivalent about measures to mitigate climate change. Moreover, Cock argues, green jobs play into the capitalist growth paradigm and will continue to exploit nature. Using South Africa as her case study, Cock argues that there is an alternative that benefits both labour and nature, epitomized in the climate justice movement, which brings together workers and their organizations into transnational solidarity networks. Cock argues that the labour movement's successful insertion of the concept of "just transition" into the United Nations Framework Convention on Climate Change (UNFCCC) in 2010 marked an important shift from the "green economy" discourse that "emphasizes growth, competitiveness and efficiency" to a discourse that places some form of justice at its centre (pp. 30–31). However, Cock also explains that the concept of "just transition" continues to be attended by great ambiguity within and among global labour movements. Labour's efforts to address issues of ecology suggest an important step forward from the old "green versus red" debate in which labour and ecology were pitted against each other in a zero-sum game.

Another important challenge facing labour in the global South has to do with the inadequacy of traditional forms of organizing in reaching women and marginalized workers. Labour in the global South is strongly characterized by casual labour contracts, informal work and marginalized workers, toiling away on the fringes of the global economy. For example, women and girls carry out two-thirds of the world's labour; yet they receive only one-tenth of the income generated (Mohanty, 2003), and trade unions have not dealt adequately with gender issues. Akua Britwum, Karen Douglas and Sue Ledwith show that the increase in women trade union members around the world has not translated into representation in leadership structures. They suggest that marginalized workers such as women, migrants and other disadvantaged groups are increasingly challenging unions to become agents of social change. They argue that "to be effective agents of change it is vital that unions themselves disrupt their own traditional male hegemony" and "that women continue to use their agency" (p. 41). Britwum, Douglas and Ledwith draw on bargaining agendas for gender from Canada, the Philippines and Turkey to show that many challenges continue to exist, but also that there is a great deal of variation between countries.

Addressing more explicit and traditional understandings of exploitation, Magoqwana and Matatu argue that new forms of structuring work come with the intensification of exploitation and increased vulnerability. Looking at South African local Government's recourse to call centres, Magoqwana and Matatu explore the way in which the labour process has changed through the outsourcing of work formerly done by government employees to call centres. Now employing over 80,000 workers, call centres have grown 8 per cent per year since 2006, yet the labour movement has not made serious inroads into this growing workforce as it is a difficult sector to organize. Magoqwana and Matatu show how the work environment has become more routinized and individualized, and is characterized by extreme forms of surveillance and management oversight. For example, workers face tough performance targets and computer-based monitoring that further depersonalize the job. Despite the perilous conditions of work, South African unions have not organized this sector adequately, and as a result of their "disregard of this new customer-centred workplace" (p. 78) only 25 per cent of South African call centres are unionized compared to the international average of 40 per cent (p. 65).

Taking the issue of union neglect of marginalized workers across the Indian Ocean, Zia Rahman and Tom Langford explore the difficult relationship between marginalized workers and trade unions in the context of Bangladesh's garment workers. Rahman and Langford show that the 3.6 million Bangladeshi garment workers have been largely ignored by trade unions since the 1980s. Despite the importance to the national economy of the manufacture of ready-made garments (RMG) – Bangladesh is the fourth largest producer of RMG in the world after China, the European Union and Turkey – its workers continue to operate under precarious conditions. Unionization "remained stagnant into the 2000s, despite the fact that employment in the industry grew by an astounding 500 per cent between 1990–91 and 2006–07" (p. 90). Rahman and Langford argue that the failure of unions to organize garment workers stems partly from the fact that the "major labour unions ... represent the interests of political parties rather than those of workers" (p. 97). However, they argue that the massive protests in the sector in 2006 not only won partial victories, but also began to raise both the status and the capacity of labour unions in the garment sector.

The intensified exploitation of both nature and marginalized workers has created serious challenges for labour, but has also provided opportunities to develop new forms of solidarity and symbolic power. The chapters in this section demonstrate that while global economic forces are crucial in determining the conditions for labour, these forces are still mediated through local and national processes, offering labour important avenues for organizing resistance.

Political movements and trade unions

Trade unions have a long history of political engagement. In the years after the Second World War, labour in the global North was incorporated into welfare state systems, providing labour with important avenues through which to shape industrial relations and social benefits (Bieler and Lindberg, 2011, p. 7). In the global South, however, the relations between trade unions and political movements have often been mediated through struggles for independence from colonial rule (in, for example, India, Kenya, Mexico and South Africa) or against authoritarian governments (as in Brazil, the Republic of Korea and Uruguay). Thus, unions in the global South have often helped to build political movements that later won places in government. Sadly, the story all too often took the same form: once in government, political movements tended to sideline their union partners as the demands of the global economy limited their capacities to act.

The chapters in this section of the volume look at the various relationships between unions and political movements in government in Brazil, Germany, South Africa and Uruguay. Exploring the challenges emerging from States' ambivalent attitudes towards unions, Ruy Braga, Jana Silverman, and Christoph Scherrer and Luciana Hachmann highlight the difficult conditions labour faces even when labour-friendly governments take power.

Braga focuses our gaze on telemarketers in Brazil, a sector which grew by 20 per cent per year between 2003 and 2009 to employ an estimated 1.4 million workers by 2011 – most of them young, Afro-Brazilian women and lesbians, gays, bisexuals, transvestites, transsexuals and transgendered people (LGBTs). Like their counterparts in South African call centres, the Brazilian telemarketers' conditions of work are characterized by precarious employment, extreme automated surveillance, physical fatigue, psychological harassment and numerous forms of sickness. Rather than just focusing on the conditions of labour that Magoqwana and Matatu highlight, Braga shows how this highly exploited "sub-proletarian" class has both looked to "Lulaism" and the State for ways to reduce social inequality and also slowly found its own voice in organizing against conditions of work. Braga argues that the extraordinary popularity of President Lula, as well as the very real connections between the State and unions that the Lula Government created, translated into shifts in the way workers saw the State and the ways in which they conducted their own struggle. In addition, he notes, telemarketers were largely apolitical and unfamiliar with trade union traditions, making it even more difficult for unions to organize them. This context, together with Lula's election victory in 2002, Braga argues, led unions to shift to "'citizen unionism', by which the union offers its associates a variety of services formerly provided by the

State, such as health-care plans and vocational training, in addition to supporting employment agencies funded by the Workers Relief Fund" (p. 116). However, in 2006 the situation began to change, with workers going on strike, developing a class consciousness and becoming more politicized. Braga suggests that the future is open to many new forms of organizing and building solidarity, largely created by the extreme forms of exploitation and increasingly fragmented workforce that have come to characterize the working environment in this sector.

Silverman offers a historical analysis of the Uruguayan labour movement, showing that the redemocratization of the country after 1985 "did not lead to a full restoration of the political and organizational capacity of the unions" (p. 125) because the adoption of neoliberal policies curtailed the role of the State in promoting labour-friendly policies and collective bargaining. Instead, the State created a "voluntary" system of bilateral labour relations that "did not take into account the inherent power inequalities between workers and employers" (pp. 125–26). Despite widespread expectations that the return to democracy would usher in an era of decent jobs, increased purchasing power and democratic unions, the era was marked by state control of labour through, for example, new restrictions on the right to strike and the introduction of neoliberal economic policies. Silverman shows that as a result real salaries declined between 1998 and 2003, massive job losses were experienced in the industrial sector and private sector unions haemorrhaged members. The situation changed in 2004 with the Frente Amplio party's election victory, which won it the majority position in government and allowed it to regulate labour relations, pass laws protecting workers and implement labour-friendly policies. As a result, social dialogue and labour rights were strengthened and the role of the state has slowly been redefined as "neocorporativist".

The next chapter shifts the focus to other forms of linkage between trade unions and parties. Brazil, Germany and South Africa raise interesting questions about relationships between trade unions and labour-friendly parties. The nature of political alliances and forms of mobilizing are vital issues, and experiments in these areas are under way in various regions of the world (for example, in many parts of Latin America). Christoph Scherrer and Luciana Hachmann investigate whether labour-friendly governments actually represent the interests of labour. They posit a degree of similarity between the cases of Brazil, Germany and South Africa, in all three of which political power passed to labour-friendly parties with long-standing relationships with progressive and relatively strong labour movements. However, while Brazil and South Africa share the experience of overcoming authoritarian regimes through popular struggles in recent times, they differ in respect of the relationship between the left-of-centre political party and the trade unions. In Brazil the trade union federation (CUT) actually provided the top leadership of the Workers' Party (PT), while in South Africa the trade union federation (COSATU) is a formal ally of the African National Congress (ANC). Germany is different again: here, the current leadership of the Social

Democrats and the trade unions do not share such decisive experiences, being separated by a generation from the common opposition to Nazism. Scherrer and Hachmann show that despite the linkages between parties and trade unions, in all three cases the left-leaning parties in government disappointed their labour constituencies in terms of macroeconomic policies in the early years of the twenty-first century. They further show that the reasons for this lie partly in economic constraints, but also, and very importantly, in issues of politics and power.

Finding alternatives: New forms of power

While the chapters in the first two parts of the volume highlight various challenges faced by workers – exploitation, informalization, marginalization, state power – they also indicate opportunities for renewal in labour organizing emerging out of these challenges. The next set of chapters, in Part III, turn more explicitly to emerging responses by labour in the global South. Growth in precarious work, including informalization, often undermines the strength and interests of organized labour; but it also holds the potential of reviving labour strategies and challenging the broader economic and political balance of power (Munck, 2002; Tait, 2005). To what extent, then, has labour in the global South embraced this possibility? While labour movements always attempt to extract as much as possible of the social surplus created through mobilization for higher wages and better working conditions, as can be seen in the recent waves of strikes around the world, many other responses are becoming evident. These are especially important in conditions of rising inequality and its devastating effects on society, with more and more people being pushed into the margins of production and consumption patterns. In these circumstances, workers both within and outside trade unions have responded in a range of creative and unexpected ways.

Among the most interesting responses are attempts by labour to find new forms of power and leverage. With rising unemployment and increasing numbers of workers pushed into precarious forms of work, new forms of power are being explored, often by the most marginalized workers and those in sectors traditionally ignored by labour movements. Labour's links to other social forces are crucial here. The quest for new forms of power also raises questions about who constitutes the working class, with wider understandings of labour increasingly finding salience in innovative movements around the world. Trade unions have a contribution to make to both debate and action in this area (e.g. innovative organizing methods, reaching out to marginalized workers, etc.), given their history as catalysts for social change and their continued role in the economic and political landscape throughout the world. It is plausible to argue that trade unionism will not "decline to the point of insignificance any time soon" (Phelan, 2006, p. 33), but it will have to build and sustain new local and global strategies.

The development of transnational linkages and networks is an important dimension of the search for new forms of power and leverage to "empower workers" (Stevis and Boswell, 2008). This endeavour includes building a sustainable global union movement and network, forging new transnational union alliances, and organizing transnational and cross-border campaigns (Harrod and O'Brien, 2002; Bronfenbrenner, 2007; Webster, Lambert and Bezuidenhout, 2008). Perhaps one of the most exciting responses to the new conditions has been the replacement of industrial production and consumption by alternative forms of production and consumption. For example, there has been an upsurge in worker cooperatives, microcredit/microfinance projects (though these pose their own challenges for informal sector workers), and local agricultural production around the world.

Bruno Dobrusin and Sarbeswara Sahoo examine examples of creative responses by workers in Argentina and India respectively. Dobrusin explores the recovered factories movement in Argentina and the links to Peronism that permeate the broader Argentine political culture. He argues that changes in labour politics, trade unions and the Peronist movement help to explain the historical roots and current characteristics of the recovered factories movement that emerged in the first decade of the new millennium. To understand the factory takeovers, he says, we must also understand their relation to the union movement: "In some cases the CTA played a substantial role in promoting and consolidating the struggle of the newly created cooperatives, while the CGT was a dominant player on the opposite side, its bureaucratized union leaders participating actively in boycotting the processes of retaking the factories" (p. 169). As Dobrusin demonstrates, the unions' role in these processes is complex and historically rooted, and important to understanding these creative responses by workers.

Turning from Argentina to India, and from recovered factories to new forms of "green livelihood", Sahoo looks at the attempts of the Self Employed Women's Association (SEWA) to fight climate change while also creating livelihoods. Whereas Cock in Chapter 2 of this volume challenged the "green economy", Sahoo takes a less critical stance, showing how SEWA has taken on the dual task of providing livelihoods for informal women workers and protecting the environment in both rural and urban areas. Sahoo explores four of SEWA's projects – smokeless cooking stoves and solar pumps; waste-pickers' cooperatives; eco-tourism; and saltpan workers' cooperatives – in arguing that informal workers have responded creatively to opportunities created by climate change. Both the Argentine recovered factories movement and SEWA's experiences suggest that workers are confronting real and multiple challenges with imagination and experimentation, responding in creative and unexpected ways.

Conclusion

The twenty-first century has brought serious structural challenges to workers and the poor, but it has also brought renewed vitality in response, with creative and innovative responses from labour evident around the world. While we have focused in this volume on struggles in the global South, many similar issues and responses are to be seen in the global North. For example, the Occupy Movement's stark framing of the 1 per cent elites versus the 99 per cent have-nots, the Arab Spring's demands for democratic transformation, and the Greek and Spanish protests against EU austerity measures all emphasize the same points. States and corporations have become disconnected from society and from the vast populations of working people around the world. The struggles we see are a response to this. Labour, which forms a significant part of the 99 per cent, is a fundamental part of the solution. In all these struggles there is an ideational component: a vision of an alternative future, one centred not on profits and exploitation, but on the well-being of humans and the natural world.

Note

[1] The GLU offers an international masters programme for trade unionists at the University of Kassel and Berlin School of Economics in Germany, the University of Witwatersrand in South Africa, the University of Campinas in Brazil and the Tata Institute in India. The GLU programme is itself part of the growing field of global labour studies and attempts to bridge the divide between academia and trade union activism.

References

Amsden, A. 2001. *The rise of the "rest": Challenges to the West from late-industrializing economies* (New York, Oxford University Press).

Bellamy-Foster, J. 2011. *The ecological rift: Capitalism's war on earth* (London, Monthly Review Press).

Bieler, A.; Lindberg, I. 2011. "Globalization and the new challenges for transnational solidarity: An introduction", in A. Bieler and I. Lindberg (eds): *Global restructuring, labour, and the challenges for transnational solidarity* (London, Routledge), pp. 3–15.

—; —; Pillay, D. (eds). 2008. *Labour and the challenges of globalization: What prospects for transnational solidarity?* (London, Pluto Press).

Bowles, P. 2011. "Globalization's problematic for labour: Three paradigms", *Global Labour Journal*, Vol. 1, No. 1, pp. 12–31.

Bronfenbrenner, K. (ed.). 2007. *Global unions: Challenging transnational capital through cross-border campaigns* (Ithaca, NY, and London, Cornell University Press).

Chun, J. 2009. *Organizing at the margins: The symbolic politics of labor in South Korea and the United States* (Ithaca, NY, Cornell University Press).

Clawson, D. 2003. *The next upsurge: Labour and the new social movements* (London, Cornell University Press).

Evans, P. 2008. *In search of the 21st century developmental state*, Working Paper No. 4, Centre for Global Political Economy, University of Sussex, Brighton.

Harrod, J.; O'Brien. R. (eds). 2002. *Global unions: Theory and strategies of organised labour in the global political economy* (London and New York, Routledge).

Hofmeyr, I.; Williams, M. 2011. "South Africa–India: Historical connections, cultural circulations and socio-political comparisons", in Isabel Hofmeyr and Michelle Williams (eds): *South Africa and India: Shaping the global South* (Johannesburg, Wits University Press), pp. 2–19.

Hyman, R. 2011. "Trade unions, global competition and options for solidarity", in A. Bieler and I. Lindberg (eds): *Global restructuring, labour, and the challenges for transnational solidarity* (London, Routledge), pp. 16–30.

Mohanty, C.T. 2003. *Feminism without borders: Decolonizing theory, practicing solidarity* (Durham, NC, and London, Duke University Press).

Munck, R. 2002. *Globalization and labour: The new "Great Transformation"* (London, Zed Books).

Phelan, C. (ed.). 2006. *The future of organised labour: Global perspectives* (Oxford, Peter Lang).

Polanyi, K. 1944. *The great transformation: The political and economic origins of our time* (Boston, Beacon Press).

Saad-Filho, A. 2005. "From Washington to post-Washington consensus: Neoliberal agendas for economic development", in A. Saad-Filho and D. Johnson (eds): *Neoliberalism: A critical reader* (London, Pluto Press), pp. 113–19.

Serrano, M.; Xhafa, E.; Fichter, M. (eds). 2011. *Trade unions and the global crisis: Labour's visions, strategies and responses* (Geneva, International Labour Office).

Silver, B. 2003. *Forces of labor: Workers' movements and globalization since 1870* (Cambridge, Cambridge University Press).

Standing, G. 2011. *The precariat: The new dangerous class* (London, Bloomsbury Press).

Stevis, D.; Boswell, T. 2008. *Globalization and labor: Democratizing global governance* (London: Rowman & Littlefield).

Tait, V. 2005. *Poor workers' unions: Rebuilding labor from below* (Cambridge, MA, South End Press).

Taylor, M. 2009. "Who works for globalization? The challenges and possibilities for international labour studies", in *Third World Quarterly*, Vol. 30, No. 3, pp. 435–52.

War on Want. 2009. *Trading away our jobs: How free trade threatens employment around the world.* Available at: http://www.waronwant.org/attachments/Trading%20Away%20Our%20Jobs.pdf [27 June 2012].

Webster, E. 2011. "The politics of labour and development: Competing paradigms in the age of globalization", keynote address presented at the Seventh Global Labour University Conference, University of Witwatersrand, Johannesburg, South Africa, 28 Sep.

—; Lambert, R.; Bezuidenhout, A. 2008. *Grounding globalization: Labour in the age of insecurity* (Oxford, Blackwell).

World Bank. 2004. *South Africa at a glance.* Country Profiles. Development Economics Central Database, 15 Sep.

PART I

COUNTERING EXPLOITATION
AND MARGINALIZATION

SOUTH AFRICAN LABOUR'S RESPONSE TO CLIMATE CHANGE: THE THREAT OF GREEN NEOLIBERAL CAPITALISM

2

Jacklyn Cock

Introduction

The ecological crisis is deepening. Despite 17 years of multinational negotiations, there is no binding global agreement on the reduction of carbon emissions. In fact, carbon emissions are rising, which means climate change will intensify and have devastating impacts – particularly on the working class – in the form of rising food prices, water shortages, crop failures and so on. Southern Africa will be the worst affected region in the world. Shifting towards a low-carbon or "green" economy will be particularly challenging for South Africa given the carbon-intensive nature of its current economy.

Very recently the South African labour movement has expressed its commitment to a "*just* transition". However, the phrase is contentious, used with very different understandings of the scale and nature of the changes involved. A just transition to a low-carbon economy could be defensive, involving demands for shallow change focused on protecting vulnerable workers; alternatively, it could require deep, transformative change to dramatically different forms of production and consumption. In this sense the ecological crisis represents an opportunity to demand the redistribution of power and resources; to challenge the conventional understanding of economic growth; and to create an alternative development path.

The crisis could also generate a new kind of transnational solidarity, wider, deeper and more powerful than anything yet seen. Moving beyond solidarities based on interests or identities, Hyman advocates a solidarity involving "mutuality despite difference", based on a sense of interdependence (Hyman, 2011, p. 26). He concludes that "the challenge is to reconceptualise solidarity in ways which encompass the local, the national … and the global. For unions to survive and thrive, the principle of solidarity must not only be redefined and reinvented: workers on the ground must be active participants in this redefinition and reinvention" (Hyman, 2011, p. 27).

19

This chapter suggests that the discourse of climate change – most clearly in its warnings of the threat to human survival – could be contributing to such a process. But it also cautions that the transition to a low-carbon or "green" economy could mean shallow change and incorporation into "green capitalism".

Green neoliberal capitalism

Capital's response to the ecological crisis generally and climate change specifically is that the system can continue to expand by creating a new "green capitalism", bringing the efficiency of the market to bear on nature and its reproduction. In effect, the climate crisis has been appropriated by capitalism as another site of accumulation: what Bond calls "climate-crisis capitalism", namely "turning a medium/long-term, system-threatening prospect into a short-term source of commodification, speculation and profit" (Bond, 2011, p. 2). Underlying all capital's strategies is the broad process of commodification: the transformation of nature and all social relations into economic relations, subordinated to the logic of the market and the imperatives of profit.

Green capitalism rests on the twin pillars of technological innovation and expanding markets, while seeking to keep the existing institutions of capitalism intact. More specifically, green capitalism involves:

- the carbon trading regime enshrined in the Kyoto Protocol to the United Nations Framework Convention on Climate Change (UNFCCC), which involves measures such as the Clean Development Mechanism (CDM) and Reducing Emissions from Deforestation and Degradation (REDD) that allow developed countries to profit from the climate crisis while avoiding the reduction of their own carbon emissions;

- appeals to nature (and even the ecological crisis) as a marketing tool;

- developing new, largely untested technologies such as "climate-smart agriculture" and "clean coal" technology in the form of carbon capture and storage, which involves installing equipment that captures carbon dioxide and other greenhouse gases (GHGs) and then pumping the gas underground;

- the development of new sources of energy such as solar, nuclear and wind, thereby creating new markets;

- the massive development of biofuels, which diverts land from food production;

- manipulative advertising in the form of "greenwash"; and

- triumphalist accounts of the potential of "green jobs" which are unsupported by empirical evidence and fail to pay sufficient attention to working conditions.

"Green jobs"

Historically, the labour movement in South Africa has neglected environmental issues. This is largely because of a widespread belief that environmental protection threatened jobs (Cock, 2007). Conversely, what is now driving trade unions into an engagement with climate change is the indirect threat posed to existing energy-intensive jobs and the possibility of new "green" jobs.

The emphasis on the creation of "green" jobs challenges the false dichotomy which portrays the relationship between labour and environment as a trade-off between jobs and environmental protection. Green jobs are at the centre of global debates on the transition to what is variously termed a "low-carbon" or "green" economy. The common element is the need for a transition to a new energy regime. However, there is ambiguity on the meaning of these terms.

The simplest definition of green jobs is those in existing and new sectors which "contribute substantially to preserving or restoring environmental quality" (UNEP/ILO/IOE/ITUC, 2008, p. 3). However, there are several problems in the current formulations of green jobs. First, many aspirational claims are made which seem inflated and are not supported by empirical evidence. As Annabella Rosenberg of the International Trade Union Confederation (ITUC) has pointed out, "the impacts of climate change on employment remain mostly unexplored by research" (Rosenberg, 2011). Insufficient attention has been paid to job losses. Some employment will be substituted, as in shifting waste handling from landfill and incineration to recycling. Certain jobs will be eliminated, as in the production of elaborate packaging materials, and many workers in existing jobs, for example electricians, or metal and construction workers, will have to be retrained. A transition to clean energy could create far more jobs than it would eliminate. However, the fact that some people could get new jobs is little comfort for the people and communities who could lose theirs – jobs in coal-fired power plants, for example.

Second, in the debate on creating a green economy, insufficient attention has been paid to the quality of green jobs (in terms of labour standards and wage levels). "Decent work" means jobs that pay at least a living wage, and offer training opportunities and some measure of economic and social security. At present, the creation of green jobs is driven more by the interests of the market than by social needs: and, as the President of the National Union of Metalworkers of South Africa (NUMSA) has pointed out in relation to the renewable energy sector, "green jobs can be as indecent as blue or brown jobs … [They] can use cheap labour, exploit women and children, use labour brokers and be dangerous in terms of occupational health and safety" (Gina, 2011).

Green jobs are at the centre of the South African Government's conception of the transition to a low-carbon or green economy.

The South African Government's response to climate change

The dominant government policy strategy is termed the New Growth Path (NGP). The document enshrining this strategy, which was released in October 2010, promised a move away from the stranglehold of the carbon-intensive minerals–energy complex towards a "green economy" marked by renewable energy and green jobs. It set targets of 300,000 additional direct jobs by 2020, with 80,000 in manufacturing and the rest in construction, operation and maintenance of new environmentally friendly infrastructure. "The potential for job creation," it asserts, "rises to well over 400,000 by 2030" (EDD, 2010, p. 13). While the NGP Framework identifies the "green economy" as important, it does not define it or specify what constitutes it.

In November 2011 the labour movement, in the form of the South African trade union federation, indicated its support for this policy thrust by signing NGP Accord 4, the "Green Economy Accord", which launched a "green partnership" and binds Government, business and labour to creating thousands of jobs by building a green industrial base. On the launch of the Accord, COSATU affirmed: "We have made a commitment through the NGP to create 5 million jobs in the next ten years. And this agreement on green jobs will make a very critical contribution to the realization of that target" (Zwelinzima Vavi, General Secretary of COSATU, cited in EDD, 2011, p. 5). While the labour movement emphasized job creation, Government ministers have emphasized the transition to a green or low-carbon economy as both a challenge and an opportunity. For example, in an interview the Economic Development minister, Ebrahim Patel, said that South Africa had to move towards a green economy as quickly as possible: "As a considerable emitter of greenhouse gases, South Africa faces the challenge of transitioning to a less carbon-intensive growth trajectory without delay."[1]

Several questions must be confronted. Are green jobs one component of a new green capitalism which is trying to avoid fundamental change through an emphasis on expanding markets and new technologies? Is the notion of a "green economy" another "false solution" which is using climate change as a new site for capital accumulation? Or are green jobs part of a "green economy" which – "based on rights, sustainability principles and decent work – can meet the challenge of a just transition" (Sustainlabour, 2011, p. 2)?

Overall, the South African Government's climate change policy is rooted in green neoliberal capitalism. This is evident in the priority it accords to profit generation, its reliance on market mechanisms (especially the promotion of carbon trading through measures such as the CDM) and its emphasis on technological innovation in expensive, high-risk schemes such as carbon capture and storage and nuclear energy. The latter is low carbon only at the point of generation: the rest of the production chain is both energy and carbon intensive, costs are excessive, safety cannot be guaranteed and nowhere has a safe storage option for high-level nuclear waste been identified.

Official policy documents lack coherence, with aspirations to reduce carbon emissions contradicted by existing government practices which involve massively expanded provision of coal-fired and nuclear energy. These practices reflect the continuing power of the minerals–energy complex, the alliance of the mining and energy sectors which have dominated South Africa's industrial development. For example, the parastatal Eskom is committed to building more coal-fired power stations, Medupi and Kusile. The World Bank's US$3.75 billion loan to Eskom to enable it to do this will increase the price of electricity for domestic consumers, worsen the country's contribution to carbon emissions and climate change, and allow continued subsidized supply of the world's cheapest electricity to large corporations, such as BHP Billiton, and the export of their profits abroad.

While another government policy document, the second Integrated Resource Plan (IRP2, 2010), introduced some energy from renewable sources into the supply mix, beyond Medupi and Kusile the IRP plans on two or three major new coal-fired plants between 2014 and 2030, and a "fleet" of six new nuclear power plants to be built by 2030. Trollop and Tyler conclude that "the IRP does not support the transition to a low energy intensive economy as is required by mitigation policy" (Trollop and Tyler, 2011, p. 18).

At the same time, South Africa has as yet no legislation requiring a reduction in carbon emissions, though the Government seems aware of the seriousness of the threat of climate change. For example, the 2011 *National Climate Change Response White Paper* warns that if international action does not limit the average global temperature increase to a maximum of 2 degrees Celsius above pre-industrial levels, "the potential impacts on South Africa in the medium to long-term are significant and potentially catastrophic". It goes on to warn that "after 2050 warming is projected to reach around 3–4 degrees C along the coast, and 6–7 degrees C in the interior. With these kinds of temperature increases, life as we know it will change completely" (Government of the Republic of South Africa, 2011, p. 9).

In 2010 South Africa's carbon emissions were about 400 million tonnes, which amounts to about 1.5 per cent of the global total. In 2009 at the multinational negotiations at the Conference of the Parties to the UNFCCC (COP-15) in Copenhagen, the Pretoria Government made voluntary commitments to a "peak, plateau and decline" trajectory. The "decline" means that "South Africa … will take nationally appropriate mitigation action to enable a 34 per cent deviation below the 'Business as Usual' emissions growth trajectory by 2020 and a 42 per cent deviation below … by 2025" (DEA, 2010, p. 2). Much publicity has been given to this commitment, but less attention to how these reductions will be made, or to the condition stipulated: that an international agreement is reached and that the financing and technology necessary to achieve this reduction are provided by the international community. Two economists have concluded that "the post 2025 plateau and decline is at least economically infeasible if not impossible within the current economic structure" (Trollop and Tyler, 2011, p. 28). Furthermore, the policy document, the NGP, does not mention the Copenhagen pledge, focusing instead on the new "green economy".

Many triumphalist claims are made about the green economy as a "major new thrust for the South African economy which presents multiple opportunities to create jobs and value-adding industries" (DTI, 2011, p. 17). It is also acknowledged that "increasing energy costs pose a major threat to manufacturing, rendering our historical, resource-intensive, processing-based industrial path unviable in the future" (DTI, 2011, p. 97). However, these claims are weakened by the compartmentalization of the green economy as distinct from the "real economy"; as "something separate and therefore different or additional to a mainstream future South African economy" (Trollop and Tyler, 2011, p. 12).

The "real economy" remains carbon intensive and environmentally destructive. As Kumi Naidoo points out, "while the NGP's (and the broader state's) commitment to 'greening the economy' focuses on the potential of environmental concerns to meet the needs of the market (through job creation and more efficient production processes), the existing deleterious effects of capitalist development on the environment continue largely unaddressed" (K. Naidoo, 2011, p. 10).

Overall, South Africa's commitments to reducing carbon emissions are vague and insubstantial. The real commitment is to economic growth. The Government's strategy perpetuates market-led economic growth models which benefit large corporations at the expense of job creation and the social needs of the majority. It will not solve the problem of climate change which threatens us all. Neither will "green capitalism". As David Hallowes comments,

> government cannot face up to what it sees coming because it remains wedded to the dominant interests of the mineral–energy complex. It remains locked in a view of the world in which economic growth constitutes the central organizing principle of development. This is not because growth is needed to alleviate poverty but because it is needed to reproduce capital … Changing the system is necessary because capitalism is not compatible with addressing climate change. (Hallowes, 2011, p. 18)

This is one of the key themes of the emerging climate justice movement in South Africa, which includes labour.

The civil society response to climate change: The climate justice movement

The civil society conference convened by COSATU in October 2010 included over 300 civil society organizations and resulted in a declaration which included a recognition of the ecological crisis. For example, "we need to move towards sustainable energy, to migrate the economy from one based on a coal to a low carbon or possibly carbon free economy. The renewable energy sector will grow, needing different skills and different locations. We have to make sure that we are in charge of this process and do not become the objects of it." There are also references to "eco-agriculture", a rejection of nuclear power, "zero-waste" and "green jobs" (COSATU, 2010, p. 6).

The notion of "climate justice" was prominent in these deliberations and has become the foundational concept in a widespread global civil society movement launched in 2007 at the Bali climate change negotiations. The movement has been steadily growing since the network Climate Justice Now (CJN) was formed that year from different strands in the women's, environmental and democratic popular movements from the global South, such as Via Campesina and Jubilee South. It is an alternative to the well-funded environmental foundations and NGOs that often lack democratic accountability and tend to ventriloquize on behalf of grass-roots communities.

The stress is on climate justice in both global and local terms. Globally, justice is a strong theme among activists who claim that a wide range of activities contribute to an ecological debt owed to countries in the global South: the extraction of natural resources, unequal terms of trade, degradation of land and soil for export crops, loss of biodiversity and so on. Locally, it is demonstrated that it is the poor and the powerless who are most negatively affected by pollution and resource depletion and will bear the brunt of climate change.

In South Africa this emphasis translates into a campaigning focus on issues such as jobs and food prices which resonate with working-class people. The consequence is that the movement has a different social base from that of past environmental struggles. Dominated by white, middle-class supporters, these were largely focused on the conservation of threatened plants, animals and wilderness areas to the neglect of social needs (Cock, 2006). The social base of the climate justice movement includes organized labour and unemployed people and, according to Standing, has a special appeal to what he terms the "precariat". This "is naturally the green class in arguing for a more egalitarian society in which sharing and reproductive, resource-conserving activities are prioritized" (Standing, 2011, p. 179).[2]

Several commentators have gone beyond this analysis to stress the unifying potential of the emerging climate justice movement in South Africa. According to Patrick Bond, "the CJ organisations and networks offer great potential to fuse issue-specific progressive environmental and social activists, many of which have strong roots in oppressed communities" (Bond, 2010, p. 3). Tristan Taylor of Earthlife Africa, Johannesburg, believes that there is potential for unity if there is tolerance for political differences and the campaign focuses on one simple idea: "'Stop climate change now.' Then the different organisations can take the idea in different political directions" (Taylor, 2011). The director of Greenpeace has also emphasized the importance of speaking with a united voice on the climate crisis. According to Kumi Naidoo (2011), "as the host of COP 17 the government of South Africa has a great opportunity to represent Africa who will be hardest hit by climate change. We must come together and speak with one voice ... Having different marches at the World Summit on Sustainable Development meant we let South Africa down."

To generate this unity, representatives from 80 different organizations across a broad spectrum of civil society, including several individual trade unions as well as COSATU, came together in Durban in January 2011 to form a coordinating committee. In the aftermath of the meeting, which has been described by a participant as "fraught" with competing claims and interests, the committee focused on a logistical unity which involved public education, providing an alternative space in Durban for civil society organizations during COP-17, and organizing the mass march on the global day of action on 3 December 2011.

This march of 12,000 people from all over the world to the site of the COP-17 negotiations in Durban was a very colourful event, with different movements – including COSATU affiliates and the COSATU General Secretary – marching in their battalions, singing and chanting slogans such as "A people united will never be defeated". However, the unity was geographical rather than ideological. Early in the march violence was initiated by some 200 people in green, labelled "Host City Monitors", who turned out to be paid members of the ANC Youth League, claiming to have been provoked by "these anti-Zuma people behind us". In response to this alleged provocation – despite an exceptionally heavy police presence – they threw stones and water bottles, tore up banners and posters, made physical threats, sang ANC songs and flourished placards such as "Zuma until Jesus comes". On another occasion in the Durban City Hall the same contingent attacked silent protestors holding placards appealing for President Zuma to "listen to the people of Africa".

The organizations participating in this march and the COP-17 process – whether inside or outside the formal negotiations – encompassed a variety of shades of "green" (meaning minimally some level of commitment to more sustainable relations between human society and nature). Overall, the main fault-line runs along the ideological division between those organizations with a "green" reform agenda (many of which belong to the Climate Action Network[3]) and those with a "red–green" anticapitalist transformative agenda (often linked to CJN). The anti-capitalist orientation of labour, particularly within COSATU, brings it closer to the CJN position. All these organizations are working on the mobilization of civil society, and most appeal to the notion of climate justice to do so. All emphasize the need for change towards the goal of a low-carbon economy, but they differ on the means of reaching it and the scale of change involved. Nor is there agreement on what a low-carbon economy would look like. Overall there are sharp divisions on five "wedge" issues:

- the role of technology;

- the value of the UNFCCC process;

- market mechanisms, particularly carbon trading;

- the expansionist logic of neoliberal capitalism as the cause of the climate crisis; and

- how our relationship to nature should change.

The main issue of contention is the reliance on market mechanisms enshrined in the Kyoto Protocol, which is viewed with a level of scepticism among CJN activists although it is the only legally binding agreement to date.[4] Generally, those organizations with a reform agenda accept market-based solutions such as carbon trading, place a heavy reliance on technologies such as carbon capture and storage, and view the UNFCCC process and the South African Government's negotiating position in positive terms. This stance is the object of intense criticism from those organizations with a transformative agenda, which stress that market-based solutions such as carbon trading are one way in which capital is attempting to appropriate the crisis and make climate change a site of capital accumulation. They are particularly critical of CDM and REDD as "unsustainable", and "unjust" REDD is particularly controversial: while some environmental groups maintain it contributes to forest preservation, others claim it involves the further commodification of nature and will benefit corporate investors while damaging the livelihoods and cultures of forest-dependent communities.[5] They are sceptical about the claims made for expensive and untested technologies, such as the "climate-smart agriculture" promoted by the World Bank and the Food and Agriculture Organization, and carbon capture and storage. There is a strong emphasis on the expansionist logic of the capitalist system as the cause of the climate crisis. Some organizations prioritize a class analysis, while many of the Northern NGOs are "class blind", for example, following the influential Mary Robinson Foundation for Climate Justice in framing climate change in the liberal discourse of human rights.[6] Others understand the issue as a stark choice between "green capitalism" and "eco-socialism".

Provisional mapping of the climate change activism terrain indicates a loose grouping around a few key nodes such as the organizations Groundwork and Earthlife Africa. The latter is now the lead organization in South Africa of the international alliance Climate Justice Now and supports a transformative agenda. The alliance Climate Justice Now South Africa (CJNSA) explicitly rejects "the false solutions based on market mechanisms such as the CDM, and REDD" (CJNSA, 2011a).[7] The CJNSA submission on the Integrated Resource Plan 2011 stated: "The IRP displays the continued power of the corporations at the centre of the minerals–energy complex to shape development to their own interests. For the people of South Africa and the environment, it is catastrophic." Another CJN position paper states:

Capitalism is not compatible with addressing climate change. It requires never ending economic growth for its survival. Growth has brought unprecedented wealth to the owners of capital, prosperity to the world's middle classes and untold misery to the majority of people particularly in the global South. Capitalism plunders the resources of the earth and of the people. It is the driving force behind ecological disruption on all scales from the local to the global. Climate change is the ultimate symptom of this renting of the earth system. (CJNSA, 2011b, p. 2)

A central node in an alternative approach is the World Wildlife Fund (WWF), an international NGO which espouses a reform agenda, supporting carbon trading, the role of the World Bank in mitigation funding, and the South African Government's negotiating position in a reform agenda. Among those adopting this approach there is an optimism that environmentally destructive capitalist activities can be corrected through political action within the system, using means such as carbon trading, taxes, technological innovation, energy efficiency and incentives to capital. The trust is on reforming or greening the present form of "suicide capitalism".

Labour's response to climate change

Clearly, workers and their organizations are an indispensable force for a transition to a low-carbon economy. As Jakopovich writes, "Environmentalists are workers and obviously potential allies in their efforts to advance workplace health and safety, and also to tackle environmental concerns of working-class communities: for workers bear the brunt of environmental degradation and destruction, both in terms of health and quality of life issues" (Jakopovich, 2009, p. 75).

For this reason, this chapter argues for building transnational solidarity networks involving labour and environmental activists. The implication is that labour needs to move away from the traditional, national-level organizational form, as well as broadening the conventional focus on jobs and workplace issues to embrace environmental issues. In South Africa this shift could build on the tradition of "social movement unionism" which involved an active engagement in community struggles. Similarly, environmentalists need to extend their traditional focus on threatened plants, animals and wilderness areas to address social needs.

A global alliance of labour and environmental activists could become a significant source of countervailing power. For example, in 2009 in South Africa two environmental justice organizations, Earthlife Africa (Johannesburg) and Groundwork, mobilized international opposition to the World Bank's US$3.75 billion loan to Eskom to build more coal-fired power stations, making connections between organizations and grass-roots communities in the global North and South. Within three months more than 200 organizations around the world (including some trade unions) had endorsed a rejection of the loan. Earthlife argued that "this loan is not about poor people or jobs or even the climate, but is benefitting vested interests" (Adam, Taylor and Peek, 2010,

p. 12), pointing out that the new power stations would increase both the price of electricity for poor people and South Africa's contribution to carbon emissions and climate change. While opposition to the loan was not ultimately successful, Earthlife officer Tristan Taylor maintains that "future World Bank funding for coal is far less likely".

To link labour and environmental activists, and to address the fear that "green jobs" are market driven, progressive forces are organizing around the notion of "climate jobs". A "million climate jobs" campaign, modelled on a British trade union campaign, is taking hold in the South African labour movement. It is based on the argument that if we are to move in a "just transition" to a low-carbon economy using renewable energy instead of coal, it will be workers who will have to build wind, wave, tidal and solar power infrastructure, and workers who will have to renovate and insulate our homes and buildings and build new forms of public transport. It is stressed that the lives of working people could improve in the process. Research findings launched at COP-17 demonstrated that 3.7 million climate jobs (jobs which reduce carbon emissions) could be created to address both the unemployment crisis and the climate crisis in South Africa. It is also stressed that climate jobs must be "decent", largely public sector jobs which promote equality and justice.

In June 2011 the central committee of COSATU – a trade union federation with 2 million members and 20 affiliate unions – endorsed the million climate jobs campaign and resolved that, "going forward, we should strengthen our participation and be more effective in the COP17 Co-ordinating Committee ... and mobilize our members for the Global Day of Action on Saturday 3 December" (quoted in COSATU, 2011).

This recognition of climate change as a developmental and social issue goes back several years. COSATU decided at its 2009 congress to increase its research capacity on climate change and at the next congress that "climate change is one of the greatest threats to our planet and our people". It noted that "it is the working class, the poor and developing countries that will be adversely affected by climate change". The congress also noted that "unless the working class and its organizations take up the issue of climate change seriously, all the talk about 'green jobs' will amount to nothing except being another site of accumulation for capitalists" (quoted in COSATU, 2011).

COSATU is influenced in its stance on climate change by the international trade union movement and organizations such as the International Labour Organization (ILO) and the United Nations Environment Programme (UNEP). Trade unions have participated in the UNFCCC since its inception, under the umbrella of the International Trade Union Confederation (ITUC), which represents 170 million workers through its affiliated organizations in 157 countries. The UNFCCC process has included rising numbers of trade unionists, albeit mostly from the developed countries.

Representatives from these organizations were present in April 2011 at the Madrid Dialogue, a gathering of trade union leaders from around the world to discuss a new low-carbon development paradigm. At this meeting the Spanish minister of the environment stressed that "the social and environmental agenda should be indissolubly joined in order for a just transition to be produced towards a new model of growth" (quoted in CJNSA, 2011b). Zwelinzima Vavi, the General Secretary of COSATU, said:

> The current economic model is heading us towards more crises, unemployment and environmental degradation … If we are serious about addressing the vulnerability of poor workers and communities, Rio+20 needs to shift from piecemeal commitments and deliver a universal social protection floor, which will ensure dignified livelihoods for all. The climate negotiations in Durban must support this effort through the protection of the poorest from a climate perspective: with ambition in terms of emission reductions and climate finance. (Quoted in CJNSA, 2011b)

In a statement which clearly prioritizes social over environmental considerations, he also said: "We will not support any form of capital accumulation that breeds inequalities – even if those forms of capital accumulation are green" (quoted in CJNSA, 2011b).

Others at this gathering expressed support for a green economy and green jobs. For example, Ambet Yuson, the General Secretary of Building and Woodworkers International (BWI), said: "A green economy based on rights, sustainability principles and decent work can meet the challenge of our societies … A just transition, such as the one unions are calling for, needs to be based on the transformation of all jobs into sustainable ones" (quoted in CJNSA, 2011b).

While capital's discourse of a low-carbon economy emphasizes growth, competitiveness and efficiency, the labour movement agrees on this notion of a "just transition". However, there is less agreement on the substantive content of the notion of a "just transition".

Different understandings of a just transition to a low-carbon economy: Paradigm shift or regime change?

Two broad approaches to this notion of a "just transition" may be identified within the global labour movement.

- The minimalist position emphasizes shallow, reformist change with green jobs, social protection, retraining and consultation. The emphasis is defensive and shows a preoccupation with protecting the interests of vulnerable workers.

- An alternative notion of a just transition involves transformative change: an alternative growth path, and new ways of producing and consuming.

In addressing climate change, the International Metalworkers Federation and the ITUC have advocated a "just transition". Their argument is that workers and affected communities need adequate social protection and access to new opportunities. This implies new labour market policies, income protection, retraining, awareness and capacity building. At the 2010 UNFCCC meeting held in Cancún, Mexico, organized labour successfully lobbied for the inclusion of the concept of a "just transition" into the UNFCCC negotiations.

The ILO defines a just transition as "the conceptual framework in which the labour movement captures the complexities of the transition towards a low-carbon and climate-resilient economy, highlighting public policy needs and aiming to maximize benefits and minimize hardships for workers and their communities in this transformation" (Rosenberg, 2010, p. 141).

However, while the concept of a "just transition" is central to ITUC policy, there are many outstanding questions. Its report *Equity, justice and solidarity in the fight against climate change* (2009) stresses the need "to create green and decent jobs, transform and improve traditional ones and include democracy and social justice in environmental decision-making processes" (ITUC, 2009, p. 10). A just transition is described as "a tool the trade union movement shares with the international community, aimed at smoothing the shift towards a more sustainable society and providing hope for the capacity of a 'green economy' to sustain decent jobs and livelihoods for all" (ITUC, 2009, p. 14).

According to Sustainlabour and UNEP, in a very influential and widely circulated document entitled *Climate change: Its consequences on employment and trade union action. A training manual for workers and trade unions,* "the appropriate measures to guarantee a fair transition for potentially affected workers" should include:

• social protection systems which "must run in parallel to adaptation efforts as they can diminish vulnerability to climate change and strengthen the social security systems, especially in developing countries";

• economic diversification policies, able to identify potential job opportunities; and

• "training and requalification programmes". (Sustainlabour and UNEP, 2008, p. 66)

The emphasis is on "the need to involve workers in climate change decision making, to establish fair transitions and to protect the most vulnerable from necessary changes to be undertaken in the world of work" (Sustainlabour and UNEP, 2008, p. 101).

The same document states: "While trade unions need to accept that changes in some sectors are necessary, they need to propose measures that prevent workers from bearing the burden of these transitions" (Sustainlabour and UNEP, 2008, p. 77). This protective discourse contrasts strongly with a transformative notion of workers carrying society forward into a completely new energy regime.

A similarly weak notion is evident in the ILO background note to the UNEP report of 2011, *Towards a green economy: Pathways to sustainable development and poverty eradication,* which states: "The structural transformation ... may also cause the contraction of sectors and enterprises which are incompatible with long term sustainable development. The management of this change needs to be fair and must ensure sufficient protection and access to alternatives for those negatively affected" (ILO, 2011, p. 5).

The majority of global trade union federations, led by the ITUC, are committed to a social dialogue model of social change. Their definition of a just transition explicitly contains the phrase "social dialogue". This contrasts with the minority World Federation of Trade Unions (WFTU) – to which some COSATU affiliates, including the National Union of Metalworkers of South Africa (NUMSA), are aligned – whose proposals around climate change frame the issue in terms of class struggle and a critique of capitalism.

In South Africa, many trade unionists emphasize the links between the climate crisis and neoliberal capitalism. A document entitled *Labour's initial response to the National Climate Change Response Green Paper 2010*, dated 28 February 2011 and endorsed by COSATU, the National Council of Trade Unions (NACTU) and the Federation of Unions of South Africa (FEDUSA), states:

> We are convinced that any effort to address the problems of Climate Change that does not fundamentally challenge the system of global capitalism is bound not only to fail, but to generate new, larger and more dangerous threats to human beings and our planet. Climate Change ... is caused by the global private profit system of capitalism. Tackling greenhouse gas emissions is not just a technical or technological problem. It requires a fundamental economic and social transformation to substantially change current patterns of production and consumption. (COSATU, NACTU and FEDUSA, 2011, p. 3)

Following discussion at a workshop on climate change convened by COSATU in Durban in July 2011 that was attended by national officeholders, representatives of the 20 affiliated unions and nine provincial structures, a Climate Change Policy Framework was adopted. Fourteen principles were agreed, on which the most controversial were:

- Capitalist accumulation has been the underlying cause of excessive greenhouse gas emissions, and therefore global warming and climate change.

- A new low-carbon development path is needed which addresses the need for decent jobs and the elimination of unemployment.

- Market mechanisms are rejected as a means of reducing carbon emissions.

- Developed countries must pay their climate debt and the Green Climate Fund must be accountable.[8]

- A just transition towards a low-carbon and climate-resilient society is required.

In the COSATU policy framework on climate change endorsed by the Central Executive Committee in August 2011, the explanation of "just transition" reads:

> The evidence suggests that the transition to a low carbon economy will potentially create more jobs than it will lose. But we have to campaign for protection and support for workers whose jobs or livelihoods might be threatened by the transition. If we do not do that, then these workers will resist the transition. We also have to ensure that the development of new, green industries does not become an excuse for lowering wages and social benefits. New environmentally-friendly jobs provide an opportunity to redress many of the gender imbalances in employment and skills. The combination of these interventions is what we mean by a just transition. (COSATU, 2011, p. 13)

It goes on to say:

> The Just Transition is a concept that COSATU has supported in the global engagements on climate change that have been led by the ITUC. The basic demands of a Just Transition are:
>
> • Investment in environmentally friendly activities that create decent jobs that are paid at living wages, that meet standards of health and safety, that promote gender equity and that are secure;
>
> • The putting in place of comprehensive social protections (pensions, unemployment insurance etc) in order to protect the most vulnerable;
>
> • The conducting of research into the impacts of climate change on employment and livelihoods in order to better inform social policies;
>
> • Skills development and retraining for workers to ensure that they can be part of the new low-carbon development model. (COSATU, 2011, p. 14)

The question is: are these not only necessary but also sufficient conditions for a just transition? To some, just transition involves shallow change focused on protecting the sectors of the workforce most vulnerable to mitigation strategies, while to others it requires deep, transformative change to ensure both sustainability and justice in the move to a low-carbon economy. For example, whereas the ITUC speaks of a "paradigm shift", some activists in one COSATU affiliate, the South African Municipal Workers Union (SAMWU), speak of "regime change". The unions' response to the *National Climate Change Response Green Paper* of February 2011, noted above, included the assertion: "Tackling greenhouse gas emissions is not just a technical or technological problem. It requires a fundamental economic and social transformation to substantially change current patterns of production and consumption." Another COSATU affiliate, NUMSA, argues that the shift to a low-carbon economy, and particularly the development of renewable energy, is being dominated by green capitalism (Sikwebu, 2012).

The President of COSATU, Sdumo Dlamini, has stressed that "we need a just transition which will not lead to job losses. We need a transition that will create jobs" (Dlamini, 2011). Fundi Nzimande, a researcher for the COSATU-aligned research organization NALEDI, says COSATU wants "just transition strategies to a green economy in which there are as few job losses as possible". She has referred to building "alliances with civil society" and emphasizes a class analysis: "We want to view climate change from a working class perspective. We want to counter the big business point of view" (Nzimande, 2011).

Overall, there are differences within the labour movement in responses to five issues:

• the substantive content of a "just" transition;

• the use of market mechanisms to reduce carbon emissions;

• the efficacy of technologies such as clean coal and carbon capture and storage;

• whether it is possible to delink economic growth from carbon emissions; and

• the scale of change necessary to address the climate crisis.

The National Union of Mineworkers (NUM), representing some 500,000 mineworkers in South Africa, is obviously particularly sensitive to job losses, and some shop stewards have expressed faith in new technology to reduce carbon emissions. By contrast, NUMSA – one of the biggest unions, representing almost 300,000 workers in energy-intensive industries – is sceptical towards the "just transition" approach. According to the NUMSA President, "the language of 'just transition' needs a class analysis. We believe that a 'just transition' can become a disarming term for the working class if we are not careful. It must always be clear that capitalism has caused the crisis of climate change that we see today. There is an urgent need to situate the question of climate change in a class struggle perspective" (Gina, 2011). NUMSA believes that a "just transition must be based in worker controlled democratic social ownership of key means of production and means of subsistence ... Without this struggle over ownership and the struggle for a socially owned renewable energy sector, just transition will become a capitalist concept, building up a capitalist green economy" (NUMSA, 2011). In 2011 NUMSA established two worker-led research and development groups, one on energy efficiency and the other on renewable energy (Sikwebu, 2012). These research groups will investigate the carbon emissions of various products and then work with groups in the community that use them. The aim is to build an evaluation of these products in relation to carbon emissions into the union's negotiating strategy.

Clearly, different affiliates will react differently to climate change policies, with marked responses especially from those directly threatened with job losses. Understanding of the issue is uneven. A recent small-scale survey of shop stewards in COSATU affiliates revealed that at least 10 per cent of the respondents were unclear about the nature of climate change, and almost a quarter (23 per cent) did not know what a "just transition" meant. Furthermore, it is unclear how much priority will be given to climate change in the context of the many other issues and planned campaigns currently being addressed by the labour movement in South Africa – issues such as labour brokers, corruption and the living wage campaign, among others.

Conclusion: An alternative developmental path

An adequate response to the climate crisis involves formulating an alternative growth path. In South Africa, given the flawed government policy and weaknesses in civil society, labour needs to take the lead in doing so. Clearly much work needs to be done, especially to build stronger alliances between the labour and environmental movements, if labour is to give priority to the climate crisis, avoid being absorbed into a green capitalism and promote a transformative understanding of a "just transition to a low-carbon economy". Such an understanding involves thinking about options which go beyond both "green" and "suicide" capitalism. According to Sean Sweeney:

> In recent years global labor has worked on the premise that the "real world" historical options are essentially two-fold. Either humanity will transition to some form of "green capitalism" where economic growth is de-linked from emissions and environmental destruction generally, or we face a "suicide capitalism" scenario where fossil-fuel corporations and major industry, agriculture, transport and retail interests are successful in maintaining business as usual. (Sweeney, 2011, p. 9)

But the notion of "green" or "sustainable" capitalism is being subjected to growing criticism (see Kovel, 2002; Harris-White and Harriss, 2006; Foster, 2009). These critiques are rooted in the understanding that *capital's logic of accumulation* is destroying the ecological conditions which sustain life. "No serious observer now denies the severity of the environmental crisis, but it is still not widely recognised as a capitalist crisis, that is a crisis arising from and perpetuated by the rule of capital, and hence incapable of resolution within the capitalist framework" (Wallis, 2010, p. 32).

At the same time there is a growing view that the notion of the "green economy" has become – like the United Nations climate negotiations – a site of "corporate capture" (Fernandes and Girard, 2011). The notion has become a key phrase in the lexicon of corporate and political elites, used to demonstrate their commitment to sustainable development, while allowing them to extend the process of commodification, the transformation of nature and all social relations into economic relations, subordinated to the logic of the market and the drive for profit.

However, a transformative understanding of a "just transition to a low-carbon economy" could be a precursor to an alternative social order. For example, it could involve:

- the collective, democratic control of production;

- the mass roll-out of socially owned renewable energy, providing decentralized energy supply with much greater potential for community control;

- the localization of food production in a shift from carbon-intensive industrial agriculture to agro-ecology, promoting not only food security, cooperatives and more communal living, but also a more direct sense of connection to nature;

- the reduction of consumption, simplifying middle-class lifestyles by reducing waste, extravagance and ostentation;

- a shift to public transport, with a concomitant reduction in the reliance on private motor cars as symbols of power and freedom;

- more sharing of resources in more collective social forms, eroding the individualism which is a mark of neoliberal capitalism;

- a shift towards a more appreciative use of natural resources, reducing the alienation from nature of many urban inhabitants; and

- the spreading of values of sharing, simplicity, solidarity and more mindful living.

This alternative social order could contain the embryo of a new kind of socialism which is democratic, ethical and ecological.

To debate genuine alternatives requires trade unions to look beyond the nation and beyond the workplace. A first and pressing task is to re-emphasize and redefine the core value of the labour movement – solidarity – which involves struggling against individualism and what has been called "the infection of self-interest" promoted by marketized social relations (Leibowitz, 2010, p. 144). It is also necessary to challenge the notion that trade unions have become largely obsolete in a globalizing world. This argument surfaces in various debilitating forms, such as the cynicism of Standing (2011), who sees a class fragmentation (involving a new elite and a growing "precariat") displacing organized labour.

Second, we need to develop a vision of an alternative social order; to be clear about the kind of future society we want to see. As Leibowitz writes, "if we don't know where we want to go, no path will take us there" (Leibowitz, 2010, p. 7). At this moment, "the deepest shadow that hangs over us is neither terror, nor environmental collapse, nor global recession. It is the internalized fatalism that holds there is no possible alternative to capital's world order" (Kelly and Malone, 2006, p. 116). Giving substantive content to the notion of a "just transition to a low-carbon economy" could be a step towards formulating such an alternative.

Notes

[1] Cited in *Sunday Times*, 4 Dec. 2011.

[2] The "precariat" is a large and growing social category characterized by insecure or no employment, minimal labour protection, no sense of secure occupational identity and few state entitlements (Standing, 2011). Standing cites no empirical evidence to support his claim that a "natural green class" is emerging. Nor does he consider how the ecological crisis is deepening insecurities among all classes and creating a "risk society" (Beck, 2001).

[3] The Climate Action Network (CAN), which includes many of the large conservation organizations, does not see capitalism as the main threat and is uncritical of carbon trading.

[4] The Kyoto Protocol promotes carbon trading, which has been described as "a cloak for the disastrous lack of action by developed countries to cut their greenhouse gas emissions and provide adequate climate finance as repayment for their climate debt to the developing world" (Friends of the Earth International, 2011). It involves the buying and selling of an artificial commodity, the right to emit GHGs, and comes in two main forms, "cap and trade" and "offsetting". The largest offset scheme is the CDM, established under the framework of the Kyoto Protocol, which allows rich countries "flexibility" in their emissions reductions by allowing them to buy those reductions from developing countries instead. What the "flexibility mechanisms" mean is that corporations are able to buy the right to pollute.

Carbon trading has failed to reduce carbon emissions but has proved to be extremely profitable for many multinational corporations. It is another manifestation of "green capitalism", which is aimed at making profits from climate change, not solving it.

[5] In response to the failure of COP-15 at Copenhagen, the Bolivian Government organized the People's Conference on Climate Change and the Rights of Mother Earth, held in Cochabamba, Plurinational State of Bolivia, in April 2010 and attended by some 30,000 participants from around the world. Participants report that there was general agreement that the cause of climate change is the expansionist logic of the capitalist system, which should be replaced by "living well" and respecting "the rights of nature".

[6] Mary Robinson, of the Mary Robinson Foundation for Climate Justice, asserts that "climate change represents ... the greatest threat to human rights that we will ever face" (meeting on climate change convened by Jayendra Naidoo, Johannesburg, 24 Mar. 2011).

[7] CJNSA is a group of individual organizations which is itself affiliated to the international alliance CJN.

[8] This fund emerged from UNFCCC negotiations to assist developing nations with adaptation and mitigation measures. Controversy centres on the role of the World Bank in its administration. The explanatory note in the COSATU policy framework on this point states: "the Fund should not be administered or dominated in any way by the World Bank. The World Bank has historically been part of the problem of climate change, not part of the solution. It continues to fund massive fossil fuel projects in at least seven different countries" (COSATU, 2011, p. 5).

References

Adam, F.; Taylor, T.; Peek, B. 2010. "South Africa's US 43.75 billion World Bank loan: Developing poverty", *Amandla*, No. 14, May–June 2010.

Beck, U. 2001. *The risk society* (London, Palgrave).

Bond, P. 2010. *South Africa prepares for conference of polluters*, unpublished paper.

—. 2011. *The politics of climate justice* (Durban, UKZN Press).

Climate Justice Now South Africa (CJNSA). 2011a. Press statement, 14 June.

—. 2011b. *CJNSA position on COP17*, 28 Nov., http://www.earthlife.org.za/wordpress/wp-content/uploads/2011/11/CJNSA-Position-on-COP17-28-Nov-2011.pdf [27 June 2012].

Cock, J. 2006. "The environmental justice movement", in R. Ballard, A. Habib and I. Valodia (eds): *Voices of protest: Social movements in post-apartheid South Africa* (Durban, UKZN Press), pp. 203–25.

—. 2007. "Sustainable development or environmental justice: Questions for the South African labour movement from the Steel Valley Struggle", in *Labour, Capital and Society*, Vol. 40, Nos. 1–2, pp. 36–55.

COSATU. 2010. Declaration of the civil society conference convened by COSATU in Boksburg, 27–28 Oct. 2010.

—. 2011. *COSATU policy framework on climate change*, adopted by COSATU Central Executive Committee meeting, Johannesburg, Aug.

—; National Council of Trade Unions (NACTU); Federation of Unions of South Africa (FEDUSA). 2011. *Labour's initial response to the National Climate Change Response Green Paper 2010*, 28 Feb., http://www.ilr.cornell.edu/globallaborinstitute/research/upload/Labours-Initial-Response-to-the-Climate-Change-Green-Paper2-2.pdf [27 June 2012].

Department of Environmental Affairs (DEA). 2010. *National Climate Response White Paper, 2010* (Pretoria).

Department of Trade and Industry (DTI). 2011. *Industrial Action Plan 2010/11–2012/13* (Pretoria).

Dlamini, S. 2011. Address to COP-17 public meeting, Durban, 7 Dec.

Economic Development Department (EDD). 2010. *The New Growth Path Framework* (Pretoria).

—. 2011. *New Growth Path Accord 4: Green Economy Accord* (Pretoria).

Fernandes, S.; Girard, R. 2011. *Corporations, climate and the United Nations* (Ottawa, Polaris Institute).

Foster, J.B. 2009. *The ecological revolution* (New York, Monthly Review Press).

Friends of the Earth International. 2011. *Our climate is not for sale: Say no to carbon trading at COP 17*, http://www.foei.org/en/resources/publications/pdfs/2011/our-climate-is-not-for-sale-say-no-to-carbon-trading-expansion-at-cop-17 [27 June 2012].

Gina, C. 2011. Opening Address to NUMSA International Seminar on Climate Change and Class Struggle, Durban, 4 Dec.

Government of the Republic of South Africa. 2011. *National Climate Change Response White Paper* (Pretoria).

Hallowes, D. 2011. *Feeling the heat in Durban: People's struggles and climate change* (Durban: Oxfam for South Durban Community Environmental Alliance).

Harris-White, B.; Harriss, E. 2006. "Unsustainable capitalism: The politics of renewable energy in the UK", in L. Panitch and C. Leyes (eds): *Coming to terms with nature* (Toronto, Palgrave for Socialist Register), pp. 72–101.

Hyman, R. 2011. "Trade unions, global competition and options for solidarity", in A. Bieler and I. Lindberg (eds): *Global restructuring, labour and the challenges for transnational solidarity* (London, Routledge), pp. 16–27.

International Labour Organization. 2011. *Promoting decent work in a green economy*, ILO background note to *Towards a green economy: Pathways to sustainable development and poverty eradication*, UNEP, 2011 (Geneva).

International Trade Union Confederation (ITUC). 2009. *Equity, justice and solidarity in the fight against climate change* (Brussels, 2009).

Jakopovich, D. 2009. "Uniting to win: Labour environmental alliances", in *Capitalism, Nature, Socialism*, Vol. 20, No. 2, June, pp. 74–96.

Kelly, J.; Malone, S. 2006. *Ecosocialism or barberism* (London, Socialist Resistance).

Kovel, J. 2002. *The enemy of nature: The end of capitalism or the end of the world?* (London, Zed Books).

Leibowitz, M. 2010. *The socialist alternative* (New York, Monthly Review Press).

Naidoo, K. 2011. Interview, Uppsala, Sweden, 13 Apr. 2011.

Naidoo, P. 2011. "New paths, old (com)promises?", in J. Daniel, P. Naidoo, D. Pillay and R. Southall (eds): *New South African Review* (Johannesburg: Wits University Press), pp. 1–17.

National Union of Metalworkers of South Africa (NUMSA). 2011. Statement from NUMSA Central Committee, 14 Dec.

Nzimande, F. 2011. Interview, Durban, 15 July.

Rosenberg, A. 2010. "Building a just transition: The linkages between climate change and employment", in *International Journal of Labour Research*, Vol. 2, No. 2, p. 141.

—. 2011. Interview, Durban, 27 July.

Sikwebu, D. 2012. Interview, Johannesburg, 7 Feb.

Standing, G. 2011. *The precariat: The new dangerous class* (London, Bloomsbury).

Sustainlabour. 2011. "The Madrid Dialogue took off", http://www.sustainlabour.org/noticia.php?lang=EN&idnoticia=132 [27 June 2012].

—; UNEP. 2008. *Climate change, its consequences on employment and trade union action: A training manual for workers and trade unions* (Madrid and Nairobi, Sustainlabour and UNEP).

Sweeney, S. 2011. "How unions can help secure a binding global climate agreement in 2011", http://www.labor4sustainability.org/post/the-durban-challenge/ [27 June 2012].

Taylor, T. 2011. Interview, Johannesburg, 7 Oct.

Trollop, H.; Tyler, E. 2011. *Is South Africa's economic policy aligned with our national mitigation policy direction and a low carbon future?*, paper presented to the National Planning Commission Second Low Carbon Economy Workshop, Johannesburg, July.

United Nations Environment Programme (UNEP). 2011. *Towards a green economy: Pathways to sustainable development and poverty eradication* (Nairobi).

—; International Labour Organization (ILO); International Organisation of Employers (IOE); International Trade Union Confederation (ITUC). 2008. *Green jobs: Towards decent work in a sustainable, low-carbon world* (Washington, DC, New York and Nairobi, Worldwatch Institute and Cornell University Global Labor Institute for UNEP).

Wallis, V. 2010. "Beyond green capitalism", in *Monthly Review*, Feb., pp. 32–47.

WOMEN, GENDER AND POWER IN TRADE UNIONS

3

Akua Britwum, Karen Douglas and Sue Ledwith

Introduction

Increasingly, women around the world are joining trade unions. However, this rise in female union membership is consistently at odds with women's representation in leadership. This lack of representation, voice and power in trade unions is significant for a number of reasons. Workers remain the focus of attack from employers and are forced to carry the burden of failures of private capital. Women carry this burden disproportionately, owing to their gendered positioning in societal and organizational cultures and structures. Thus women are placed precariously and insecurely in labour markets, dominating informal sectors especially. This positioning is also partly responsible for women's difficulties in joining trade unions, while unions themselves also use this as an excuse for their low levels of organizing activity among women and other marginalized groups. Nevertheless, newly diverse labour forces, including women, migrant workers and other previously marginalized groups, are becoming more and more vocal in their demands for recognition and representation in labour movements, and in a period of sustained ideological attack, trade unions cannot credibly maintain their important place in the global community as agents of social change if their own internal decision-making bodies do not reflect the full range of their constituencies.

To be effective agents of change it is vital that unions themselves disrupt their own traditional male hegemony, and of equal importance that women continue to use their agency in this project. Women trade unionists (mainly) have been discussing these issues and increasingly mounting challenges and developing strategies for change. In this they are supported by scholars and researchers providing data, analysis and ideas. Unions, too, are putting gender equality measures in place and formally out-lawing discriminatory practice, often in line with legal and rights frameworks. Such work challenges long-held assumptions that women are averse to union membership and lack a capacity for power, including capabilities in leading their unions. In this chapter we examine the "women and power" question in unions, addressing both women's power deficit and their prospects for holding power. First, we briefly survey the relationship between gender relations in society and in labour markets, and how the gender order is replicated in trade unions. Then we move to focus on women within their trade unions, exploring factors that account for their continued subordinate roles in unions, the role of power and gender, and ways in which gender may be central in agendas for change.

We pursue these themes through an unusual study which draws its strength from two aspects. First, the researchers are an international team of trade union colleagues from 11 countries across six continents: Africa, Asia, Australia, Europe, Latin America, and North America.[1] Most are graduates of or teach on Global Labour University (GLU) masters programmes. Second, the researchers are both "insiders" and "outsiders". All are directly or indirectly linked to trade unions or trade union inclined research institutes and/or university departments in their respective countries, and are actively engaged in labour movements; yet the demands of our positioning as researchers calls for a certain distancing that also makes us outsiders. This unique combination of seemingly contradictory positions provides us with a vantage standpoint as participant observers. Our research has been taking place since 2009, and is continuing.

Gendered labour markets

Women's participation in the labour market is influenced by their historical treatment in both paid and unpaid work. Theoretical developments around gender and class, as well as race and sexuality, have stressed the fragmentary and fluid nature of subjectivities, insisting that identities are constructed by, and embedded in, the different places, spaces and times of particular lives.

For women workers these identities have been shaped through the standard employment relationship, a gendered contract based on the idea of a male breadwinner and female caregiver and characterized by one job, one place, one working career. This "unencumbered" worker was the favoured type of employee, protected in the labour market and by the professional and managerial classes of both genders (see Cass,1995; Broomhill and Sharp, 2005; Chapman, 2005; Young, 2005; Vosko, 2010). Thus at a personal level women and men have very different material and temporal experiences of paid work. Generally, male labour force participation rates tend to be around 75–90 per cent and are fairly steady, whereas women's vary over their life cycle as they move in and out of the labour market, working part time and then full time, and/or holding several short-term and part-time jobs as family life allows. This locates women in a narrow range of jobs which mirror and reproduce their ascribed family role of caring and servicing. Everywhere women dominate the "five Cs" of caring, cashiering, catering, clerical and cleaning, mainly in service and public sectors in formal labour markets, and in precarious work in both formal and informal sectors. Gender relations permeate all aspects of economic, social and political life, constructing economies and societies as gendered cultures and structures (Çağatay and Erturk, 2004, p. 5).

Now, as globalization fragments work and workforces, restructuring and the demands of flexibility have seen women's labour force participation rates continuing to rise, in most of the countries in our study reaching 50 per cent of the workforce, with high proportions of women dominating informal sectors and precarious work. Often, women are not replacing male workers but are increasingly competing with them, pushing down already meagre earning levels. In addition, the negative fallout from earlier Structural Adjustment Programmes imposed by the international financial institutions continues to affect labour forces adversely. In these shifts we see the rise of the "precariat" (Standing, 2011), a hybrid of the proletariat and the precarious worker, toiling in insecure, casual jobs – often several simultaneously – and usually without rights: conditions long familiar to women, migrant workers and other minority groups, especially those in informal sectors and in the global South. This growth of precarious employment has come to be referred to as the "feminization of work" (Fudge and Owens, 2006, p. 11). Women also comprise a significant group working in agriculture, domestic work and export processing zones (EPZs), where exclusion from state rights, including health care and occupational safety, and from trade union protection, is routine.

These are all forms of work that challenge the very notion of traditional trade union organization, historically strongest in primary and extractive sectors such as mining, iron and steel, and in big factories and workplaces with large, stable workforces, mainly male. Indeed, the International Union of Food, Agricultural, Hotel, Restaurant, Catering, Tobacco and Allied Workers' Associations (IUF) sees the development of precarious work as a deliberate strategy to restrict workers' ability to organize and challenge issues such as poverty, insecurity and unsafe working conditions through collective bargaining (IUF, n.d.).

We move now to unpack these issues, starting with women's positions and roles in labour movements.

Women in trade unions

Even though recent research informs us that women's membership of trade unions is increasing at higher rates than men's (Yates, 2006, 2010; Pillinger, 2010;), this has not yet resulted in a corresponding increase in the numbers of women in union leadership roles, demonstrating that a male hegemony in trade union leadership persists. This is not surprising. Since trade unions are integral to labour markets, it follows that occupational and industrial gender patterns and gender relations are all reproduced in unions.

The trend in trade union membership overall is one of decline, but within that there is also evidence of considerable change within the membership demographic, with increases in women, migrant workers and those from minority ethnic groupings – the previously marginalized (see e.g. Moore, 2011). In Europe women are making up an increasing proportion of trade union members in most union centres and countries for which data are available, suggesting that their membership is tending to hold up better than men's in union organizations that are shrinking, and that they are making up a greater proportion of growth in organizations that are expanding (Carley, 2009). But outside Europe and the English-speaking countries it is difficult to find statistical data on membership generally, let alone by gender.

Nevertheless, we do know that women are still not represented proportionally in leadership positions and authority roles in their unions. This gender leadership deficit is also a democratic deficit, and is of major concern. Worldwide, women account for less than a third of those in the highest decision-making bodies (ILO and ICFTU, 1999). The European Trade Union Confederation's 8 March 2011 survey reports that only a few confederations, most of them in the Nordic countries, have women delegates to national general committees or councils in proportion to their membership (ETUC, 2011). Briskin (2012) writes that although there is limited systematic documentation in Canada and the United States, recent US scholarship speaks to the low numbers, and the Canadian Labour Congress (CLC) comments: "People are worried that we're starting to slide backwards." In New Zealand, the rise in women holding elected positions in union leadership is so slow as to have been described as "glacial" (Parker and Douglas, 2010, p. 444).

So, as re-emphasized recently by the ETUC, "improving the gender balance in union leadership and decision-making structures remains a fundamental challenge for the trade union movement" (Pillinger, 2010, p. 7). Central here are the issues of gender power relations and sexual politics in unions.

Gender and power in unions

Franzway (2001) asserts that the politics of gender represent the greatest barrier to women in their unions, and she and colleague Mary Margaret Fonow identify how the dynamic and changing circumstances of sexual politics, in which gender relations contest and shape political opportunities and social identities, produce the resources and capacities for political action (Franzway and Fonow, 2009, p. 2).

Unpacking these power relations, Harriet Bradley (2007, pp. 188–89) addresses two key questions which go to the heart of gender politics in trade unions: "Who holds power and in whose interests is it exercised?" Bradley discusses power in terms of resources which can be employed by groups and individuals to achieve their ends. In particular, she examines how men as a group are able to access and control some of the most crucial power resources: physical, positional/status, economic and symbolic. We are interested in how men do this and how women fare in the process.

Bradley sees power as multidimensional, which can allow for complexities and variations, while also incorporating agency. She develops a model of different types of power resource. Men as a group control the most crucial of these – physical power, positional power, economic power and symbolic power – though there are some, such as sexual power and domestic power, which women can also use to their advantage (Bradley, 2007, p. 189). Altogether, the command of such resources represents a formidable armoury in the struggle for control, where gendered power is seen as the capacity of one sex to control the behaviour of the other.

These struggles also tap into discussions of women challenging union oligarchies (see e.g. Healy and Kirton, 2000), whereby lay leaders (mainly male), once elected, tend to retain their positions by using their expertise and the union's resources to stave off challenges to their power (Kelly and Heery, 1994). We can recognize some of these outcomes of gendered power dynamics in the "patriarchal dividend" (Connell, 1996, p. 162): the benefits that have accrued to men from unequal shares of the products of social labour, such as being on the right side of the gender pay gap (Williams, 2007, p. 294). These are outcomes of Lukes's (1974) conceptualization of "power over", a traditional model of dominance and control whereby one party (in gender politics, usually heterosexual men) seeks to influence another party regardless of the latter's agency or interest. More useful for us is the concept of a "power to" approach of resistance, which seeks to place power with the individual – and also, in our union project, with the collective – to exercise their own agency; what Bradley refers to as women's ability to control certain types of resources and use them as countervailing bases of resistance and challenge. We are especially keen to explore the dialectics involved here; as Foucault observed, "where there is power there is resistance" (1979, p. 95).

Levesque and Murray (2010) propose shifting from a "power to" to a "capacity to" approach, while a cooperative approach is described by Berger (2005) as "power with", reflecting an empowerment model where dialogue, inclusion, negotiation and shared power guide decision-making. On the one hand, we can see gender relations in unions as being about a frontier of control. On the other, asks Burrell (1992, pp. 74–75), even if patriarchy and power are present in cross-gender interactions, does this mean that it is impossible for the sexes to cooperate in the face of common problems, since both women and men are oppressed and impoverished?

Challenge and strategies

Feminist scholarship has argued for a more inclusive, equity-based trade union agenda to transform unions and thus influence social agendas (Kirton and Healy, 1999; Kainer, 2006). A significant element necessary to orchestrate such a shift is a reconsideration of the role of gender power relations in decision-making processes within unions and its impact on internal gender democracy. Discussions about union gender democracy usually focus on the persistence of male dominance and conclude that unions are embedded in a system of power relations that supports the status quo by ordering union structures and operations to serve male interests (Creese, 1999; Curtin, 1999; Deslippe, 2000; all in Britwum, 2010, p. 7). Strategies to unsettle and disturb these are discussed now.

Unions' own moves towards closing the gender democracy deficit have been invested in equality strategies approached from two interrelated directions, which together represent an ongoing dialectic of gender power relations. Excluded groups, mainly women, organizing autonomously and also in coalitions with progressive men, have made demands on their unions for strategic change. Strategies generally involve three main approaches for addressing both structural and cultural gender and equality democratic deficits in unions: organizing women into membership and encouraging them into activism; affirmative action such as electoral systems to encourage women, including reserved seats and gender quotas; and gender mainstreaming, the inclusion and integration of those from oppressed groups into mainstream structures and processes.

Structural measures have mainly focused on the numbers, for example gender quotas and proportional representation. Culture remains the place where informal power relations grip most strongly, but they are slippery and cannot be easily dealt with through the "normal" or "formal" channels of union rules and procedures. Measures here overlap to some extent with the structural measures and involve women and other diversity groups having their own committees, conferences, dedicated officers and support systems. They also entail autonomous organizing, for example in women's groups and education programmes, which can be risky and are frequently contested (Briskin, 1993). Unions have been equivocal about putting in place such measures, which raise complex feelings among and between the genders, and are continuously resisted on the grounds of being separatist and divisive of traditional (read "masculine") solidaristic union values.

Such contestation involves the use of power, especially status and authority, sexual power and collective homosocial organizing. There is much at stake when women resist, muster their collective agency and develop a capacity to challenge gender politics, thereby upsetting and interfering with the existing order. Here women's groups have a central role in raising awareness and developing consciousness and skills, as well as generating collective strategies for carrying gender agendas for change into the union mainstream (Colgan and Ledwith, 2000; Parker, 2003, 2006; Kirton and Healy, 2004). We agree with the contention of Cornfield (1993, p. 345) that "insurgency" inside unions is most likely to be successful where women are organized into caucuses, networks or structures which allow women as a social group to harness the union's resources to attain and exercise power.

While much of the concern about the absence of women from leadership roles is focused on senior positions, leadership in active grass-roots and community unionism is also important, although less readily visible: local unions that are embedded in external and community networks are more likely to play a strong role in the workplace (Yates, 2006). Perhaps the best known of these is SEWA, the Indian Self Employed Women's Association, organizing in the informal sector, "the unprotected labour force of our country", over 94 per cent of whom are women (SEWA, n.d.). SEWA's strategy is one of "struggle and development", and in SEWA, leadership is done cooperatively.

Forming horizontal and local alliances, including with social movements, organizing the traditionally unorganized, and adopting direct action as a means of raising the profile of worker action in the public milieu while simultaneously disrupting entrenched vertical leadership regimes (Voss and Sherman, 2000; Voss, 2010) are all important strategies. This "power with" approach to democratic determination provides the space for an inclusive politics of difference, opening up opportunities for diverse groups of workers to be included in unions' decision-making processes, to pursue social and economic justice for workers and to reframe union legitimacy (Fraser, 2000; Young, 2002; Kainer, 2006; Dufour and Adelheid, 2010).

We find the analysis of institutional decision-making processes by Iris Marion Young (1990, 2002) useful in disrupting historical approaches to decision-making. Young challenges the notion of "representation", arguing that discharging this responsibility adequately rests on understanding *difference*. Suppression of difference obscures diversity, thus constructing political engagements on the basis of the dominant culture, imposing a discipline centred on "sameness" and thus "deny[ing] recognition" (Fraser, 2000, p. 109) of the other. To be effective in practice, differences have to be respected; but at the same time a system of transversal politics (Yuval-Davis, 1997) can be implemented, whereby women and members of other groups from different constituencies may remain rooted in their own membership and identity, while at the same time being prepared to shift into a position of exchange with those from different groups with different interests in pursuit of a common agenda.

Fung and Wright (2001) suggest that these sorts of alternative, cooperative community decision-making deepen democratic processes – they use the term "Empowered Deliberative Democracy" – by engaging people with a myriad of technical skills, community commitment and access to resources in a consensus-based decision-making process. There are similarities here with the autonomous organizing discussed above and a Freirean dialogical pedagogy of gender conscientization; an essential ingredient of the gender challenge to traditional trade unionism on the road towards a gender politics of inclusion and equity.

Women's agency: Individual and collective strategies

Meanwhile, however, although gender conscientization of women moving into activist and leader positions is essential, on its own it is not sufficient. Building a "capacity to" element into our model, we draw on a proposal by Sue Ledwith (2009) about the development of a feminist/gender counter-hegemony which seeks to challenge and then shift the axis of masculine hegemonic control in trade unions. Taking a Gramscian approach, this involves two groups of intellectuals/thinkers: "movement activists", including feminist and sister-traveller activists in trade unions, communities, social movements, NGOs and civil society; and "movement thinkers", including gender and feminist researchers and activists engaging with and working with trade unionists in gender and labour movements locally, nationally and internationally, and in a range of ways, such as joint research projects, round tables and international e-networking. Our GLU gender and trade unions research group encompasses both, and thus is an active contributor to this gender and trade unions counter-hegemonic project.

Research methods and issues

Our methods triangulate, involving a range of quantitative and qualitative data collection tools. For the quantitative data we developed a series of templates to be completed by colleagues in their own countries, as far as possible. These covered labour markets broken down by gender, between full- and part-time workers, and between private and public sectors. The resulting data are inconsistent but sufficient to give us a broad picture at this stage, as well as identifying gaps.

Others also have such problems – as the European Industrial Relations Observatory comments, such a process "is also sometimes contentious and sensitive for unions themselves, and features numerous methodological and conceptual problems" (Carley, 2009, p. 2) – for instance, how trade unions and union membership are defined and how the data are gathered. Such issues make the examination of national trade union membership figures problematic; the difficulties are magnified when an international comparison is attempted, and again when we ask for gender breakdowns.

To try to overcome these problems we developed a second series of templates to collect data about gender and trade unionism: these addressed gender proportions in membership and in a range of leadership positions, and attendance as delegates at conferences. In addition, we collected information about trade union equality structures and positions. Since the numbers alone do not tell the full story about the social and political struggles confronting women in unions, we also carried out individual and group interviews that enabled us to interact directly with women activists, especially those in union leadership positions. In a smaller but more detailed study in three countries, colleagues examined the Bargaining Agenda for Gender (BAG): we are aware of the potential for change here that can flow from having women in leadership roles.

Using these methods, we found that even just asking the questions in our own unions can be a powerful move in challenging the inertia of the status quo. In Nigeria, for example, GLU colleague Joel Odigie reported that no gender data had been collected, but in future the Nigerian Labour Congress (NLC) will be collecting data by gender – because he asked the question.

Further, as a response to the unreliability of gender data, our GLU gender and trade unions research group (RG) has set up its own database. This will collect gender information from our RG members across six continents and 11 or more countries, with the intention of providing regular reliable data over time. We intend to publish this annually, initially on the GLU website,[2] and see its potential as a powerful tool to mark out gendered space in international labour movements. It is a tangible example of, initially, "capacity to", with the potential of moving to a position of "power to", changing the debates about gender and visibility in trade unions. It is also a mark of the unique capacity of the GLU RG members who, as union insiders, are able to access union information through a range of channels and methods. Likewise, by publishing this initial account of power and gender in our unions, we can see the RG members as both "movement activists" and "movement thinkers", actively challenging traditional union oligarchy and hegemony. Group members, in addition to their varied positions within the trade union research nexus, operate within the feminist position that insists on connecting theory to practice. Our participation in this research group has affirmed our political commitment to a gendered and feminist agenda for change.

Findings

Notwithstanding the gaps in our data, in all the countries in our study increasing proportions of women can be seen to be moving into work and into trade union membership. Even when overall unemployment increases women's work, often shifting it to part-time work, their labour force participation tends to hold up, along with their union membership. Within this general pattern, union membership is generally more robust in public sectors and service work in both formal and informal sectors, largely as a result of the predominance of women working in the "five Cs" noted above.

In almost all the countries covered by our research, female union densities were lower than male, ranging from a low of 8 per cent in the Republic of Korea to a high of 46 per cent in Australia, where the female presence in the public sector is high and growing. There were also sectoral differences: as colleagues Boniface Phiri and Crispen Chinguno report respectively from Zambia and Zimbabwe, women teachers make up just over half their unions' membership, although they do not reach proportionality in senior positions. Nevertheless, among women in Zambia, participation in the union is increasing, largely due to growing awareness of women's rights. Generally there was higher density of union membership among women in the industrialized countries of the global North. This is not surprising, since women are highly concentrated in precarious work and informal sectors, especially in the global South, where trade union organization is weak.

Table 3.1   Percentages of women on trade union decision-making
bodies, 2009

Country	Union	Percentage of women in:				
		Membership	National executive	National council	National conference	Conference delegations
Brazil	CONTRAF/ CUT	53	0	50	29	36
Canada	CUPE	67	–	13	51	51
Ghana	GTUC	30	20	33	–	–
Republic of Korea	KCTU	27	10	28	28	–
Zambia	ZaCTU	–	0	0	–	–
	ZNUT	52	–	–	–	–
Zimbabwe	ZiCTU	20	33	17	–	–
	ZIMTA	52	33	27	27	27

Key: CONTRAF/CUT: Bank workers' union confederation, Rio de Janeiro; CUPE: Canadian Union of Public Employees; GTUC: Ghana Trades Union Congress; KCTU: Korea Confederation of Trade Unions; ZCTU: ZaCTU: Zambia Congress of Trade Unions; ZNUT: Zambia National Union of Teachers; ZiCTU: Zimbabwe Congress of Trade Unions; ZIMTA: Zimbabwe Teachers Union.

Data from our countries clearly show women's lack of proportional representation in positions of power in trade unions, in spite of the policies of gender equality formally espoused by their unions. Women are generally missing from top trade union leadership positions irrespective of the proportion of membership they constitute. Thus, trade unions with a majority of women members are just as likely as trade unions with a minority of women members to have few women in leadership positions. Table 3.1 shows, for example, that the Canadian public sector union CUPE and teachers' unions in Zambia and Zimbabwe all had predominantly female memberships and yet had only a minority of women in decision-making roles. Of all the unions covered in our study, CUPE had the highest proportion of female membership (67 per cent); yet women constituted only 51 per cent of conference delegates and filled just 13 per cent of union leadership roles. In the Zimbabwean teachers' union ZIMTA women made up just 33 per cent of the national executive and 27 per cent of conference delegates.

There were instances where the proportion of women in leadership positions was slightly higher than the proportion of women in the membership. This was the case in Ghana and the Republic of Korea, where success had been achieved through affirmative action provisions. Women were, however, in the minority in conference delegations in all the unions studied except CUPE.

In respect of the particular positions occupied (see table 3.2), the Republic of Korea and Zimbabwe were exceptional in having women holding high union office at

Table 3.2 Senior office-holders in selected trade unions and confederations, by gender, with percentages for women

Country	Union	Union position										
		President	Vice-President	Treasurer/Trustee	General Secretary	Assistant/Deputy Secretary	Lead Organizer	Education	Provincial/regional leaders	Local/branch representatives	Other officers	Union staff
Brazil	CONTRA/CUT	M	M	M	M	–	M	–	–	–	2W, 40%	–
	CONTRAF/CUT	M	M	W	M	M	M	M	–	–	2W, 25%	–
Canada	CUPE	–	–	–	–	–	–	–	1W, 10%	48% W	–	–
Ghana	GTUC	M	M	–	M	M	–	M	–	–	–	–
Korea, Rep. of	KCTU	M	2W, 50%	3W, 50%	M	M	4W, 22%	2W, 50%	–	–	15W, 32%	–
South Africa[1]	COSATU 19% leaders women	M	M	W	M	M[2]	–	10% W	11% W	–	Organizers: 22% W	–
Turkey[3]	–	–	–	–	–	–	–	–	13W, 7.6%	–	70W, 10.8%	–
United Kingdom[4]	TUC	M	–	–	M	W	–	W	–	–	–	55% W
Zambia	ZaCTU	M	M	2W, 50%	M	–	–	–	–	–	–	–
	ZNUT	M	M	1W, 25%	M	1W, 50%	–	–	–	–	–	–
Zimbabwe	ZiCTU	M	2W, 33%	M	M	M	M [CEO]	W	–	–	3W, 30%	24W[5], 49%
	ZIMTA	M	W	M	M	M	M	–	1W, 11%	–	2W[5], 22%	15W[6], 27%

Key: CONTRA/CUT: National Confederation Financial Sector Workers; CONTRAF/CUT: Bank workers' union confederation, Rio de Janeiro; CUPE: Canadian Union of Public Employees; GTUC: Ghana Trades Union Congress; KCTU: Korea Confederation of Trade Unions; COSATU: Confederation of South African Trade Unions; TUC: Trades Union Congress; ZaCTJ: Zambia Congress of Trade Unions; ZNUT: Zambia National Union of Teachers; ZiCTU: Zimbabwe Congress of Trade Unions; ZIMTA: Zimbabwe Teachers Union.

Notes:

M = male; F = female.

[1] Gender Report to the COSATU National Conference March 2012; Tsomondo 2011. [2] First deputy president is M. Second deputy president is W. [3] National data compiled from 2009 statistics of the Ministry of Labour and Social Security of Turkey. [4] See TUC 2011 Equality Audit. [5] Women employed by ZiCTU are mainly support staff. Of 11 heads of departments, seven are men and four women. [6] One woman is the AIDS coordinator.

51

confederation level as vice-presidents. Women in leadership positions were, however, more likely to be in subordinate roles such as treasurer or organizer (CONTRAF/CUT, KCTU and ZiCTU). It was notable that in some unions/confederations seats were reserved for women, but only as secondary office-holder: in Ghana, for example, Akua Britwum reported that the second vice-chairperson must be a woman, a provision that generates the assumption that this is as high as a woman can aspire.

In South Africa, too, Constance Tsomondo (2011) confirms that union gender representation reproduces women's labour market position, with women mainly found in education, health, and commercial and catering services. Women are scarce in union leaderships, occupying only 19 per cent of leadership positions by 2004; even in unions where the majority of members are women, those in influential positions are still mostly male. Women are mainly found as administrators, positions that lack influence and are not involved in policy-making, whereas men are the organizers and office-bearers.

Union equality structures

As can be seen in table 3.3, all the unions covered had in place some form of equality structures: in all cases there were national women's committees, and in five regional or local women's committees as well. Most also had national women's conferences. In Brazil the banking unions also had structures for other forms of inequality, relating to race, ethnicity and disability. In three countries (Brazil, Ghana, Nigeria) there were 30 per cent women's quotas.

The existence of women's equality structures, however, does not guarantee an automatic promotion of women's interests in their trade unions, or their resourcing. When we asked about the effectiveness of these measures, only in Brazil and the Republic of Korea were they found to be effective. In the case of the Brazilian bank workers' union CONTRAF/CUT, Jo Portilho reports that the women's structures had been able to exert pressure for the inclusion of equality provisions in all collective agreements of the union, while Kim Mijeoung writes that in the Republic of Korea the promotion of women's structures at confederation level has filtered down to all the affiliate industrial unions. The position of women's structures in the remaining unions, however, is best captured in the pronouncements of interviewees who described them as "moribund" and unable to challenge the male hegemony in the union. "Most do not function nationally – no meetings are held." The ineffectiveness in two African cases was attributed to the fact that the "women's structures have no budget".[3]

Table 3.4 shows the main barriers impeding women in their unions, and the successes that have been achieved. The barriers can be summarized as emerging mainly from what the report from Zambia described as the "hardwired" masculine and patriarchal union culture which encouraged sexual harassment, male hostility towards women, resistance and men's unwillingness to share power, while also contributing to

Table 3.3   Women and trade union equality structures, 2009

Country	Union	National women's officer	National women's committee	National women's conference	Targets for women's representation	Regional/local women's committees	Gender policy
Brazil	CONTRA/ CUT	N	Y[1]	–	Y[2]	–	–
	CONTRAF/ CUT	N	Y[3]	–	Y[4]	–	–
Canada	CUPE	–	Y[5]	Y	N	–	–
Ghana	GTUC	Y	Y	Y	Y[6]	Y	Y
Korea, Rep. of	KCTU	Y	Y	Y	Y	–	–
Nigeria	NLC	Y	Y	Y	Y[7]	Y	Y
South Africa[8]	COSATU	Y[9]	Y	Y	–	–	Y
United Kingdom[10]	TUC	Y	Y	Y	Y	–	Y
Zambia	ZaCTU	Y[11]	Y	–	–	–	Y
	ZNUT	–	Y	Y	–	Y	Y
Zimbabwe	ZiCTU	Y	Y	Y	Y	Y	–
	ZIMTA	Y	Y	Y	Y	–	–

Key: CONTRA/CUT: National Confederation Financial Sector Workers; CONTRAF/CUT: Bank workers' union confederation, Rio de Janeiro; CUPE: Canadian Union of Public Employees; GTUC: Ghana Trades Union Congress; KCTU: Korea Confederation of Trade Unions; NLC: Nigerian Labour Congress; COSATU: Confederation of South African Trade Unions; TUC: Trades Union Congress; ZaCTU: Zambia Congress of Trade Unions; ZNUT: Zambia National Union of Teachers; ZiCTU: Zimbabwe Congress of Trade Unions; ZIMTA: Zimbabwe Teachers Union.

Notes: [1] Made up of national commission of gender, race, sexuality and disability. [2] 30 per cent quota for women for affiliates and confederation. [3] Made up of national commission of gender, race, sexuality and disability. [4] Target available for membership on the National Executive Council. [5] National Equality Committee. [6] 30 per cent quota in all union events and reserved seat; second vice-chairperson. [7] 30 per cent quota and special seat. [8] Source: Tsomondo, 2011. [9] Titles are "gender" throughout. [10] Source: TUC, 2011. Affiliates vary, e.g. quite often the national structures and officers encompass other diversity groups, defined by e.g. race/ethnicity. All the largest unions have structures for ethnicity/race, disability and sexuality as well as women. [11] Gender desk.

women's perception that union leadership positions were really only for men. Females were deemed not to be real union leaders. The most frequently recurring barrier identified was the belief that union leadership was a male preserve. From this culture flowed problems for women such as the lack of union education programmes and the practice of holding union meetings outside working hours, which then impinged on women's "domestic burden". This was a particular problem in the case of the Zambian teachers' union, where, although women formed a majority of the membership, they were not yet in a position to gain access to power. The responsibilities of the home were raised several times as a major barrier to women's participation, hammered home by the absence of support for women in this role.

Table 3.4   Successes and barriers for women in their unions

Country	Union	Barriers	Successes
Canada	CUPE		Data on gender, race, ethnicity and disability
Ghana	GTUC	Male hostility and resistance Sexual harassment Women's domestic burden Apathy Women's value of usefulness of unions Distance between women and their union	Gender quotas and special seats Gender desk Gender policy Women's committees
Republic of Korea	KCTU	Patriarchal culture Men unwilling to share power No trade union course for women No support for women as caregivers	TU gender quota system Monitoring and review Women's committees in all affiliates; quotas for education and training
Nigeria	NLC	Lack of political will Male resistance	Special seats Quotas for education and training Women's committees
Philippines	Survey across several unions	Time Women's domestic responsibilities	Assuring women's representation in union decision-making Women's committees Quotas for women in leadership positions Appointment of gender equality officers
Turkey	Interviews and discussions with women outside the workplace	Anti-women legislation Male-dominant union structures Women's low labour market participation Sexual division of labour at home	Increase in the number of unionized women in some sectors, e.g. health services Greater media coverage of women in unions
Zambia	ZNUT	Union constitutional provisions Dominant perception that union positions are male	Women's committees Gender policy
Zimbabwe	ZiCTU ZIMTA	Holding union meetings outside work hours	

Key: CUPE: Canadian Union of Public Employees; GTUC: Ghana Trades Union Congress; KCTU: Korea Confederation of Trade Unions; NLC: Nigerian Labour Congress; ZNUT: Zambia National Union of Teachers; ZiCTU: Zimbabwe Congress of Trade Unions; ZIMTA: Zimbabwe Teachers Union.

It is perhaps striking that these barriers can be interpreted as emerging from collective masculine power resources, including economic power (lack of support systems for women), positional and symbolic power (which maintains men in senior roles), and sexual resources (especially sexual harassment and sexual bribery: what is often described by African women as 'pull her down' sexual politics). Conversely, it is women as individuals who have to cope with what is often experienced as powerlessness. However, when we look at the successes achieved – affirmative action provisions such as quotas and special seats for women in union decision-making structures, women's committees backed by gender policies and units – these have all been the result of women acting collectively to push their unions to put these in place, sometimes in alliances with powerful men. Even so, as our male colleague reports from Zambia, the Women's Committee has been in existence for over a decade, which brings its effectiveness into question. In addition, not all national unions have created gender desks to support and provide technical expertise to the women's committees, except at the federation (ZaCTU).

There is a general view that women's committees remain isolated and sometimes parallel to the main union structures they are intended to integrate with. They are still perceived as typical "women's structures", largely used for campaigns and appeasement rather than for integrating women into the mainstream. The women's committees are run by women and all their activities exclusively target women, which further works to isolate them. In some cases, the committees have no specific budgetary allocations and are funded on an ad hoc basis.

Unions and the Bargaining Agenda for Gender (BAG)

Since we are interested in making the links between gender and unions and the impact of union activity on the material working lives of the female membership, we also examined collective bargaining agendas – what we call the Bargaining Agenda for Gender or "BAG". We wanted to see what was in that BAG beyond women's pay and conditions of work. In discussing the BAG we need to differentiate between what was on the bargaining agenda, what actually reached the bargaining table, and what did or did not end up in agreements about women's pay and conditions at work.

The BAG reports cover only three countries: Canada, the Philippines and Turkey. Nevertheless, the detailed research undertaken, particularly in the Philippines and in Turkey, provides some revealing insights.

Canada

The Canadian research by Patricia Chong concerned CUPE, the country's biggest public sector union. CUPE's efforts at bringing women's issues on to the union bargaining agenda were the result of a two-year membership consultation by its

National Women's Task Force. Over 7,000 members were asked about the "status of women in our workplaces, society and within the union" through surveys and face-to-face discussions. The report produced as a result of the consultation was presented at the 2007 CUPE national convention.[4] There were 54 recommendations, grouped into the following six categories:

- bargaining to support women;

- applying equality throughout the union;

- education and training for women;

- leadership development for women;

- more effective union meetings and ways to involve members;

- creating a more representative union structure.

This survey was followed two years later with a Women's Equality Conference with the twin goals of building "bargaining strength to advance women's equality" and setting "achievable goals on bargaining issues for women" (CUPE, 2008). The conference report, "Recipes for setting the table: Getting what you want in bargaining", highlighted areas considered "critical for women's equality", which covered minimum pay, job retention, pensions, work–life balance, and elimination of violence and harassment in the workplace (CUPE, 2009, p. 1).

In addition, CUPE creatively provides a recipe for achieving equality in these areas through an ingredients list of information and "a bowl of facts", about workplace issues, and concludes with recommendations as to how to build collective strength. It also offers "Recipes for setting the table: Collective agreement language", a collection of terminology actually used in union contracts, gathered from various localities, on issues affecting women such as "child rearing", "pensionable service", "violence in the workplace", "employment equity" and "flexible hours". There is also a collection of materials for members presented under the title "Bargaining equality: A workplace for all", covering issues such as disability, harassment and violence that are of particular concern to groups of marginalized women like Aboriginal and LGBT workers.[5]

The CUPE research, then, gave us information on who decided what was to go in the BAG, and how it could be negotiated. We have to move to the Philippines to find out more about what happens at the negotiating table, and afterwards.

Philippines

Our research colleagues in the Philippines, Ramon Certeza and Melisa Serrano, carried out a large questionnaire survey, and interviewed seven officers of national federations and 12 local union leaders. Their findings identified how advances in the promotion and protection of women's rights have resulted from several interacting factors:

a strong women's movement; legislation promoting gender equality and rights of women (e.g. law on anti-sexual harassment); and a strong ILO gender and women's rights programme. These have combined to impact on women's involvement in collective bargaining. Their BAG study found that the top three items on women's list of demands were maternity leave, pay equality and menstrual leave. The downside was that these three priorities were also among the top six items which were most likely to be traded off for other bargaining proposals. The survey showed that women were a minority in union bargaining teams, comprising only 20 per cent of team membership. About 70 per cent of the unions responding to the study had no provisions to ensure that women were represented on their bargaining teams. As a result, unions with bargaining teams led by men tended to focus more on wage increases and other direct economic measures in the collective agreement and were less likely to see gender-/women-related proposals as important.

In the absence of a strong BAG presence, employers were highly likely to resist agreeing to provisions that they saw as costs, such as menstrual leave, special leave for women, day-care services and facilities, pay equality, breastfeeding facilities and maternity leave beyond what is stipulated by law. It will therefore be in management's interests to resist, or at least not encourage, the incorporation of women in bargaining teams. Except for reproductive health and protection against sexual harassment, all other gender-/women-related proposals in collective bargaining were always traded off by the union against other bargaining proposals. Protection against sexual harassment, and, to a lesser extent, reproductive health and equality of opportunities for training and education, are likely to be less costly and to offer opportunities for direct payback.

However, women's absence from direct BAG negotiations did not deprive them of the chance to influence the content of issues covered in union bargaining. Their active participation in organizing drives increased the likelihood of their demands being featured in union bargaining agendas: there are many Philippine unions that have strong gender equality programmes at the workplace, and reproductive health is one of the issues that some unions are pursuing through their national agendas.

Turkey

In Turkey the difficulties involved in accessing women in their unions or at the workplace, in part owing to anti-union legislation, led our researcher, Gaye Yilmaz, to organize small tea parties in cafes where the women could freely discuss their concerns. Her report concerns women leaders in the health sector, where women predominate. Although in Turkey there is a framework of legal rights which includes protection for pregnant women, maternity leave for female workers, paid time off for nursing/breastfeeding, and mandatory provision in workplaces with over 100 women employees for babies and children up to the age of six, in practice these are not always implemented. Among Turkish unions interest in pressing for these rights varies. KESK, the only one of the three main confederations which is seen as gender sensitive, and also as a militant union, has scored notable success: for example, it has doubled the time off for mothers nursing babies for up to four months, and increased the time off for caring for infants to six months. Women have a weak presence in Turkish union negotiating teams: all but five of the women reported that there were no women represented on negotiating teams, and they strongly supported change.

Discussion and conclusions

While the data reported here are partial and concern a range of not always comparable material, nevertheless we think there is sufficient evidence to provide a basis for examining gender power relations in the unions covered in our study.

These relations are complex and comprise a fluid set of interactions involving labour market positions of women and men, union structures, culture and ideologies, individual and collective agency, and the ability to access and use power resources. These relations ebb and flow as forces for women come up against powerful male hegemonic resistance.

We can see the influence of differing labour market positions in the global South and North, whereby higher union density in countries like Australia, Canada and the United Kingdom reflect a greater female presence in formal labour markets. Although women's relative position in their own labour markets may be circumscribed and increasingly precarious, nevertheless there is in these countries a longer history of industrialization, unionization and feminization, facilitating the construction of sophisticated gender and equality structures and bargaining frameworks. In countries of the global South, where a strong presence in the informal labour market and the absence of rights are the norm for women, their task is harder and the road longer.

Nevertheless, in some of the more precarious places the combination of women's agency and the resources of external donors from the global North supporting women's projects – as in Ghana – offers a model of how such coalitions can muster sufficient power resources to counter the inertia of homosocial masculinity. In Ghanaian unions such alliances have been able to put in place comprehensive gender structures and support mechanisms such as women's education programmes, both developing a gender consciousness among women and enabling them to move into leadership positions. In the Philippines such external influences were also significant. There, advances for women are the result of several interacting forces, including a strong women's movement, legislative rights and a strong external ILO gender programme. Development of such measures has provided space, visibility and voice for women, which, together with a growing awareness of women's rights, represent significant accumulations of and strategic use of women's power resources to address the democratic gender deficit.

Structural gains are also evident in a number of cases where collective agency is at play internally. In Brazil and the Republic of Korea affirmative action programmes such as gender leadership quotas have been established. In addition, radical union ideologies have been important both in motivating the establishment of gender structures and in achieving material outcomes – as in Brazil, and in Turkey where the militant union KESK is seen as gender sensitive and has made gains for mothers in provision for the care of their babies and infants.

There is another important issue that needs raising, even though our research was not specifically aiming to discuss it: namely, when women do reach senior roles, are those women buying into the gender agenda? Other research shows that this is not necessarily the case, for although women are elected into reserved positions, it is not realistic to see women as a single interest group always supporting feminist or gender agendas (Colgan and Ledwith, 2000). Also, they are not usually elected only by women, and are likely in their positions to represent a broader constituency of both women and men. Research has shown that if oppressed social groups are to gain real power, there is an additional need for gender political consciousness among women office-holders and new radical democratic frameworks (McBride, 2001). Political knowledge and skills can be developed at women's courses – although our research found that these were often not available – and within women's groups, as discussed above, which may also provide the springboard for radical strategies.

Action research is in itself a powerful method of consciousness raising and indeed organizing. Several of the research team found that by setting up meetings and asking questions they were able to pass on information, for example about bargaining rights. This form of empowerment is also an important way of developing gender democracy from below, among grass-roots and community groupings. As we saw, women interviewees in the Philippines discovered for the first time, from the researchers, what their union gender policy was in relation to collective bargaining. In Turkey the women had not previously thought about the possible impact of having women in negotiating teams, nor were they aware that such teams might by right be gender balanced. The women told our colleagues how helpful the research had been: the questions posed had helped them to think about gender issues more than they had ever done previously. In Canada, CUPE is vocalizing the importance of the gender discourse and claiming the language of gendered workplace demands.

Against such gains, however, must be weighed the power of masculinized resistance. In some countries, economic power has been used to block budget allocations for women's education. In others, women's advances in union structures have been limited to certain secondary positions, reinforcing beliefs among both women and men that real leadership is a male preserve, and women's is the domestic sphere. A further significant inhibitor that circumscribes women's position and role is that based on the discourse that women's self-organizing prevents their integration into the union mainstream, as so forcefully expressed in the Zambian case, for example. It includes "hardwired" masculine and patriarchal union cultures which encourage the "pull her down" syndrome when women reach positions of power. In collective bargaining, too, where a third party, the (usually male-dominated) employer, is present, there is a pincer movement, even collusion, between the accumulated power of the masculinized union and the employer. In such circumstances the malestream power in sexual politics is stronger than the forces of collective women's agency.

These power resources are fluid and unstable, and our study has shown how gender resistance and challenges both open up and limit the spaces for women. While some gender gaps may have been closing, male hegemony has managed to hold on to power in both structure and culture in unions. Yet there is evidence from the study that, where radical union ideology combines with women's collective agency in a counter-hegemonic journey, an inclusive "power with" approach can recognize difference and can address the democratic gender deficit. It is this dialectic that could open up further space both to women's capacity for power and to the ability of unions to develop gender solidarity in the face of global neoliberalism, which increasingly oppresses and impoverishes both women and men. While this may sound overly optimistic, we see it as the greatest challenge for twenty-first-century labour movements.

Acknowledgements

As the writers of this chapter, we wish to acknowledge the continuing input, as well as the formal reports already compiled, from the whole research team, with special thanks to Patricia Chong who got the team going and coordinated so much of the work:

Australia	Karen Douglas
Brazil	Jo Portilho
Canada	Patricia Chong
Ghana	Akua Britwum
Republic of Korea	Kim Mijeoung
Nigeria	Joel Odigie
Philippines	Ramon Certeza, Melisa Serrano
South Africa	Janet Munakamwe
Turkey	Gaye Yilmaz
United Kingdom	Sue Ledwith
Zambia	Boniface Phiri
Zimbabwe	Crispen Chinguno

We also thank all our union colleagues who so readily completed questionnaires, answered questions and took part in discussions. We hope they will be able to use our findings to further the gender project in their unions.

Notes

[1] See the list of contributors at the end of this chapter.

[2] http://www.global-labour-university.org [accessed 4 June 2012].

[3] Reports from Crispen Chinguno, Zimbabwe, and Boniface Phiri, Zambia.

[4] http://cupe.ca/nwtf [accessed 2 June 2012].

[5] http://cupe.ca/bargeq [accessed 2 June 2012].

References

Berger, B. 2005. "Power over, power with, and power to relations: Critical reflections on public relations, the dominant coalition, and activism", in *Journal of Public Relations Research*, Vol. 17, No. 1, pp. 5–28.

Bradley, H. 2007. *Gender* (Cambridge, Polity Press).

Briskin, L. 1993. "Union women and separate organizing", in L. Briskin and P. McDermott (eds): *Women challenging unions* (Toronto, University of Toronto Press), pp. 89–108.

—. 2012. "Merit, individualism and solidarity: Revisiting the democratic deficit in union women's leadership", in S. Ledwith and L. Hansen (eds): *Gendering and diversifying union leadership* (London, Routledge).

Britwum, A. 2010. "Reconciling class and patriarchy: Female unionists and union governance in Ghana", in Ghana Research Advocacy Programme (G-RAP), *Experiences, contesting spaces, renewing commitments* (Accra). Available at: http://www.g-rap.org/docs/gender/gender_forum_2010/britwum_ao-01.pdf [30 May 2012].

Broomhill, R.; Sharp, R. 2005. "The changing male breadwinner model in Australia: A new gender order?", in *Labour and Industry*, Vol. 16, No. 1, pp. 103–27.

Burrell, G. 1992. "Sex and organizational analysis", in A. Mills and P. Tancred (eds): *Gendering organizational analysis* (London, Sage), pp. 71–92.

Çağatay, N.; Erturk, K. 2004. *Gender and globalization: A macroeconomic perspective*. Working Paper No. 19, Policy Integration Department, World Commission on the Social Dimension of Globalization (Geneva, International Labour Office).

Canadian Union of Public Employees (CUPE). 2008. "Setting the table: Bargaining women's Equality Conference", 15 Sep. Available at: http://cupe.ca/bargaining/nbc [2 June 2012].

—. 2009. "Recipes for setting the table: Getting what you want in bargaining", Feb. Available at: http://cupe.ca/updir/Recipes_for_Setting_the_Table.pdf [2 June 2012].

Carley, M. 2009. *Trade union membership 2003–2008* (Dublin, European Industrial Relations Observatory (EIRO)). Available at http://www.eurofound.europa.eu/docs/eiro/tn0904019s/tn0904019s.pdf or http://www.eurofound.europa.eu/eiro/studies/tn0904019s/tn0904019s.htm#hd1 [30 May 2012].

Cass, B. 1995. "Gender in Australia's restructuring labour market and welfare state", in A. Edwards and S. Magarey (eds): *Women in a restructuring Australia* (Sydney, Allen & Unwin), pp. 38–59.

Chapman, A. 2005. "Work/family, Australian labour law, and the normative worker", in J. Conaghan and K. Rittich (eds): *Labour law, work, and family: Critical and comparative perspectives* (Oxford, Oxford University Press), pp. 79–97.

Colgan, F.; Ledwith, S. 2000. "Diversity, identities and strategies of women trade union activists", in *Gender, Work and Organization*, Vol. 7, No. 4, Oct., pp. 242–57.

Connell, R. 1996. "New directions in gender theory, masculinity research and gender politics", in *Ethnos*, Vol. 61, Nos. 3–4, pp. 157–76.

Cornfield, D. 1993. "Integrating US labour leadership, union democracy and the ascent of ethnic and racial minorities and women into national union offices", in *Research in Sociology of Organizations*, Vol. 12, pp. 51–74.

Creese, G. 1999. *Contracting masculinity: Gender, class, and race in a white-collar union, 1944–1994* (Toronto, Oxford University Press).

Curtin, J. 1999. *Women and trade unions: A comparative perspective* (Aldershot, Ashgate).

Deslippe, D. 2000. *Rights not roses: Unions and the rise of working class feminism 1945–80* (Champaign, IL, University of Illinois Press).

Dufour, C.; Adelheid, H. 2010. "The legitimacy of collective actors and trade union renewal", in *Transfer: European Review of Labour and Research*, Vol. 16, No. 3, pp. 351–67.

European Trade Union Confederation (ETUC). 2011. *4th Annual ETUC 8 March Survey 2011.* Available at: http://www.etuc.org/IMG/pdf/8_March11_analysis_FINAL_EN.pdf [4 June 2012].

Foucault, M. 1979. *The history of sexuality*, Vol. 1 (London, Allen Lane).

Franzway, S. 2001. *Sexual politics and greedy institutions* (Melbourne, Pluto Press).

—; Fonow, M.M. 2009. "Queer activism, feminism and the transnational labor movement", in *The Scholar and Feminist Online*, Barnard Center for Research on Women, Vol. 7, No. 3, Summer, pp. 1–9. Available at: http://www.barnard.edu/sfonline [30 May 2012].

Fraser, N. 2000. "Rethinking recognition", in *New Left Review*, No. 3, May–June, pp. 107–20.

Fudge, J.; Owens, R. 2006. *Precarious work, women, and the new economy* (Oxford, Hart).

Fung, A.; Wright, E.O. 2001. "Deepening democracy: Innovations in empowered participatory governance", in *Politics and Society*, Vol. 29, No. 1, March, pp. 5–41.

Healy, G.; Kirton, G. 2000. "Women, power and trade union government in the UK", in *British Journal of Industrial Relations*, Vol. 38, No. 3, pp. 343–60.

International Labour Office (ILO); International Confederation of Free Trade Unions (ICFTU). 1999. *The role of trade unions in promoting gender equality and protecting vulnerable women workers*, First Report of the ILO–ICFTU Survey (Geneva, ILO).

International Union of Food, Agricultural, Hotel, Restaurant, Catering, Tobacco and Allied Workers' Associations (IUF). n.d. Available at: http://www.iuf.org [30 May 2012].

Kainer, J. 2006. *Gendering union renewal: Women's contributions to labour movement revitalization*, Gender and Work Database. Available at: http://www.genderwork.ca [10 June 2012].

Kelly, J.; Heery, E. 1994. *Working for the union* (Cambridge, Cambridge University Press).

Kirton, G.; Healy, G. 1999. "Transforming union women: The role of women trade union officials in union renewal", in *Industrial Relations Journal*, Vol. 30, No. 1, March, pp. 31–45.

—; —. 2004. "Shaping union and gender identities: A case study of women-only trade union courses", in *British Journal of Industrial Relations*, Vol. 42, No. 2, pp. 303–24.

Ledwith, S. 2009. "Encounters between gender and labour politics: Towards an inclusive trade union democracy", in M. Ozbilgin (ed.): *Equality, diversity and inclusion at work* (Cheltenham, UK, Edward Elgar), pp. 272–86.

Levesque, C.; Murray, G. 2010. "Understanding union power: Resources and capabilities for renewing union capacity", in *Transfer: European Review of Labour and Research*, Vol. 16, No. 3, pp. 333–50.

Lukes, S. 1974. *Power: A radical view* (London, Macmillan).

McBride, A. 2001. "Making it work: Supporting group representation in a liberal democratic organization", in *Gender, Work and Organization*, Vol. 8, No. 4, Oct., pp. 411–29.

Moore, S. 2011. *New trade union activism* (Basingstoke, Palgrave Macmillan).

Parker, J. 2003. *Women's groups and equality in British trade unions* (Lampeter: Edwin Mellen).

—. 2006. "Towards equality and renewal: Women's groups, diversity and democracy in British unions", in *Economic and Industrial Democracy*, Vol. 27, No. 3, Aug., pp. 425–62.

—; Douglas, J. 2010. "Can women's structures help New Zealand and UK trade unions' revival?", in *Journal of Industrial Relations*, Vol. 52, No. 4, pp. 439–58.

Pillinger, J. 2010. *From membership to leadership: Advancing women in trade unions. A resource guide* (Brussels, European Trade Union Confederation).

Self Employed Women's Association (SEWA). n.d. Available at: http://www.sewa.org/ [30 May 2012].

Standing, G. 2011. *The precariat: The new dangerous class* (London, Bloomsbury).

Trades Union Congress (TUC). 2011. *TUC Equality Audit 2011* (London).

Tsomondo, C. 2011. *"Struggling to get the position and struggling to keep it": How women become trade union leaders*, MA thesis, GLU, University of the Witwatersrand, Johannesburg.

Vosko, L. 2010. *Managing the margins: Gender, citizenship, and the international regulation of precarious employment* (Oxford, Oxford University Press).

Voss, K. 2010. "Democratic dilemmas: Union democracy and union renewal", in *Transfer: European Review of Labour and Research*, Vol. 16, No. 3, pp. 369–82.

—; Sherman, R. 2000. "Breaking the iron law of oligarchy: Union revitalization in the American labor movement", in *American Journal of Sociology*, Vol. 106, No. 2, Sep., pp. 303–49.

Williams, C. 2007. "Masculinities and emotion work in trade unions", in F. Colgan and S. Ledwith (eds): *Gender, diversity and trade unions: International perspectives*, digital ed. (London, Routledge), pp. 292–311.

Yates, C. 2006. "Challenging misconceptions about organizing women into unions", in *Gender, Work and Organization*, Vol. 13, No. 6, Nov., pp. 565–84.

—. 2010. "Understanding caring, organizing women: How framing a problem shapes union", *Transfer: European Review of Labour and Research*, Vol. 16, No. 3, pp. 399–410.

Young, B. 2005. "Globalisation and shifting gender governance order(s)", in *Sowi-online*, No. 2. Available at http://www.jsse.org/2005/2005-2/pdf/globalization-young.pdf [27 June 2012].

Young, I.M. 1990. *Justice and the politics of difference* (Princeton, N.J, Princeton University Press).

—, 2002. *Inclusion and democracy* (Oxford, Oxford University Press).

Yuval-Davis, N. 1997. *Gender and nation* (London, Sage).

LOCAL GOVERNMENT CALL CENTRES: CHALLENGE OR OPPORTUNITY FOR SOUTH AFRICAN LABOUR?

4

Babalwa Magoqwana and Sandra Matatu

Introduction

The South African call centre industry has been steadily growing over the years. Fostered as a means of curbing escalating unemployment, the industry was predicted to contribute more than 100,000 jobs (directly and indirectly) to the national economy by 2009 (TradeInvestSA, 2007). A 2007 report by the Global Call-centre Industry Project at the University of the Witwatersrand revealed that South Africa's call centres are concentrated in Johannesburg (51.8 per cent), followed by Cape Town (38 per cent), Durban (7.9 per cent) and then the Eastern Cape Province (1.6 per cent) (Benner, Lewis and Omar, 2007). It also reported that only 25 per cent of these call centres surveyed were unionized, a lower figure than the international average of 40 per cent unionization of call centres. These unionized call centres offered better working conditions and higher wages (Benner, Lewis and Omar, 2007). Public service call centres tend to be unionized and small and to handle inbound calls, leading to better working conditions than in their outsourced counterparts. Arguably, the outsourced centres tend to pose more threats to unionization in this industry owing to the flexible nature of their employment practices (Shire, Holtgrewe and Kerst, 2002; Benner, Lewis and Omar, 2007).

From the industrial relations perspective, the biggest challenge for the unions in this industry has arguably been the individualistic nature of call centre work and its reward system (Bain and Taylor, 2000, 2002, 2004), both of which inhibit collective action. In view of this challenge, the routine, controlling, intense nature of call centre work should be taken into account in the bargaining process. The service management school (Frenkel et al., 1999; Korczynski et al., 2000; Korczynski, 2003) argues that unions need to adapt to the new capitalist consumption model and be part of the solution at the front line by extending their involvement beyond the bread-and-butter issues of pay and conditions to include the delivery of customer services, which seems to be the primary cause of stress among the call centre operators.

This chapter contributes to the sparse literature on employment conditions at local government call centres. It highlights the concerns arising from working conditions associated with call centre work and outlines the challenges and opportunities for public sector trade union strategies illustrated by the case of the South African Municipal Workers Union (SAMWU). The chapter is based on research conducted at the front line in the City of Johannesburg Metropolitan Municipality call centre, supplemented by data from the Nelson Mandela Bay Metropolitan Municipality (NMM). SAMWU forms the majority union in both municipalities. The study is exploratory in nature, owing to the paucity of prior research in this area: very little South African literature is available on the study of trade unions and call centres, especially in the local government sector. This chapter will shed some light on this issue, using material from the two metropolitan municipalities, and will thereby contribute to extending our understanding of the labour process at local government call centres. Initial findings confirm concerns that the call handling section of South African local government is beset by serious problems such as high levels of stress, high turnover of staff, understaffing, lack of training, unequal wages among employees and lack of communication at all levels of the organization.

Methodology

This chapter draws on qualitative data obtained from Joburg Connect (the City of Johannesburg metropolitan call centre) in 2010 and 2011. Qualitative data were collected through semi-structured in-depth interviews with over 30 participants, including call centre operators, trade union officials, shop stewards, managers and municipal officials.[1] Different interview questions were designed for managers, supervisors and operators respectively. The overarching aim of these interviews was to collect detailed data on the history, objectives, development and outcomes of the local government call centres. The interviews lasted between 45 and 90 minutes and focused on each individual's perceptions and experiences of the call centre workplace. Non-participant observation was also undertaken in call centres for over six weeks, during which researchers talked to operators, supervisors, shop stewards and managers. The aim of the observation was to capture the dynamic and interactive nature of the call centre labour process in action, to explore participants' responses to it, and thereby to establish a detailed picture of the process. Detailed field notes were taken during and after the observation, and were transcribed as soon as possible. Focus group discussions were also used to explore participants' responses in greater depth by stimulating group interaction and to tease out some of the less clear responses from the individual interviews.

The City of Johannesburg forms the epicentre of South Africa's financial, business and information services. It is the biggest metropolitan municipality in terms of both population and contribution (13 per cent) to gross domestic product (GDP). Johannesburg was the first city to be restructured along neoliberal lines immediately after the democratic elections of 1994. In order to expand services to cover areas previously racially segregated and lacking basic provision, while at the same time addressing the City's severe financial crisis, the City Council introduced the iGoli 2002 transformation plan. The main objectives of this plan were to decentralize operations, stabilize the City's finances and promote administrative efficiency. This involved, among other things, the creation of utilities, agencies and corporatized entities (UACs). Among South African city authorities, Johannesburg Council has completely separated its utilities functions from the City Government bureaucracy. Though they remain wholly owned by the City, they have their own chief executive officers just like private companies. Johannesburg's commanding position as the hub of economic and political power in the country makes it a role model in municipal business operations, which in turn means that this model is likely to be exported not only around the country but possibly into the southern African region more widely.

The City of Johannesburg was chosen as the focus for this study because of its socio-historical and political position in the country. The metropolitan population consists of approximately 3.2 million people, of whom 72 per cent are Black, 17 per cent White, 6.5 per cent Coloured (mixed race) and 3.7 per cent Asian (mainly Indians). The City, whose racialized inequality reflects the greater South African social problem, has some of the biggest low-income formal townships in the country, for example Soweto, Alexandria, Diepsloot, Ivory Park and Orange Farm. The northern suburbs are mainly occupied by white and affluent communities who benefited from services provided by the apartheid Government. The inner city is characterized by slums where service delivery is poor or absent (Smith, 2006). Data gathered through the municipality's regular customer service surveys helps in assessing the population's perceptions about the city and satisfaction with service delivery.

In 2001 the then Mayor, Amos Masondo, launched the "One Number, One City, One Vision" campaign and opened up Joburg Connect at Proton House in Roodepoort. Joburg Connect is the single biggest council call centre in the country, with more than 120 workstations.

The Johannesburg data are supplemented by data collected between 2007 and 2009 in NMM, which are used for purposes of confirmation or comparison. Though smaller than Joburg Connect, the NMM call centre showed many similarities with the larger institution in terms of working organization and labour process.

Public call centres: A product of the New Public Management

The first call centres came into being over 35 years ago when the travel and hospitality industries decided to centralize their reservation operations to cope with growing consumer demand. Today, they are the norm in the retailing, telecommunications, entertainment and travel industries, and in public sector service delivery. Call centres are not uniform. Differences exist in relation to several variables: size, industrial sector, market, call complexity and cycle time, the nature of operations (inbound, outbound or combined), management style and priorities, the configuration of technological integration of telephones and computers, and the effectiveness of representative institutions – including trade unions (Bain and Taylor, 2001). The most significant differences are in work organization and call complexity, especially the distinctions that arise from an emphasis on, respectively, quantity or quality. Table 4.1 presents the contrasting characteristics of call centre operations focused respectively on quantity and quality. These elements are not necessarily exclusive and both may exist in an operation.

Call centres in the public sector have been inspired by the neoliberal concept of the sovereign customer. They reflect the influence of the New Public Management (NPM), which introduced private sector managerial styles of business operation, with emphasis on flexibility, performance management systems and privatization, into the public sector. The introduction of call centres in the public service was intended to close the digital divide and encourage active citizenship: arguably, they play a role in improving social inclusion by redressing citizen exclusion from information and services, and foster participatory democracy by encouraging citizens to exercise influence on the provision of services. According to these ideas, the citizen as "customer" should not just be a recipient of service but should be able to participate in policy formulation. However, the concept of customer in the public sector inherently excludes the masses of those who are deemed unable to pay for services, especially in the developing world (Hague, 2001, p. 69). Parkin's (1979) notion of "a shift from collective to individual exclusion" relates to the physical distance placed between service and citizen by the introduction of public call centres. Public call centres are arguably the "masks" of political leaderships that seek to remove the masses from face-to-face interaction in dealing with basic services. This raises questions about the purported ability of the call centres to open up access to participatory democracy for the masses.

According to the international literature, the ostensible focus of public call centres is less on the reduction of costs and more on customer satisfaction. Owing to the nature of the target market in size and orientation, they are inclined to emphasize the quality rather than the quantity of service delivery outputs, a contradiction noted by Korczynski (2001). They are part of the interconnected network linking different departments and citizens and, as Glucksman (2002, p. 796) observed, they are not "self autonomous workspaces" but part of the whole production-to-consumption system. They handle enquiries with regard to various basic needs, including water and electricity accounts, refuse collection, health and emergency services. Their advantages are that they deal with large volumes of enquiries, relieve citizens of the need to spend time and money travelling, do away with physical queuing, and reduce the time spent in face-to-face

Table 4.1   Characteristics of call centre operations focused on, respectively, quantity of calls handled and quality of service provided

Focus on quantity	Focus on quality
Simple customer interaction	Complex customer interaction
Routinization	Individualization/customization
Targets hard	Targets soft
Strict adherence to scripts	Flexible or no scripts
Tight call handling times	Relaxed call handling times
Tight "wrap-up times"	Customer satisfaction a priority
High percentage of time on-phone/ready	Possibility of task completion off-phone
Statistics-driven	Statistics modified by quality criteria
Volume	Value

Source: Bain and Taylor, 2001, p. 118.

customer interaction. However, they have also been labelled the "new sweatshops of the service economy" or "white-collar factories", driven by standardization and rationalization (Fernie and Metcalf, 1998; Knights and McCabe, 2003). They are staffed mainly by experienced public servants who have been moved into the new environment (Bain, Taylor and Dutton, 2005; Huws, 2009; Pupo and Noack, 2009).

The literature on call centres can broadly be divided into the pessimistic and the optimistic. The pessimistic strand has been largely influenced by Fernie and Metcalf (1998), who saw this sort of work through a Foucauldian perspective. On the basis of their study in the private sector, they saw call centres as the epitome of assembly line production, with management using electronic surveillance to exercise total control over the labour process. Silent surveillance through call recording makes it hard for operators to know whether any conversation is being recorded or listened to or not, and so makes direct supervision redundant as the operators are constantly under surveillance. Poynter (2000) endorses this view, arguing that new forms of service work embody practices once the preserve of assembly line and manual employees, routinizing and deskilling professional work. The form of organization once characteristic of manual labour has rapidly diffused within industries previously associated with white-collar workers and "mental" labour (Poynter, 2000, p. 151). This new deskilled pool of labour does not need either qualifications or extensive training.

The optimists, most of whom are to be found in the new service management literature, argue that the call centres are producing more empowered, semi-professional, highly skilled and committed employees, delivering customized service (Schneider and Bowen, 1999). Most of these optimistic accounts are endorsed by the business practitioners who seek to spread call centre services. Taylor and Bain (1999) emphasize the variation of the call centres in size, market orientation and so forth. In observing the labour process of call centre work, many authors have described it as "deskilling" what was "a complex set of tasks"; however, Taylor et al. (2005) argue that not all call centres are monotonous and deskilling, and that some are based on a quality of service principle which stresses employee discretion in decision-making. Service quality varies across the industry, depending on many factors such as size, sector and the nature of the functions performed.

Many commentators associate aspects of call centre work with bad customer service (Blunden, 2003). Some note that workers are increasingly treated as "human robots" in these "McJobs" (Korczynski, 2001, p. 79), and portray contemporary service work as fake, invasive, demeaning and highly routinized (Korczynski, 2001, p. 80). Front-line workers experience "emotional alienation", being required to hide their unpleasant emotions and always put the customer first (Taylor, 1997). Prevalent physical problems associated with call centre work include repetitive strain injury, sleeplessness, voice loss and hearing problems. In working conditions, low pay, close supervision, surveillance, monotonous work, boredom and unsociable hours are common (Richardson, Belt and Marshal, 2000, p. 363). Some scholars have noted high turnover and employee absenteeism in call centres as coping or resistance strategies against these "dehumanising" working conditions (Mulholland, 2004).

Unionization at call centres

Non-standard employment arrangements are characteristic of call centres in many parts of the world. These forms of employment are commonly categorized as precarious work because they are insecure, unprotected and poorly paid. Generally, where employment is precarious, union representation is non-existent, very low or discouraged by the employer (Tucker, 2002). Shire, Holtgrewe and Kerst (2002) noted that increased flexibility in working arrangements within the service sector reflects an attempt to challenge the traditional collective restraints through a "liberal employment model" which seeks to avoid the unions. Little knowledge has been gathered about the role of trade unions in call centres, with research dominated by an almost exclusive focus on work organization and management control. The unionization of call centres has been seen as inhibited by the nature of the job, which is based on individualistic work organization and reward systems. Call centre operators are tied to their desks, deal with numerous calls and are mostly under heavy supervision, which makes them hard to organize. The individualizing nature of call centre working conditions, epitomized by individual contracts, results in workers feeling discouraged about unions and union membership (Webster and Omar, 2003; Stewart, 2005). Performance rewards are strongly determined by individual call monitoring: the more calls the operator handles, the better. Bain and Taylor (2000) have contested the "myth" of the decline of collective resistance within call centres. They argue that call centre workers use their oppositional attitude and subversion to resist in these individualized workplaces.

Gorz (1982) suggests that individualism could be the starting point in rejecting the current working order: "This rupture can only come from the individuals themselves. The realm of freedom can never arise out of material processes; it can only be established by a constitutive act which, aware of its free subjectivity, asserts itself as an absolute end in itself within each individual" (Gorz, 1982, p. 74). Gorz's idea of individual agency has arguably been prevalent in the call centre industry, noticeable through high turnover throughout the industry. This exit option has been seen as the main resistance strategy applied at the individual level. According to Gorz's description of the neo-proletariat (Gorz, 1982, p. 69), call centre workers are part of the non-class that can only resist the capitalist production system by breaking away to liberate themselves from work. In a later publication Gorz (1999) suggested that if trade unions see their only task as that of defending the interests of those with stable jobs, they run the risk of deteriorating into a "neo-corporatist, conservative force, as has occurred in many Latin American countries". Instead, they should engage with societal issues affecting the whole working class.

The youthful profile of call centre operators and empathy with their customers seem to pose additional challenges for union organization in this industry. Wray-Bliss argues that in "privileging customer relations over industrial relations, frontline staff may be interpreted as contributing to the declining political visibility and viability of unions" (2001, p. 46). Korczynski (2003) expands this view with the notion of "communities of coping", where capitalist consumptions supersede the collective class solidarity propounded by Marx. According to this neo-Weberian perspective, the presence of abusive and irate customers prompts the emergence of informal "communities of coping" among workers to assist them to cope in this contradictory environment in which they sometimes empathize with customer complaints. These "communities of coping", which are embedded in the "collective emotional labour" shared by these front-line workers, then create a potential solidarity from which trade unions can emerge (Korczynski, 2003, p. 71). Korczynski posits that trade unionism at the front line should not be concerned solely with bread-and-butter issues of pay and conditions but should also "acknowledge the enmeshing of consumption and production that occurs in the service work. A potentially potent sustaining ideology for trade unionism in the service economy becomes the aim of simultaneously civilising production and consumption – seeking to create not only decent jobs, but also decent services to deliver to customers" (2007, p. 579). This means that trade unionism at the front line can grow out of customer service issues, easing the strain both on front-line workers and also on customers. The concept of "customer-oriented bureaucracies" (COB) supports the notion that, in service work, the presence of the customer has sociological significance. Worker satisfaction and customer satisfaction are interrelated. Therefore, trade unions can usefully expand their scope beyond the basic issues of pay and conditions.

Local government call centres

Within South African municipalities, call centres are a recent phenomenon. Their introduction was motivated by the Government's quest for a more customer-centred service delivery plan in compliance with the Batho Pele ("People first") framework outlined in the 1998 White Paper on Local Government (see Batho Pele, 2000). Since the introduction of Batho Pele, government philosophy in public administration has shifted, giving centre stage to the recipients of services as customers. NPM reforms have been adopted, entailing the introduction of private sector business principles into the management and delivery of public services. Performance management systems, for example, have become mandatory for municipalities, under arrangements set out in various pieces of legislation.[2] These systems are viewed as a means through which municipalities can improve organizational and individual performance to enhance service delivery, and also as a means of promoting a responsive and performance-based culture.

The Municipal Systems Act (2000) stipulates that local municipalities should treat their residents as consumers. Chapter 6 of the Act states that the "municipality must facilitate a culture of public service and accountability amongst staff ... [and] give members of the local municipality full and accurate information about the level and standard of the municipal services they are entitled to receive". Call centres are a means by which the Batho Pele principle of access to information and services for "customers" is being realized. It is worth noting that call centres serve a different purpose from that of customer care centres. The call centre allows residents from anywhere to call in with their queries and complaints, whereas the customer care centres are walk-in centres located in different parts of the municipality to offer services that cannot be resolved over the phone, for example rectifying incorrect bills.

Within most municipalities, call centres are designed to answer queries from citizens about utilities accounts, water bills, emergency services, natural disasters, service cut-offs and so forth, using an automatic call distributor (ACD) and interactive voice response (IVR). At Johannesburg Metropolitan Municipality, for example, organizational and structural transformation has transformed a network of helpdesks into a fully fledged call centre. This shift has been accompanied by expectations that these public call centres should have better working conditions and be less "alienating" than if outsourced private operating call centres were used.

Call centre organization: The case of Joburg Connect

Joburg Connect is the largest call centre in South African local government and a role model for other metropolitan municipalities. It has 120 workstations, most of which (70 per cent) are occupied by black women between the ages of 20 and 38. It operates around the clock, seven days a week and 365 days a year. Its main purpose is to centralize service access for customers, deal with queries by telephone, and handle complaints in a standard and speedy fashion. The call centre is divided into two sections: Emergency Connect and Care Connect. Emergency Connect operators receive calls relating to life-threatening emergencies and dispatch ambulances, police, fire engines and rescue vehicles in response. Care Connect is a customer relations call centre used to assist the public with queries about municipal services, for example billing issues, meter reading and traffic fines.

Findings revealed that in 2010–11 each Joburg Connect operator dealt with up to 200 calls per shift, which means that one operator spent less than three minutes on each call. During the day shift there are 96 workers (80 per cent capacity), whereas on the night shift there are fewer than 20 (17 per cent capacity). However, these statistics have been changing as a result of inaccuracies in water statements and bills issued to customers. This topic will be discussed later in the chapter, under the causes of stress in the call centre. Call centre operators are employed under full contract by the City, which is a different arrangement from that typical of contracts in the separate utilities call centre, which is run on commercial lines. However, the higher incentives and pay in the utilities call centre are envied by those working in the City call centre.

Customer service centres such as Joburg Water, City Power and Joburg Metro Police Department run in parallel with the City call centre. These call centres are not linked, which has posed a challenge from the outset; nor are they situated under the same roof, though they use the same IVR number in connecting all calls.[3]

Working conditions

Stress

It is well known that the call centre industry the world over is beset by high levels of stress and high staff turnover, exacerbated within the local government context by the experience of poor service delivery at the local level. Both Joburg Connect and NMM call centre workers noted that they experienced considerable stress. A primary cause of this was the continuing shortage of staff in both call centres. Joburg Connect has been experiencing high turnover, and some of the terminated contracts were not immediately replaced by new ones owing to financial difficulties. "The whole municipality is a mess; we are currently operating on less than 60 per cent capacity … because the municipality refuses to replace those budgeted vacancies" (JC, SM 1). This comment was echoed by other managers and agents within the Joburg Connect call centre, and the lack of capacity was visible during the researchers' visits to the call centre. The NMM call centre was operating at almost full capacity, with usually 20 call centre operators in the electricity section and a few open spaces waiting to be filled. A supervisor here explained: "We usually call on our casuals during the peak periods … as the call centre gets busy around pay days and during natural disasters" (NMM, Supervisor 1).

On top of understaffing, another major challenge within the call centres was absenteeism owing to high levels of sick leave. In both municipal call centres studied, this proved to be a tactic operators used to relieve pressure and stress. Most admitted that they take sick leave not because they are physically ill, but because the work is too stressful. "People who take leave outnumber the ones at work. Some maybe are lazy, but most are bored; it's not nice to come to work and call centre work is stressful" (JC, CCO 2).

The levels of stress that lead to absenteeism on this scale are partly the result of poor communication within the organization. Working conditions have worsened as expectations of service delivery on the part of the councils have risen. Local government call centres, though (relatively) small and unionized, are stressful places to work because the operators are seen not as call handlers, but rather as the "face of inefficient service delivery". The abuse they receive from irate customers is not based only on "bad customer service" but is also about service delivery itself. Because of the lack of communication between the back office and the call centre, operators have to answer for things about which they are not informed, and so they sound "inefficient" to members of the public. Having to deal with irritated customers and protect the council's decisions makes this job stressful for workers. Moreover, call centre workers become identified not only with the municipality but with the public sector as a whole. One worker at Joburg Connect seemed to have accepted these relations with customers, saying: "Threats and angry customers are part of our job" (JC, CCO 1). However, some workers in the NMM call centre who were accused of inefficiency and blamed for the national Government's faults regarded the insults and abuse from the public as racist. One agent quoted a customer as saying: "All of you Thabo Mbeki government people, you don't know what you are doing there … You are so incompetent" (NMM, CCO 2).

It is clear from the research that call centre workers are not just "answering the phone": they have become "fire extinguishers" or "shock absorbers" who have to smooth the relationship between the customer and the council. As customers call the municipality, irritated about services and angrily searching for answers, they are met with a voice that has to assure them that all is going to be well. "When the council makes a decision that is very unpopular, we get more frustrated callers … which we understand, but it's not our fault" (JC, CCO 2).

This was evident when the energy supply company Eskom increased tariffs by 30 per cent in 2009, a move exacerbated by an inefficient billing system and power supply problems. Call centre workers bore the brunt of customer dissatisfaction and had to be spokespersons not only for the municipality but also for Eskom, which ended up not answering calls to its own office. The burden on call centre operators was worsened by the lack of communication between the back office and front-line workers.

Workers' voices and accents were among the key factors contributing to the stress they experienced. Operators identified their accents as the source of attack and abuse by customers who immediately accused them of incompetence. "When they listen to your name and accent, then you get it" (NMM, CCO 3). The same point was emphasized by an NMM customer care manager, who argued for training in voice and telephone etiquette for workers. One of the operators explained that when she complained about the lack of training: "You know us, hey … from disadvantaged education background; when you get here and deal with English and Afrikaans speaking customers you tend to be intimidated and not want to answer the calls" (NMM, CCO 2).

Lack of training

There are no fixed criteria for recruitment, as long as candidates have knowledge of the job and some basic customer service experience. Most of the managers seemed to think that age was a big problem with call centre operators who had worked in the "old culture of the organization", which posed a challenge to the current "customer-oriented" municipality. A top manager in the NMM stated: "The biggest challenge is changing the attitudes of the employees towards this new customer-oriented approach … It is easy to deal with new recruits, but the old staff has to be retrained and it is hard to retrain those people" (NMM, SM 2).

One of the most common and effective ways of changing attitudes and culture in an organization is through extensive training and development. In the local government call centres, most of the managers were trained in the new customer care approach; but they are not the ones who sit at the desk dealing with customers every day. Joburg Connect operators complained that their training was not sufficient to deal with the current water and electricity billing software crisis, which had become a source of grievance to both customers and operators. "The impact of billing … basically call volumes have skyrocketed because of incorrect bills. This has frustrated the staff members, which results from a frustrated customer; this saw a backlog in our calls and increased abandonment rate. Response times have tended to be longer" (JC, SM 2).

It is acknowledged by the managers that the inaccurate statements given to customers have worsened working conditions in the call centre and further increased the turnover of staff. This problem is not restricted to Johannesburg, as the billing system in most municipalities is linked directly to the call centre's function. Customers anywhere, infuriated by the inaccuracy of their statements or by having their electricity cut off, turn angrily to the first person they face representing the municipality and insult them.

Poor communication between the front and back offices

Though managers seek to control workers, there is always space for resistance by employees. Dropping the call of an irate customer, putting it on loudspeaker and letting the customer talk unattended, or "working to rule", thus restricting both the information and the courtesy given to the customer, are the most common forms of resistance. This kind of behaviour by call centre operators has been provoked by poor communication between different departments of the municipalities and/or between the departments and the call centre. According to one NMM manager, "Front-line office should work well with back-office but there is lack of communication between the two which makes call centre work very difficult … People work in silos here" (NMM, SM 3).

One instance of this failure to communicate concerned an appearance by the director of the NMM electricity department on a radio programme the night before the researchers visited the call centre. Answering questions about electricity supply on a Port Elizabeth based radio station, he apparently gave the call centre number for more enquiries. The issue he was questioned about on the radio was not about electricity faults, but about the poor quality of service delivery. The call centre then received a high volume of calls from people about their lack of access to electricity. After answering one of these calls, a supervisor, looking lost and shocked at the same time, was very embarrassed that she had not known about the radio appearance: "When did Mr Sompete[4] go to this station? How come he never told us about this [shaking her head]?" (NMM, Supervisor 2).

Joburg Connect workers have gone as far as saying: "Customers teach us lots of things that are not communicated to us by the management" (JC, CCO 2). Poor communication forms one of the sources of frustration and pressure in the call centre environment as the primary task of staff members is the dispersal of information. "You know what is happening in the call centre, the customer teaches you lots of things. You then pretend as if you know because you are trying to cover up for the municipality, and then you run to the supervisor who knows nothing as well because there is no communication between the supervisors and the managers" (JC, CCO 3).

Communication should be a priority in a call centre in order to avoid customers becoming angry and embarrassing or abusing operators. As things stand, the operators are insulted for their lack of knowledge and for being purely message-takers, who cannot actually help at all. The most interesting observation on this topic was that poor communication was not only evident within the organization, but was also reported to apply to the union representatives who were supposed to inform and protect the call centre operators. Some of the operators felt isolated from and even on occasion compromised by their union.

Union collective action and limitations on worker participation

According to Omar (2008), it is very difficult for call centre workers to strike owing to the "individualized" nature of their jobs. Collective action is constrained by individualized employment contracts and the nature of the work carried out (Benner,

Lewis and Omar, 2007). Although workers at one of the call centres operated by the private communications company Telkom did attempt a strike, the calls were simply redirected to another call centre within Telkom. Thus workers in the call centre industry are at a disadvantage, for employers can easily avoid the impact of a strike (Omar, 2008). Some limited action has been taken. In Joburg Connect, workers participated in a strike organized by SAMWU in October 2007, leaving the call centre operating with 50 per cent of the staff; and an operator in the NMM said: "We do strike, but only during lunchtime, and picket, but we cannot leave our workstation as this is considered as the emergency services" (NMM, CCO 3).

Most of the workers interviewed identified loyalty and job protection as the major reasons for joining the union. Despite these reasons, the union was deemed invisible in the call centres. Although many operators wanted to participate in union activities, their opportunities to do so were limited by the nature of their jobs and time constraints. One of them even suggested that "if meetings were during the time where all of us can make it, I'm sure we will be able to participate ... but in our job it is impossible for all of us to attend [or] even to picket when there is a strike because we are more like essential service ... If we go picketing, we'll have to go during lunchtime and get back to work" (NMM, CCO 3).

Unions will need to deal with call centres differently from other working environments because of the unique working conditions. They should address issues relating to gender, shift work, transport home after late night shifts, the stress associated with management's time control and training to deal with stress. Greater SAMWU visibility in call centres could also assist in building trust among union members, some of whom termed their shop stewards "shop stupid" because of their perceived ineffectiveness.

When asked about the role of call centres in the municipality with regard to service delivery, one SAMWU organizer said: "In South Africa, people cannot afford R10.00 prepaid electricity. How do you expect these people to call a call centre and wait for a long time without money? Call centres are a convenience for the rich and a nightmare for the poor ... How can you become a customer still struggling for the basic needs? Water is not a luxury; it's a necessity" (SAMWU, EC 1).

A representative of the SAMWU Gauteng Provincial structure went further: "Call centres are just message-takers who cannot help you or provide any feedback. They are just glorified PAs of other departments; there is no link between call centres and the other municipal entities" (SAMWU, GP Rep. 1). Both these respondents pointed to the "uselessness" of call centres – not only to the public, but also to the workers themselves, who lack any capacity to assist the public.

SAMWU officials appeared to lack knowledge of how much local government is now being conducted through call centres. It is, moreover, a matter of urgency that they conduct their own research about the number of call centre workers within their union. Hitherto, this category of workers has been largely ignored, because they are not present in every municipality. They are treated as front desk or reception staff, differing only that they are specialized in dealing with telephone enquiries (SAMWU, GP Rep. 2).

This deficiency was recognized by another union official who acknowledged that this group of workers has never been explicitly covered by the union, which historically has focused on organizing blue-collar workers within the municipality. "Maybe this is the start of the conversation about this section of workers. We need to set up a national approach and put it in our agenda, even in the bargaining council. They are [a] unique section of workers within SAMWU. Maybe they have been overlooked; nothing much has been done by the union" (SAMWU, JHB 1).

The union is facing a number of challenges with regard to the reforms in local government entailed by programmes such as iGoli 2002. Poor relations between the union and the managers of the utilities were mentioned by several speakers. This tension was observed by Barchiesi (2007, p. 64), who noted that utility managers tended to be ambivalent towards collective bargaining and unions in general. This attitude might also lead to inter-union conflicts and competition as the utilities attract unions from outside local government boundaries. For example, the South African Transport and Allied Workers Union (SATAWU) recruits bus drivers in local government, who may also be members of SAMWU. "SATAWU and SAMWU ... though we are under COSATU [Congress of South African Trade Unions], these unclear jurisdictions affect the strength of union organizations as we now fight for members ourselves ... We have a court case tomorrow directly linked to this issue" (SAMWU, JHB 2).

Similarly, while the Communication Workers Union (CWU) organizes workers in the communication industry, since the call centres are part of local government they fall under SAMWU. One of the senior SAMWU officials was very confident that SAMWU would remain pre-eminent in local government, dismissing the threat from other unions:

> SATAWU and CWU can never take over from our jurisdiction because each union has its own constitution stipulating exactly where it will start in terms of the jurisdiction ... For example, there are police in local government, but that is POPCRU's [the Police and Prisons Civil Rights Union's] territory. We can't go just because they are on local government ... The scope for each union is defined – whether public or private – call centre is the function of local government, so they will need to prove a demarcation dispute at the CCMA [Commission for Conciliation, Mediation and Arbitration] to prove that it is their jurisdiction. (SAMWU, JHB 1)

The new customer-centred workplace within local government seems to present both new challenges to and opportunities for mobilization. One SAMWU representative recognized the impact of the new customer-driven ethos on both working conditions and citizens in general in pointing out:

Customerization worsens the working conditions of municipal workers because they now seek to maximize profit with less workers to increase revenue and impressive fiscal policies. For example, we've got this case now here [showing me a document about the working hours and conditions in the local government]. Library workers are now required to work on Saturdays as well and given that day during the week without pay. This was done without consultation with the union, but we oppose that. Workers are supposed to be given a choice whether to work on a weekend or not and paid for the overtime they worked. This business rule of more [work] with fewer workers is wrong. (SAMWU, EC 1)

Echoing this point, one worker complained: "We work Monday to Monday and sometimes get the day off during the week. When you start questioning this, they just say read the contract" (NMM, CCO 1).

Given this noticeable deterioration in employment conditions offered by the formerly "secure and fair" employer, SAMWU needs to move beyond its traditional concerns and probe the growing number of socio-political questions which have strengthened its course in history. Von Holdt (2002) and Barchiesi (2007), however, seemed pessimistic about the prospects for social movement unionism within the democratic dispensation buttressed by labour's alliance with the ruling party. The radicalism and militancy of SAMWU that were apparent in its opposition to privatization (see Barchiesi, 2007) seem to have diminished. Nevertheless, through engaging with service delivery SAMWU can provide support and relief to the call centre workers who have been abused by angry citizens. Shortcomings in service delivery, moreover, do not only affect call centre operators at work, for they too are service users. For this reason they sometimes express sympathy with customers.

A case in point was the billing crisis of 2010/11, when Johannesburg City Council came under media attack after issuing inflated water and electricity bills. Workers were then blamed by the senior managers who denied the existence of a crisis in the municipality, arguing: "It is not really accurate to say we have a billing crisis, but rather to say we have a customer-service challenge … If you say billing crisis, you get the impression we have cash-flow problems, and that was never so … until we re-establish our credibility with customers, that will remain a problem."[5]

The silence of SAMWU throughout this crisis was heavily criticized by both shop stewards and operators, who pointed to the close relations between SAMWU and municipal officials as the source of compromise on issues relating to the workers. Close political ties with the ruling party were then cited by senior SAMWU officials themselves as the diluting force in their struggle for the workers. For example, before and during the introduction of Project Phakama in the City of Johannesburg,[6] SAMWU at first resisted but later accepted the decision by the council to implement the project. This generated great disappointment with the union among call centre operators, who argued that union self-interest had separated the leadership from the rank and file: "The workers were seriously compromised in this whole period …

SAMWU never tried enough to stop the implementation of the Phakama Project" (JC, CCO 1).

Barchiesi (2007) rightly observed the weakening of the union through its alliance with the ruling party, casualisation and fragmented collective bargaining due to municipal restructuring. Though the wages of call centre workers in Johannesburg municipality are regulated at the national level under the South African Local Government Association bargaining council, inequalities have been noted, with the utilities call centre paying more and offering better working conditions and benefits. After the implementation of Phakama, this meant call centre workers performing the same tasks in the same building were paid differently because some were working for utilities and some were not. This affected morale among the call centre workers and collective solidarity among SAMWU members within the workplace: "The major challenge, as I have mentioned, it's salaries. The city pays less than these utilities, and the terms of employment and conditions of work are completely different. For example, they enjoy a 13th cheque and paid maternity leave, but the union can't do anything at this level; such things need to be addressed at the national bargaining council" (SAMWU, JHB 2).

This finding was confirmed by Joburg Connect operators, who argued that utilities offered career opportunities not available to those in the City call centre as well as better pay and benefits: "The [utilities] employees get paid more than the City employees. There is growth there; not more than two years in call centre. Here, there are people who have been here since it started and they will say the old staff does not want to work ... Managers of those entities open up doors for them and recommend their staff members" (JC, CCO 3).

Recommendations for union organization and representation

SAMWU's apparent lack of knowledge of the number of workers working in call centres and the issues affecting them reflect the union's disregard of this new customer-centred workplace. As a majority union, with the politicized nature of workplaces in South Africa working to its advantage, SAMWU nevertheless cannot be complacent. It needs to conduct its own research about the number of local government call centres, which appears to be growing as metropolitan municipalities across the country convert their helpdesks into fully fledged call centres.

SAMWU did seem to be aware of the lack of training and development among this group of workers. These matters should be included among collective bargaining issues, for training and development can boost workers' confidence and lower their stress levels. Also lacking are counselling services, which are vital for psychologically abused workers and could improve both attendance and morale among the demoralized workforce. SAMWU could further engage the municipality to secure better working conditions for call centre workers, who appear to be particularly vulnerable to health and safety problems (Taylor et al., 2003). All these issues could be raised with the employer by SAMWU, along with the matter of clear job descriptions to improve workers' performance.

SAMWU's initiative in putting pressure on the municipality to bring contract workers into permanent employment in 2007 should be acknowledged. This is a significant step towards increasing the number of union members. The atypical contracts governing call centre workers make them vulnerable to poor wages. When wage issues are pursued by the union, the needs of this category of workers should be addressed. In the Johannesburg municipality, call centre operators working for the utilities refused to be treated as part of the Joburg Connect call centre, because they enjoyed better working conditions and wages. This discrepancy needs to be abolished, as all these operators belong to the same union; doing so will increase a sense of unity among SAMWU members in the same or similar jobs.

Call centre workers are not easily accessible to the union. The strict working hours make it difficult for workers to attend union meetings. SAMWU should improve and extend its communication channels between these workers and union representatives. These should include routine union inspections of the workplace and visibility in worker canteens during break times. Call centre workers' low expectations of the union may change if the union makes itself accessible and provides information on workers' rights and benefits.

The union should work on its image, conveying a message relevant to the needs of call centre workers. It also needs to address recent allegations of corruption and mismanagement of funds, said to have influenced the Johannesburg branch against participating in the 2011 strike. SAMWU's challenge in "representing the changing municipal workforce" has been noted by Barchiesi (2007, p. 71), and many observers have confirmed the growing representation of managers within the union, which may challenge the union's capacities and loyalties: "SAMWU has neglected its duties; unions want to retain members and not to expose them … nepotism, bedroom promotions are all part of the frustration here" (JC, CCO 4). The feeling of being compromised for the sake of the union's political gains further spreads these negative sentiments among the rank and file.

Call centre workers are situated at the intersection of customer, council, citizen and service delivery. This means that the union's campaigns have to encompass all elements of this nexus. While some of the issues highlighted above relate to technical matters, most of the discontent among this group of workers seems to relate to socio-political questions. This brings us back to the question of community unionism or social movement unionism. SAMWU's militancy, though neutralized by the political alliance with the ruling party, may prove to be a key in addressing the current stresses on call centre workers. The union's strategy should include confronting citizen service delivery issues (community-based concerns) as well as worker grievances about their experiences of working in call centres (workplace struggles). The negative effects of socio-political problems experienced by the citizen translate into the call centre worker's experience of work. Therefore a deliberate widening of the union's scope of action would yield broader results.

Conclusion

As government elevates the customer as sovereign, trade unions should be responsive to the experience of call centre workers. The precarious nature of public call centre work limits unionization and demands new union strategies to organize and represent the growing numbers of call centre workers. The issues of high stress levels, high turnover, understaffing, unequal wages and lack of communication from all levels of the organization require a comprehensive trade union strategy. Call centre work is individualizing not only labour but also the citizen by removing direct contact with the politicians accountable for service delivery. This is why we argue that, in responding to the issues raised by call centres, trade unions will need to revise their community unionism approach and deal with service provision problems in order to improve the well-being of call centre workers. Given the rising number of public sector call centres, more research needs to be conducted within this sector. Little literature exists on public call centres in South Africa, and so this chapter is explorative and descriptive. In the light of the global trend towards the increasing use of call centres, the working conditions of call centre workers are likely to continue to be a cause for concern. More work needs to be done in studying public call centres as a unique workplace attached to the bureaucracy, distinct from those in the commercial sector and requiring different tools of analysis to capture the labour process.

Appendix 4.1   List of interviewees (with pseudonyms used)

Municipality/union	Position	Number	Name	Date of interview
NMM	SM	1	Thamsanqa	02/10/08
NMM	SM	2	Andile	02/10/08
NMM	SM	3	Ondela	08/09/08
NMM	Supervisor	1	Jessica	11/09/08
NMM	Supervisor	2	Ngwanya	04/08/08
SAMWU	SAMWU EC	1	Chumile	05/08/08
SAMWU	SAMWU NMM	2	Mphumzi	06/08/08
NMM	CCO	1	Kago	04/08/08
NMM	CCO	2	Carol	04/08/08
NMM	CCO	3	Rhonda	04/08/08
JC	SM	1	Felicia	04/08/10
JC	SM	2	Amandla	06/08/10
JC	CCO	1	Kromotso	09/08/10
JC	CCO	2	Kholiswa	09/08/10
JC	CCO	3	Thuli	04/07/11
JC	CCO	4	Sqhamo	05/07/11
SAMWU	SAMWU JHB	1	Denson	11/08/10
SAMWU	SAMWU JHB	2	Vusumzi	11/08/10
SAMWU	SAMWU GP Rep.	1	Mahlubi	04/07/11
SAMWU	SAMWU GP Rep.	2	Petros	05/07/11
SAMWU	Shop Steward JC	1	Mandla	06/07/11

Key: NMM = Nelson Mandela Bay Metropolitan Municipality; SAMWU = South African Municipal Workers Union; JC = Joburg Connect; SM = Senior Manager; EC = Eastern Cape; CCO = Call Centre Operator; JHB = Johannesburg; GP = Gauteng Province; Rep. = Representative.

Notes

[1] A list of the interviewees quoted in the text, with explanations of abbreviations used, is provided in appendix 4.1.

[2] Municipal Systems Act 32 of 2000, Municipal Planning and Performance Management Regulations 2000, Municipal Finance Act 53 of 2003 and Municipal Performance Regulations for Municipal Managers and Managers Directly Accountable to Municipal Managers of 2006.

[3] At the time of writing, the call centres from different utilities were being integrated under Programme Phakama, which seeks to unify the revenue services and billing system under one database.

[4] Not his real name.

[5] Roland Hunter, Executive Director, Finance and Economic Development, City of Johannesburg, quoted in *Mail and Guardian*, 3 Feb. 2011.

[6] This collection of initiatives uses a comprehensive software program to streamline operations across the metropolis.

References

Bain, P.; Taylor, P. 2000. "Entrapped by the 'electronic panopticon'? Worker resistance in the call centre", in *New Technology, Work and Employment*, Vol. 15, No. 1, pp. 2–18.

—; —. 2001. "Seizing the time? Union recruitment potential in Scottish call centres", in *Scottish Affairs*, Vol. 37, Autumn, pp. 104–28.

—; —. 2002. "Ringing the changes? Union recognition and organisation in call centres in the UK finance sector", in *Industrial Relations Journal*, Vol. 33, No. 3, pp. 246–61.

—; —. 2004. "No passage to India? UK unions, globalisation and the migration of call centre jobs", paper presented to the Work, Employment and Society Conference, Manchester, 1–3 Sep.

—; —; Dutton, E. 2005. "The thin front line: Call handling in police control rooms", paper presented to the 23rd International Labour Process Conference, Glasgow, 21–23 March.

Barchiesi, F. 2007. "Privatization and the historical trajectory of 'social movement unionism': A case study of municipal workers in Johannesburg, South Africa", in *International Labour and Working-Class History*, Vol. 71, No. 1, pp. 50–69.

Batho Pele. 2000. *Service delivery improvement guide*. Available at http://www.dpsa.gov.za/batho-pele/docs/BP_HB_optimised.pdf [30 May 2012].

Benner, C.; Lewis, C.; Omar, R. 2007. *The South African call-centre industry: A study of strategy, human resource practices and performance*, Global Call-centre Industry Project, Society, Work and Development Institute, Witwatersrand University, Johannesburg.

Blunden, D. 2003. *Music to your ears? The impact of call-centres on public library service*, Master's thesis, University of Sheffield, UK. Available at: http://s3.amazonaws.com/zanran_storage/dagda.shef.ac.uk/ContentPages/833862123.pdf [26 June 2012].

Fernie, S.; Metcalf, D. 1998. *(Not) hanging on the telephone: Payment systems in the new sweatshops* (London, Centre for Economic Performance, London School of Economics and Political Science).

Frenkel, S.; Korczynski, M.; Shire, K.; Tam, M. 1999. *On the front line: Organization of work in the information economy* (Ithaca, NY, and London, Cornell University Press).

Glucksman, M. 2002. "Call configurations: Varieties of call centre and division of labour", in *Work, Employment and Society*, Vol. 18, No. 4, pp. 795–811.

Gorz, A. 1982. *Farewell to the working class* (London, Pluto Classics).

—. 1999. *Reclaiming work: Beyond the wage-based society* (Cambridge, Polity Press).

Hague, S. 2001. "The diminishing publicness of public sector under the current mode of governance", in *Public Administrative Review*, Vol. 61, No. 1, pp. 65–82.

Huws, U. 2009. "Working at the interface: Call centre labour in a global economy", in *Work, Organisation, Labour and Globalisation*, Vol. 3, No. 1, pp. 1–8.

Knights, D.; McCabe, D. 2003. "Governing through teamwork: Reconstituting subjectivity in a call and processing centre", in *Journal of Management Studies*, Vol. 40, No. 7, pp. 1587–619.

Korczynski, M. 2001. "The contradictions of service work: The call centre as customer-oriented bureaucracy", in A. Sturdy, I. Grugulis and H. Wilmott (eds): *Customer service control, colonisation and contradictions* (London, Macmillan), pp. 79–101.

—. 2003. "Communities of coping: Collective emotional labour in service work", in *Organization*, Vol. 10, No. 1, pp. 55–79.

—. 2007. "Service work, social theory and collectivism: A reply to Brook", in *Work, Employment and Society*, Vol. 21, No. 3, pp. 577–88.

—; Shire, K.; Frenkel, S.; Tam, M. 2000. "Service work in consumer capitalism: Customers, control and contradictions", in *Work, Employment and Society*, Vol. 14, No. 4, pp. 669–87.

Mulholland, K. 2004. "Workplace resistance in an Irish call centre: Slammin' scammin' smokin' an' leavin'", in *Work, Employment and Society*, Vol. 18, No. 4, pp. 709–24.

Omar, R. 2008. *Call centres: A new contested terrain for unions in South Africa*, paper presented at the South African Sociological Association (SASA) Conference, Stellenbosch University, 7–10 July.

Parkin, F. 1979. *Marxism and class theory: A bourgeois critique* (London, Taylor & Francis and New York, Columbia University Press).

Poynter, G. 2000. "Thank you for calling: The new ideology of work in the service economy", in *Sounding Issue*, Vol. 14, Spring, pp. 151–60.

Pupo, N.; Noack, A. 2009. "Standardising public service: The experiences of call centre workers in the Canadian federal government", in *Work, Organisation, Labour and Globalisation*, Vol. 3, No. 1, pp. 100–13.

Richardson, R.; Belt, V.; Marshal, N. 2000. "Taking calls to Newcastle: The regional implications of the growth in call-centres", in *Regional Studies*, Vol. 34, No. 4, pp. 357–69.

Schneider, B.; Bowen, D.E. 1999. "Understanding customer delight and outrage", in *Sloan Management Review*, Vol. 41, No. 1, pp. 35–45.

Shire, K.; Holtgrewe, U.; Kerst, C. 2002. "Re-organising service work: An introduction", in U. Holtgrewe, C. Kerst and K. Shire (eds): *Re-organising service work: Call centres in Germany and Britain* (Aldershot, Ashgate), pp. 1–18.

Smith, L. 2006. *Neither public nor private: Unpacking the Johannesburg Water Corporatization model*, Paper 27, Social Policy and Development Programme, United Nations Research Institute for Social Development (Geneva).

Stewart, P. 2005. *Employment, trade union renewal and the future of work: The experience of work and organisational change* (London, Palgrave Macmillan).

Taylor, P.; Bain, P. 1999. "'An assembly line in the head': Work and employee relations in the call centre", in *Industrial Relations Journal*, Vol. 30, No. 2, pp. 101–17.

—; Baldry, C.; Bain, P.; Ellis, V. 2003. "A unique working environment: Health, sickness and absence management in UK call centres", in *Work, Employment and Society*, Vol. 17, No. 3, pp. 435–58.

Taylor, S. 1997. "Empowerment or degradation? Total quality management and the service sector", in R. Brown (ed.): *The changing shape of work* (London, Macmillan), pp. 171–202.

TradeInvestSA. 2007. *Call centres and BPO set for exponential growth in Gauteng.* Available at: http://www.tradeinvestsa.co.za/news/982204.htm [27 June 2012].

Tucker, D. 2002. *Precarious non-standard employment: A review of the literature* (Wellington, New Zealand Department of Labour).

Von Holdt, K. 2002. "Social movement unionism: The case of South Africa", in *Work, Employment and Society*, Vol. 16, No. 2, pp. 283–304.

Webster, E.; Omar, R. 2003. "Work restructuring in post-apartheid South Africa", in *Work and Occupations*, Vol. 30, No. 2, pp. 194–213.

Wray-Bliss, E. 2001. "Representing customer service: Telephones and texts", in A. Sturdy, I. Gruelis and H. Willmott (eds): *Customer service: Empowerment and entrapment* (Basingstoke: Palgrave), pp. 38–59.

WHY LABOUR UNIONS HAVE FAILED BANGLADESH'S GARMENT WORKERS

5

Zia Rahman and Tom Langford

Introduction

The manufacture of ready-made garments (RMG) for global markets took hold in Bangladesh in the 1980s because the country had wage levels among the lowest in the world and a huge reserve army of labour available for exploitation, and its policy-makers were averse to introducing labour standards and allowing unionization of this sector because of a fear of losing foreign currency earnings. The Bangladeshi public's perception of the existing union movement as corrupt was used to justify the resistance to further unionization. Consequently Bangladesh soon became a preferred manufacturing location for many outsourcing transnational apparel companies (Dannecker, 2002; Kabeer, 2004; Rock, 2001a; Siddiqi, 2004). Here we see an illustration of the race-to-the-bottom thesis of globalization. The ruling elites in Bangladesh were able to pursue such policies effectively because of their control of an overdeveloped State, a product of colonialism (Alavi, 1979).

By 2010/11 there were 5,150 garment factories in Bangladesh employing 3.6 million people (see table 5.1). Yet labour unions in Bangladesh largely ignored the RMG sector in the 1980s and efforts at unionization since 1990 have had very limited success. This chapter explains why labour unions have failed Bangladesh's garment workers over the past 30 years. It is based upon a review of the historical literature, extensive documentary research, and in-depth interviews with labour union officials, industrial relations experts and garment workers conducted by the first author in Dhaka in 2007.

Over the past three decades the RMG sector has become crucial to Bangladesh's economy. In 2007 Bangladesh became the fourth largest RMG-producing country in the world after China, the EU-27 and Turkey (Mirdah, 2010). In the same year, Bangladesh ranked fifth in the list of RMG exporters to the United States. The RMG

Table 5.1   The garment industry in Bangladesh: Numbers of factories
and employees, 1983/84 to 2010/11

Year	No. of garment factories	No. of employees (000)	Year	No. of garment factories	No. of employees (000)
1983/84	134	40	1997/98	2 726	1 500
1984/85	384	115	1998/99	2 963	1 500
1985/86	594	198	1999/2000	3 200	1 600
1986/87	629	283	2000/01	3 480	1 800
1987/88	685	306	2001/02	3 618	1 800
1988/89	725	317	2002/03	3 760	2 000
1989/90	759	335	2003/04	3 957	2 000
1990/91	834	402	2004/05	4 107	2 000
1991/92	1 163	582	2005/06	4 220	2 200
1992/93	1 537	804	2006/07	4 490	2 400
1993/94	1 839	827	2007/08	4 743	2 800
1994/95	2 182	1 200	2008/09	4 925	3 500
1995/96	2 353	1 290	2009/10	5 063	3 600
1996/97	2 503	1 300	2010/11	5 150	3 600

Source: Bangladesh Garment Manufacturers and Exporters Association (BGMEA), http://www.bgmea.com.bd [accessed 21 June 2012].

sector contributes a staggering 78 per cent of Bangladesh's foreign exchange earnings, keeps many associated service businesses going and provides employment to millions of workers, approximately 80 per cent of them women, who otherwise would be hard pressed to find waged labour (BGMEA, 2012; Khan, 2008).

When transnational apparel companies first contracted production in Bangladesh, the country's textile sector did not meet international standards and did not produce related accessories such as zippers, buttons, threads and labelling, so that Bangladeshi entrepreneurs had to import fabrics and related accessories from other countries. Therefore, for a long time the RMG industry in Bangladesh depended upon its one and only so-called comparative advantage: cheap and abundant female labour (Kabeer, 2004). Every year since the 1980s, thousands upon thousands of young rural women have migrated to major Bangladeshi cities and been absorbed into the burgeoning RMG factories (Ahmed, 2004; Kabeer, 1991, 2004; McCarthy and Feldman, 1983). These rural-to-urban migrants have tended to be illiterate and deferential towards male authority figures, and have continued to think of the rural areas they come from as their permanent homes. Gender is therefore an integral dimension of the story of labour unions in the RMG industry in Bangladesh, even though it is not an analytical focus of this chapter.

The remainder of this introduction summarizes our argument, which is then presented in more detail in the following three sections of the chapter. Those three sections, respectively:

- establish an understanding of the various historical forces that shaped labour unions in Bangladesh up to the 1980s;

- identify the causes for the failure of labour unions to organize and represent the interests of the RMG proletariat over the past three decades; and

- assess the implications of the massive wave of protest by Bangladeshi garment workers in 2006 for the current status and capacity of labour unions in the sector.

Labour unions first developed in Bangladesh in the jute and cotton textile industries during the British colonial period.[1] These unions provided stability for the colonial enterprises. However, they soon became part of the broader anti-colonial movement dominated by left and nationalist political parties. This process represented a particular type of politicization of labour unions: factory-based trade unionism was virtually absent and unions were key organizations on the national political stage.

Political unionism, dominated by the left political parties, and the labour unions' prominence in the jute and textile industries continued even after the end of colonial rule. However, the tradition of left political unionism was challenged in the 1960s by the military dictator General Ayub Khan. He introduced factory-level unionism as part of an anti-communist campaign and with the aim of extending the military regime's hegemony over the working class (Ahmad, 1969; Siddique and Akkas, 2003; Umar, 2006). After Bangladesh gained independence from Pakistan in 1971, all its industries were nationalized (Akash, 1998; Sobhan and Ahmad, 1980). This led to the politicization of labour unions by the ruling party (Hossain, 2005; Umar and Kabir, 1978), a pattern that persisted during the two major military regimes that existed between 1975 and 1990 (Ahmed, 1995). Whereas the leftist parties prior to the 1960s had used politicized unions to promote their oppositional political agendas, the ruling parties of recent decades have used politicized unions to support their hold on power.

During the first military regime after independence (1975–81), the country's economic policy based on nationalization was abandoned in favour of a neoliberalism that flourished during the second military regime (1981–90), led by General Ershad (Ahmed, 1995; Akash, 1998). It was during this latter period that garment manufacturing began to shift to Bangladesh. At this point the labour movement was incapable of mounting organizing drives. During the period of military dictatorship, many of Bangladesh's radical political unions were replaced by unions attached to the ruling party, which were characterized by corruption, nepotism and the development of a self-interested labour aristocracy (Ahmed, 1995). This situation created a very negative image of labour unionism among urban, educated citizens and civil society groups, and as a result the conscience constituency for progressive labour union activism has been very small since the 1970s. At the same time, because of the neoliberal economic policy introduced by the military regimes, the private sector became the engine of growth and private entrepreneurs did everything in their power to prohibit union activities. Furthermore, the mass media propagated both the ruling elites' views and the sentiments of the urban, educated middle class in favour of union-free development of the RMG industry. In addition, the State indirectly supported private sector employers by not enforcing regulations on labour standards.

Unionization of RMG workers remained stagnant into the 2000s, despite the fact that employment in the industry grew by an astounding 500 per cent between 1990/91 and 2006/07. However, it seemed likely to receive a big boost after a massive and chaotic protest by thousands of RMG workers in Dhaka in May 2006. This mass action occurred in sympathy with worker actions at two factories. At F.S. Sweater, workers had gone on strike on 10 May 2006 because of the non-payment of wages. Two of the strike leaders were arrested on 18 May and the next day a worker was shot and killed by the police. Meanwhile, workers at a second factory, Universal Knitting Garments Ltd, had been locked out on 18 May after management suddenly refused to engage in negotiations with their union representatives. On 22 May over 5,000 workers protested outside the Universal Knitting gates, joined by many other garment workers on their lunch breaks. Together the two independent, leftist unions involved in the F.S. Sweater and Universal Knitting disputes organized nine separate protest rallies on 23 May 2006 in order to mobilize as many sympathizers as possible. These protest rallies were repressed by management security forces throughout Dhaka, thus provoking militant counter-action by numerous groups of workers. The entirety of Dhaka City and its adjacent areas became a battlefield because the workers were extremely militant and enraged, and as a result normal life ground to a standstill. On 23 May approximately 16 factories were burnt, 50 factories were vandalized, 200 vehicles were ransacked and a worker was killed (Cheng, 2006). Such militant mass action had never previously been seen in the Bangladesh RMG industry.

The Bangladesh Garment Manufacturers and Exporters Association (BGMEA) initially called this movement a conspiracy against the booming industry. However, the gravity of events soon prompted them to meet with the Sramik Karmachari Okkyo Parishad (SKOP), the umbrella organization of the country's national labour federations, and the Government. After three meetings of a tripartite committee, an historic memorandum of understanding was signed on 12 June 2006 whereby the BGMEA accepted all the unions' demands, including an increase in wages, an appointment letter for all workers, a weekly day off, female maternity leave, withdrawal of all disciplinary cases against workers, and the right of trade unions to represent garment workers. On 22 June another agreement was signed between the BGMEA and 16 garment workers' unions highlighting the same concessions.

In the end, however, the May 2006 movement was only partially successful. Its greatest success was in challenging the previously unquestioned ownership rights of the RMG factory proprietors. This was first seen when the frightened owners took to the streets on 23 May to defend their property. It also represented the first time that the Government had become a party to an agreement between employers and unions. A third success of the movement was the formation of a minimum wage board that raised the minimum wage for garment workers by over 75 per cent. Nevertheless, much of the promise of the May 2006 labour movement remains unrealized to this date (August 2012). Some RMG factories, particularly those in the export processing zones (EPZs), have implemented the terms of the tripartite agreement, but the majority of factories have not. Although the State was for the first time a signatory of an agreement between the BGMEA and garment workers' labour unions, it has not taken steps to ensure the full implementation of the agreement. The two leftist unions that helped to organize the strikes at F.S. Sweater and Universal Knitting continue to be marginalized by the State, employers and other unions. Finally, the collaborationist unions affiliated with the BGMEA acted to undercut the workers' initial demand in 2006 for a minimum wage of 3,000 taka (BDT) (much higher than the BDT1,662.50 that was eventually implemented in October 2006).[2] The final section of this chapter considers what it would take for labour unions to break this impasse and begin making significant and continuing contributions to the welfare of Bangladesh's RMG proletariat.

Labour unions as shaped by colonialism, the anti-colonial struggle and military dictatorships

Labour movements and labour unions in Bangladesh were shaped and strongly influenced by the two centuries of British colonial rule in the Indian subcontinent, lasting from 1757 until 1947. In colonial India, the expanding cotton industry in Bombay and jute industry in Bengal were the early sites for labour movements (Ahmad, 1969; Basu, 1993; Read, 1931; Saha, 1978; Sharma, 1963). The labour organizations that formed in colonial India had five distinctive characteristics. First, they were largely organized as the arms of leftist or nationalist political parties engaged in anti-colonial politics. As a consequence, the early labour unions in India were unable to develop a distinctive labour philosophy like Revisionism in Germany or Fabianism in England (Basu, 1993; Saha, 1978; Sharma, 1963). Second, most of the membership did not strongly identify with labour organizations because the new industrial working class maintained an unbroken link with its rural origins and thus was slow to develop the urban industrial proletarian culture that is crucial for any working-class organization. As Read noted:

> The effect of the Industrial Revolution [in Europe] was to create very rapidly a permanent urban population, completely cut off from the countryside, dependent for their work, homes, health and recreation on the cities. In India, even after eighty years and more of industrial organization in the chief centers, the factory population still continues to ebb and flow from village to city, and from city to village, preferring with the wisdom of the east the fields and open skies to the city alleys and the street lamps. (1931, p. 4)

Third, caste, ethnic and religious stratifications were superimposed on the newly developing capitalist relations, making it difficult to create united labour organizations. For instance, during the heyday of industrialization in colonial India there were many riots between Hindus and Muslims even when workers of the two religious groups shared a similar class situation.[3] Fourth, the workers lacked previous experience of organizing (that is, there were few rural popular movements at the time), and most of them lacked formal education (Das, 1923); indeed, the 1931 Royal Commission of Labour noted that the almost universal illiteracy of the industrial proletariat posed significant barriers to labour organization (Read, 1931, p. 52). Finally, the ethos of the feudal period was reproduced when powerful elites acted as the saviours of the poor masses in the absence of legal rules and regulations to ensure justice and rights (Etienne, 1979). Extreme allegiance of the worker towards the proprietor created a paternalistic *ma–bap* relationship.[4] Overall, these five factors during the colonial period tended to create a transient, divided and dependent working class, and labour organizations that neglected the day-to-day exploitation and oppression of workers.

The politicization of labour was particularly prevalent in the decade just prior to the independence of India. During this period, three new labour federations were established as alternatives to the All India Trade Union Congress (AITUC). Hussain Shahid Suhrawardy formed the Bengal National Chamber of Labour (BNCL) in 1937, when he was labour minister in the Muslim League Government in Bengal, as a pro-Government labour organization acting as an arm of the incumbent regime. Similarly, and also in 1937, when in power in the seven Hindu majority provinces, the Indian National Congress formed the Indian National Trade Union Congress (INTUC) (Ahmad, 1969; Sharma, 1963). Finally, in 1941 M.N. Roy formed the Indian Federation of Labour (IFL) in order to promote India's involvement on the side of the Allies in the Second World War.[5] It is noteworthy that each one of these three newly formed umbrella labour organizations was organized under the aegis of a ruling party, and in all three cases their main purpose was to help sustain the political line and power of the respective ruling party rather than to concentrate on the well-being of the working class. This legacy of a multiplicity of politicized labour unions, as well as recurring conflicts among competing labour elites, is one of the key historical consequences of the colonial period.

The formation of Pakistan as a nation in 1947 was very peculiar, since historically West and East Pakistan were divided by distinctly different patterns of language, ethnicity and culture. On the whole, while the political leadership in West Pakistan was conservative and absolutely served the interests of the feudal elites, the leadership of East Pakistan was relatively liberal and connected to the rising middle class. While the majority of the West Pakistani people followed a relatively orthodox Islamic ideology, East Pakistani people were relatively secular; while the mother tongue of West Pakistan was Urdu, East Pakistani people spoke Bengali; and while historically West Pakistan had a conservative and relatively homogeneous cultural ethos, East

Pakistan had a diverse and humanitarian cultural heritage (Ahmad, 1975; Umar, 2004). After independence, West Pakistan became the power locus of Pakistan; conservative and feudal values dominated every sphere of society, and East Pakistan became in effect an internal colony of West Pakistan (Ahmad, 1975; Hossain, 2005; Mamoon and Ray, 1998; Sobhan, 2003; Umar, 2004). The period immediately following the creation of Pakistan was also marked by the emergence of US hegemony and the Cold War between the United States and Soviet Union, throwing the world into turmoil. The ideology of the ruling elites in Pakistan was in line with US economic and political policies, and these elites started suppressing the communists and other radical politicians in Bengal (East Pakistan) where progressive politics were relatively strong (Ahmad, 1969; Umar, 2004).

From 1947 the main labour leadership in Pakistan was in the hands of so-called liberals who were directly or indirectly associated with the ruling Muslim League. Hence the nature and actions of labour unions and labour movements during the early years of independent Pakistan were influenced by state patronage. The number of labour movements grew significantly in these years: about 250 unions were formed in which 200,000 workers registered with the Registrar of Trade Unions (Ahmad, 1969, p. 42). However, during these years labour unions were permeated by politicization, nepotism, corruption, splits and the cult of leadership. Furthermore, the labour leadership was dominated by conservatives; indeed, the main labour federation, the All Pakistan Confederation of Labour (APCOL), was guided and directed by the then labour minister, Dr Abdul Motaleb Malik. It is interesting that within three years of independence many labour federations, claiming to represent the workers of East Pakistan, were formed because of personal and political conflicts among leaders. This was the period when the main labour unions were preoccupied with state patronage and labour leaders were mainly concerned with personal gain rather than the interests of the workers. Another significant feature is that the major labour unions were led by people belonging to middle-class and professional groups who took unionism as a career; no leadership was developed from among the workers themselves (Ahmad, 1969; Umar, 2004).

During the late 1950s, labour organizations were directed and organized by the major political parties and hence labour movements became even more politicized. For example, in 1956 when the Bangladesh Awami League (or Awami League for short) came to the fore in East Pakistan, many labour leaders and workers joined this new party since it seemed to be a labour party (Ahmad, 1969). In 1958, after martial law was declared by General Ayub Khan, all kinds of trade union politics were banned and a large number of labour leaders and workers were arrested (Ahmad, 1969; Hossain, 2005; Umar, 2006). Even so, leftist labour leaders tried to reorganize various unions during the martial law period. The Awami League, as the emerging popular party at that time, also initiated various political movements against the military dictator and the continuing oppression of East Pakistan by West Pakistan; many of those political movements were organized and launched by labour leaders and workers (Ahmad, 1969; Mamoon and Ray, 1998; Ziring, 1992).

Between 1966 and 1969, Pakistan was in a serious political crisis. On the one hand, the military dictator tried to consolidate his regime by repressing political leaders, students, labour leaders and workers; on the other hand, oppositional groups launched a series of concerted street protests that eventually forced the military dictator to hand over power to another general, Yahiya Khan. In November 1968, the charismatic political leader Maulana Bhashani urged the rural poor to *gherao* (surround or blockade) various corrupt government officials in the rural areas, and since then *gherao* movements have become popular tools of protest in Bangladesh. During the anti-Ayub movement in 1969, the urban industrial workers applied this *gherao* strategy to intimidate and coerce the employers, with the support of other social forces, especially students (Ahmad, 1969; Mamoon and Ray, 1998; Umar, 2006). It is therefore understandable that the nationalist political struggle, headed by the Awami League's charismatic leader Sheikh Mujibur Rahman, dominated labour struggles between 1969 and 16 December 1971, when Bangladesh secured its independence.

There were three additional important features of labour politics in East Pakistan between 1947 and 1971. First, both the International Confederation of Free Trade Unions (ICFTU) and the American Federation of Labor–Congress of Industrial Organizations (AFL-CIO) were very active in Bangladesh. As a result, the East Pakistan Federation of Labour (EPFL) became affiliated to the ICFTU. When the EPFL acrimoniously split into three factions in 1960, "each one of them declared that the others had taken thousands from employers, from the ICFTU funds and from the AFL-CIO" (Ahmad, 1969, p. 50). Hence both trade union bureaucracy and trade union imperialism were important elements of labour politics. Second, as political movements and labour movements converged, the development of independent labour unions was seriously hampered. Third, despite repressive measures against labour unions including a ban on strikes, workers continually launched strikes (Umar, 2006).

At the point of Bangladesh's independence in 1971, both the nationalist Awami League and its leftist competitor, the National Awami Party, had their own strong labour unions that supported the paths taken by their respective political parties. In a broad sense, the multiplicity of labour unions, the power of the labour aristocracy, trade union imperialism, the politicization of labour unions, the close connections between the State and labour unions, and the cult of labour leaders all emerged under the Pakistani regime with numerous historical antecedents in the colonial period. Yet in spite of all the negative elements that developed during the Pakistani regime, leftist labour organizations such as the Chatkal Sramik Federation and Purba Pakistan Sramik Federation played significant roles in organizing various militant labour movements and achieving numerous labour rights after 1961.

Taking power in 1972 after the successful war of independence, the Awami League Government introduced a socialist economic policy, leading to the nationalization of more than 90 per cent of the country's enterprises (Akash, 1998; Sobhan and Ahmad, 1980). A progressive labour policy was announced in which workers' participation in management was initiated and a Workers' Management Council was formed in all nationalized industries (Siddique and Akkas, 2003; Sobhan and Ahmad, 1980). However, the authoritarian state bureaucracy and the right-wing members of the ruling party obstructed the implementation of this "Yugoslavian style" self-management policy. In 1975 the Government squeezed workers' rights by incorporating all the labour unions within a single organization, treated as an integral part of the socialist Government. Some commentators have argued that government leaders moved to politicize and incorporate labour unions for their own political interests in this period (Bhuiyan, 1991; Hossain, 2005; Umar and Kabir, 1978). As a result, corruption, nepotism and inter-union rivalry continued. Later that year the Awami League Government was ousted in a brutal military coup, in which the founder of the country, Sheikh Mujibur Rahman, and 18 of his 20 family members were assassinated.

After the coup, in 1975, General Ziaur Rahman (also known as General Zia or Zia) assumed the de facto authority of the State. Trade union politics were banned under martial law. Since Zia wanted to do politics, he formed a political front and later a political party, namely the Bangladesh Nationalist Party (BNP). In 1977, he lifted the ban on trade union politics and introduced a mandatory registration system for all labour unions. Henceforth the registration of 30 per cent of the employees in a workplace was required to form a union (Akkas, 1999; Hossain, 2005). Furthermore, registration could only be obtained by the labour front of a political party (Taher, 1998, p. 69). In 1979, General Zia formed his own labour front which directly served the interests of the BNP. General Zia created an environment in which inter-union rivalry became the norm; corruption and nepotism became permanent features in Bangladesh labour politics. Furthermore, he bought the allegiance of many political and labour leaders, mostly those of the right and pro-Beijing left (Ahmed, 1995; Akkas, 1999; Hossain, 2005; Siddique and Akkas, 2003).[6] He also introduced a privatization policy prescribed by the World Bank and IMF and sold many nationalized enterprises to supporters of the ruling party at undervalued prices (Ahmed, 2004; Akash, 1998). Labour movements during the Zia regime ground to a standstill.

This was the political context in which transnational corporations began to outsource the manufacture of RMG to Bangladesh in the early 1980s.

Labour unions' failures in the RMG sector since 1980

General Ziaur Rahman's time in power ended in 1981, when he was assassinated during an unsuccessful military coup. In 1982 another general, H.M. Ershad, captured power from the BNP and ruled the country until 1990, when a mass student movement toppled his regime. Like his predecessor, General Ershad formed a new political party, Jatiyo Party. Ershad followed the neoliberal policies of his predecessor, and as a consequence several more state-owned organizations were sold to private owners at very cheap prices, following the Structural Adjustment Programme prescribed by the IMF (Akash, 1998). In order to consolidate his power, General Ershad spent large sums of state money on the formation of labour, student and youth fronts. In fact, a number of the leaders of General Ziaur Rahman's BNP simply transferred to the newly formed political party of General Ershad. These political leaders threw off any semblance of political principle and immersed themselves in the politics of money, power and corruption (Ahmed, 1995; Hossain, 2005; Mamoon and Ray, 1998).

Throughout the Ershad regime, progressive labour leaders initiating various anti-military movements were repressed by harsh measures while the ruling party labour front grew in stature by incorporating veteran opposition leaders. Labour unions were used as one of the main arms of the military dictatorship. Inter-union rivalries, corruption and nepotism spread throughout public enterprises while competition over lucrative trade union positions and offices, even to the extent of opponents being killed, became a permanent feature of the labour unions in nationalized enterprises in Bangladesh (Akkas, 1999; Siddique and Akkas, 2003; Talukder, 1997). Nonetheless, an oppositional labour movement eventually emerged, protesting against various anti-labour acts by the Ershad regime. A significant step occurred in 1984 when major labour unions in the country formed SKOP and initiated a range of actions against anti-labour measures (Hossain, 2005; Rock, 2001b). Nevertheless, the focus of oppositional unions was on action at the political level, and the nascent RMG sector was largely ignored. Furthermore, the unity of the oppositional labour movement was soon thereafter shattered when two of its central leaders joined the Ershad Government as Cabinet members and the labour unions sponsored by the Awami League stopped participating in SKOP. Later in the 1980s all labour unions once again worked through SKOP. It should be noted, however, that between 1984 and 1990 SKOP did not realize even one of its demands: the military regime would sign agreements but would never enact them (Hossain, 2005).

Since the autocratic Ershad regime was forced from power in 1990 by powerful student movements, democratic means have been used to select governments in Bangladesh. From 1991 to 1996, and from 2001 to 2006, the BNP ruled the country; the Awami League held power from 1996 to 2001, and returned to power once more in 2009 after a brief period of caretaker government. It is interesting that although both the Awami League and BNP claim allegiance to democratic norms and practices, neither of the parties has made any remarkable contributions towards the welfare of the workers. When either party was in power, many agreements were signed with labour union federations but most of them remained unrealized. Since both parties support an open market economy, their policies towards workers and unions are very similar. In fact, during each of the parties' period in office, the respective ruling party's labour front became very powerful and everything was carried out in accordance with the party line. As a result, during the period of democratic governance over the past 20 years, the major labour unions in Bangladesh have continued to represent the interests of political parties rather than those of workers. It is disturbing to note here that the major labour unions in Bangladesh had become so myopic and obsolete by 2002 that when the Government closed a 50-year-old nationalized jute mill and snatched away the employment of 30,000 workers, no fruitful resistance was mounted (Rahman and Langford, 2010, p. 55).

Garment manufacturing in Bangladesh is governed by two separate regulatory regimes. The majority of the RMG factories exist outside the EPZs, have Bangladeshi owners and are covered by the regulations of the Bangladesh Labour Law of 2006. Two main state agencies are responsible for enforcing these regulations: the Directorate of Labour (DL) and the Office of the Chief Inspector of Factories and Establishment (CIFE). Both of these agencies are widely regarded as being financially corrupt and under the influence of factory owners. Union leader Lovely Yesmin recounted an example of such corruption. As a child and a young adult she worked for Sparrow Apparels in Mirpur. In response to a repressive work environment that included physical harassment and forced overtime, Lovely Yesmin and her supervisor, Ms Jaheda Begum, decided to organize a union in the late 1980s. They were success-ful in registering the union with the DL. However, when the newly formed union submitted an eight-point set of demands to Sparrow Apparels just two days after getting their union registration, they faced ruthless obstruction from the owner and management. According to Ms Yesmin, the owner employed a number of repressive measures, including hiring local thugs. The unionists learned that the owner was able to organize these repressive measures quickly because he had been given information about the union from someone at the DL office. Lovely Yesmin explained the nexus between the corrupt state officials and factory owners: "What happens in our country is that the Joint Director of Labour or the Office of the Factory Inspector actually do not work in favour of the workers; they maintain a liaison with the owners. … Initially they [DL officials] wanted our organization to be formed or the union to be registered but they supplied all the information to the owner later on."[7]

A second major problem with the enforcement of the Bangladesh Labour Law in the RMG sector is that the Office of the CIFE lacks the resources to carry out its mission. In 2007 this office was responsible for inspecting 22,000 factories, including those in the RMG sector, all over Bangladesh. However, at that time it employed only 48 factory inspectors. In an interview the Chief Inspector indicated he had urged the Government to provide funds to hire an additional 315 people. After a struggle that lasted three years, the Ministry of Establishment approved the hiring of only 146 personnel and subsequently the Ministry of Finance cut the number to 59 – and this number included all positions, not just factory inspectors.

The second regulatory regime covers the small minority of RMG factories that are located in one of the eight EPZs in Bangladesh. Much of the investment in the

EPZs has been made by foreign investors, and the EPZs were established with a legal prohibition on trade unionism (Fair Labor Association, 2005; ILO, 1998). In contrast, in the RMG factories outside the EPZs trade unionism was allowed in principle (as Lovely Yesmin's account of registering a union at Sparrow Apparels in the late 1980s revealed) but nevertheless strongly opposed and repressed when it took practical form (Khan, 2001; Rock, 2001b; Zaman, Arefin and Ahmed, 2002). Indeed, there was only one political party/labour union that was active in organizing garment workers during the 1980s – a pro-China leftist party, the Bangladesh Workers' Party, which was more interested in recruiting workers for its own political purposes than in trying to build a solid basis for the mass unionization of the sector. Furthermore, throughout the 1980s, no NGOs, philanthropic organizations or international groups were active on the questions of labour rights and the exploitation of garment workers.

Within this closed opportunity structure, there were occasional worker protests at particular factories but no organized protest movements aided by established labour unions. The occasional protests were spontaneous and often quite militant: common actions included factory blockades, destruction of the means of production, sit-in protests, processions and mass meetings in front of the factories. Such spontaneous protests occurred because the workers in the industry generally suffered from oppressive and often unsafe working conditions, poor wages and poor benefits.

Towards the end of the 1980s, some union registration drives were launched after local working-class leaders communicated with the leaders of union federations. In addition, international organizations, especially the Asian American Free Labor Institute (AAFLI) – now called Solidarity Center (SC) – aided various individual factory leaders and developed the Bangladesh Independent Garment-Workers Union (BIGU). Despite the infusion of such outside resources, however, most of the union drives were ruthlessly suppressed by local musclemen employed by the factory owners or by the state police, both of whom often used physical torture against union activists. In addition, union drives were undercut by various deceitful strategies, including short-term increases in wages, bonuses or overtime rates, and buying off union leaders by awarding them a promotion or even a straightforward bribe.

The fire at the Saraka Garments factory in December 1990, which killed 27 people, blew the lid off this bleak, repressive situation. Thousands of workers came out into the streets and an opportunity arose to unite the disconnected local leaders working in the RMG industry. Therefore, even though the main pattern in the industry throughout the 1980s and into the 1990s was a lack of working-class resistance and protest, the 1990s saw an increasing number of localized protest movements under the banners of various unrecognized factory-based unions. The main organizing tactic of the unions was to organize street protests outside garment factories. In addition, some unions placed demands directly before the BGMEA on issues such as the length of the working week and overtime pay. However, these attempts at negotiation failed. A prime example of the unions' inadequacy is the repetitive sequence of agreements that the Bangladesh Garment Workers Unity Council (BGWUC) has made with the BGMEA regarding the same issues time and again. The typical pattern of negotiation follows this course: the BGWUC announces a tough set of demands, and the BGMEA is reluctant even to negotiate; the workers' organization then follows up with a contentious action like a strike, upon which the BGMEA is eager to make an agreement; and then after things settle down, the BGMEA shows no interest in implementing the agreement. This pattern has been repeated with monotonous regularity since 1997. It is noteworthy that the BGWUC's demands have never amounted to anything more than the implementation of Bangladesh's labour laws. The failure of the unions to get the BGMEA to implement agreements is, therefore, an indication not only of labour's impotence but also of the State's complicity in the suppression of workers' rights. Our contention is that labour leaders in the RMG industry often launch negotiations with the BGMEA not because they expect to improve the lot of workers but to justify their own existence.

The persistent general weakness of the mainstream union movement in Bangladesh is a key reason why unions have failed the nascent garment proletariat. The contemporary characteristics of the mainstream labour unions – their political subservience, corruption, nepotism, lack of a democratic union culture and domination by a trade union bureaucracy – are the product of historical forces that are ultimately connected to the overall underdevelopment of Bangladesh in the capitalist world-system. In tandem with the weakness of mainstream unions has gone the relegation of progressive trade unionism to the margins of Bangladeshi society between the 1960s and 1980s when the RMG industry was becoming established; as a consequence, progressive unions were in no position to organize anything but small pockets of the huge RMG workforce.

The unfavourable political opportunity structure for labour unions and the State's shameless subservience to the interests of capital are two other general factors that help explain unions' failure in this sector from 1980. The State's anti-worker actions in the RMG sector have included the routine suppression of spontaneous workers' protests by the police; the failure to hire enough factory inspectors to enforce employment and occupational standards; and the prevalence of state officials who are willing to accept bribes from owners.

As noted above, beginning in the 1990s a number of labour unions became active among the garment proletariat, although union attempts to negotiate with owners on behalf of workers were uniformly unsuccessful right up to the May 2006 uprising. During these years industrial relations in the sector were marked by the refusal of RMG owners and the Government to respect the collective bargaining process, and by the timid responses of labour unions to the prevarications of the owners. It is important to note, however, that the ever-increasing mass of workers was accumulating valuable experience of capitalist relations of production in the 1980s and 1990s and right up to the eve of the 2006 uprising. What this meant is that even though the majority of the female labour force presented themselves as uninformed about their basic rights and intimidated by authority figures,[8] they were developing a practical (as opposed to a discursive) class consciousness that could readily be mobilized in a strike wave; indeed, this is exactly what occurred in May 2006.

The lack of outside support and internal divisions in the labour movement itself are two further reasons why labour unions have failed the garment proletariat in Bangladesh. Historically, civil society in Bangladesh has meant the sophisticated, urban, educated middle class that has been the main participant group in broad political movements. However, up until recently there have been no prominent organizations that link this urban middle class to the RMG proletariat. The labour fronts of the major political parties could have taken on this role, but never did. As a consequence, during the course of the spontaneous protests that marked the early years of the industry, workers had to rely upon contributions from passers-by on the street to sustain their collective actions. It is little wonder that worker resistance was fleeting rather than sustained.

In recent years some support for workers has flowed into the RMG sector from international labour organizations and from both international and Bangladeshi NGOs. This has not been a uniformly positive process. For instance, the support provided by the SC, itself backed by the AFL-CIO, may well be tainted since it appears to promote the protectionist interests of US manufacturers and labour unions. The SC directly funds BIGU and indirectly funds the Bangladesh Garment and Industrial Workers Federation. Two local NGOs, Karmojibi Nari and the Awaj Foundation, also sponsor their own labour unions (Bangladesh Garment Sramik Jote and the United Garment Workers Federation, respectively). Furthermore, some NGOs have undercut labour unions by taking on union-like roles and others unintentionally undermine the willingness of workers to volunteer freely for union activity by paying those same workers for participation in NGO seminars. On the other hand, however, domestic NGOs such as the Bangladesh Institute of Labour Studies and Bangladesh Legal Aid and Service Trust, and international NGOs such as Oxfam, have provided significant boosts to the efforts of resource-starved Bangladesh unions.

Finally, internal weaknesses and divisions have limited the effectiveness of Bangladesh labour unions in the RMG sector. First, it is indeed peculiar that there are so many separate unions and alliances of unions,[9] given the generally accepted motto of the labour movement that "in unity there is strength". This multiplicity of organizations is not, in our view, a by-product of differences in political ideology and strategy; rather, each alliance is based on the personal interests of its leader in terms of fame, career advancement and resources. This point is supported by the extraordinary fact that the federations are identified in Bangladeshi society by the leaders' names rather than the official names of the organizations. Another reason for the proliferation of federations is that there exists a variety of international organizations, local NGOs and employers' organizations, all of which prefer to sponsor their own respective labour union allies rather than face the uncertainty of dealing with an independent union federation.

The existence of so many alliances leads to many conflicts among union leaders in Bangladesh. Indeed, we believe that the reason labour unions were unable to consolidate gains after the May 2006 garment worker uprising lay in inter-union rivalry, mistrust and lack of respect. Another negative consequence of this situation is that unions have to expend a much higher proportion of their limited resources on basic organizational survival than they would if there were a smaller number of larger unions in the sector.

Second, the diverse backgrounds of the labour leaders are a compounding source of division. Some of the leaders have almost no education, coming directly from the factory, while a number have higher degrees and lack any direct working-class experience; this second category includes many of the country's prominent national labour leaders. In interviews in 2007, the first author of this chapter observed that many of the labour leaders who lacked formal education seemed to be jealous of their counterparts who had higher degrees, social status and prominence. At the same time, veteran labour leaders with advanced education tended to ignore and dismiss those new leaders who had come from the shop floor because of the latters' perceived lack of knowledge and sophistication.

Third, although internal divisions are an important factor, the lack of finance is the number one problem for labour unions. It means that they do not have the means to run independently and are forced to form alliances with organizations that can offer material help (either local NGOs or international organizations of some type). This situation creates additional rivalry among the unions, since they are in competition for outside help. The only exceptions to this pattern are the unions based on left ideology that depend on well-wishers' donations. It must be noted that even unions with a sizeable number of members cannot avoid the problem of a lack of funds. This is because most garment workers are so poor that they cannot afford to pay any union dues.

Implications of the May 2006 mass uprising by garment workers

The broad details of the May 2006 uprising were sketched in the introduction to this chapter. This concluding section provides additional details and analysis, and identifies the strategic actions that hold out the most hope for advancing the interests of Bangladesh's garment workers in the coming years.

The May 2006 movement of garment workers was so powerful and widespread that it eventually had an impact on the Dhaka EPZ area; indeed, strikes and other forms of unrest occurred in various EPZ factories in early June, during the second week after the main uprising. The owners responded by closing their EPZ factories from 4 June for an indefinite period of time. However, on the initiative of the

Government, the Bangladesh Export Processing Zone Authority, owners and workers met and agreed to a number of concessions, including the historic provision of trade union rights for workers in an EPZ; as a result, production resumed about a week later (Cheng, 2006).

The workers' movement of May 2006 received widespread public sympathy and attention. The representative of the ILO in Bangladesh, various international and local NGOs, and many prominent Bangladeshi civil society leaders supported the demands of the unions (Rashid, 2006), especially an increase in a minimum wage that had been frozen since 1994 (Cheng, 2006).

Contemporary social movement theory can be used to help explain how this movement emerged and flourished. Within such an adverse political opportunity structure, where plant-level dispute mechanisms were completely absent and repression levels were high, the initial factory movements could not have developed in the way they did without help from external organizations (in this case, two unions with ties to leftist political organizations).[10] For the same reasons, extreme militancy was the only hope for successful labour action. In terms of the mobilization of resources, the initial factory movements depended upon the limited resources of rank-and-file workers supplemented by the relatively limited resources of the radical unions. One important political resource of the two unions was their close working relationship, which allowed them to coordinate the protests on 23 May 2006 in order to obtain maximum effect. The explosion of consciousness and mass action on that day, however, cannot be explained using resource mobilization concepts – it better fits the model of working-class mobilization theorized by Rosa Luxemburg and the later industrial relations scholar John Kelly (1988).

In conclusion, while we recognize that recommending an emancipatory model for Bangladesh's RMG workers is not easy, we think three complementary strategies are well worth pursuing. First, contemporary garment workers and their union leaders require enormous institutional support and resources to build their organizations and capacities for political action. Our suggestion is that capacity training and awareness education should be the number one priority during quiet periods of class struggle. What is needed is a network of proletarian schools that teach literacy while simultaneously helping workers to better understand the character of class relations in the garment industry and to build rank-and-file networks. For this sort of project, resources from domestic and international NGOs and genuine internationalist working-class organizations would be essential.

Second, when it comes to achieving gains for garment workers it is evident that soft, non-confrontational approaches are totally ineffective in Bangladesh; unless the State and the owners receive a severe and alarming blow from mobilized workers, they ignore even the most basic and reasonable demands. The power of mass, contentious protest by the working class was demonstrated by the movement that burst out after the tragic Saraka Garments fire in 1990 and by the upsurge in protest in May 2006.

Third, although militant mass protests have yielded dramatic concessions from factory owners and the Government, such concessions have been difficult to consolidate after labour relations have returned to "normal". This indicates that the Bangladesh Government must be pressured to reform the labour relations system such that (1) independent unions are no longer ignored and repressed, and (2) employers are required to engage in meaningful collective bargaining. Although domestic organizations need to take the lead in promoting such demands, international organizations can make significant contributions to such a pressure campaign.

It is true that there is always a risk in attempting to build militant movements because the dominant elites and their supporters (a large section of the educated middle class, some NGOs and think-tanks, and even some labour organizations) continuously argue in favour of peaceful movements and against any militancy. The position of the NGOs on this strategic matter is understandable, given that these organizations are very dependent upon Western organizations for financial support. Nonetheless, it is our argument that until the State changes its elite-centred policy, until the owners change their feudal mindset and unhesitatingly abide by the labour laws and ILO Conventions, and until international labour organizations are free from any hidden protectionist agendas, militant movements are essential to the successful pursuit of workers' demands. If the militant kind of labour movement can be roughly classified as the Marx–Polanyi type of movement, then the only remedy for the exploitation and repression that ails the RMG proletariat in Bangladesh at this point is just such a militant movement.

Notes

[1] Bangladesh (then known as Bengal) was part of the British colony of India until 1947. In 1947, after 200 years of British rule, India gained independence and was divided into two different states: India and Pakistan, the latter divided into East and West Pakistan. Until 1971, Bangladesh was named East Pakistan. In 1971, after a nine-month armed struggle for independence from West Pakistan, Bangladesh appeared on the world map as an independent State.

[2] The minimum wage was raised on 27 July 2010 from BDT1,662.50 to BDT3,000; this is the only significant improvement achieved by RMG workers since the 2006 protests. It is not surprising, then, that factory-level protest movements are currently a common feature in the RMG industry in Bangladesh.

[3] Hindu–Muslim riots were very common in colonial India, and were exploited by the colonial rulers to "divide and rule" the people whenever needed. After the British invaded India, defeating the Muslim ruling class, Muslims tended to be very hostile towards the British, while Hindus were more likely to cooperate and take the resulting benefits. The conflicts spread not only among the elites but also among the masses and industrial workers. This inter-communal antagonism was fomented by the British rulers and as a result became one of the main barriers to working-class solidarity in India. A lower-caste Hindu assassinated Gandhi, a pioneer in defending working-class interests, because he did not subscribe to this communalism and consequently opposed Hindu–Muslim conflict.

[4] Sharma (1963, p. 27) quoted a very revealing exchange concerning this feudal *ma–bap* (mother–father) relationship: "The personnel officer of one firm asked a worker representative who was demanding a long list of free amenities, including free shoes, 'But why free shoes?' The worker replied, 'Shahib, the company is our father and our mother.'"

[5] The AITUC did not support Indian participation in the Second World War because of its official opposition to British colonial rule. For supporting the colonial Government's war role, the IFL received INR13,000 per month (Sharma, 1963).

[6] For instance, Kazi Jafar Ahmed, once famous as a pro-Beijing leftist student and trade union leader, became the country's education minister during the Zia regime. In the 1980s, under General Ershad's regime, Mr Ahmed became Prime Minister (Ahmed, 1995; Hossain, 2005; Mamoon and Ray, 1998).

[7] First author's interview, 2007.

[8] These tendencies were strongly apparent in four focus group discussions with garment workers conducted by the first author in 2007.

[9] In 2007 there were four major alliances of unions active in the RMG industry, each with between eight and 16 affiliated unions. Independent unions active in the industry sometimes form temporary alliances with one another.

[10] The two radical unions were the Bangladesh Garment Workers Union Federation (active at F.S. Sweater) and the Bangladesh Garment Workers Trade Union Centre (active at Universal Knitting). The latter is the labour front of the Communist Party of Bangladesh.

References

Ahmad, K. 1969. *Labour movement in East Pakistan* (Dhaka, Progoti).

—. 1975. *A socio-political history of Bengal and the birth of Bangladesh* (Dacca [Dhaka], Zahiruddin Mahnud Inside Library).

Ahmed, F.E. 2004. "The rise of the Bangladesh garment industry: Globalization, women workers, and voice", in *NWSA Journal* [now *Feminist Formations*], Vol. 16, No. 2, pp. 34–45.

Ahmed, M. 1995. *Democracy and the challenge of development: A study of politics and military interventions in Bangladesh* (Dhaka, University Press Ltd).

Akash, M.M. 1998. *Privatization and its implication for labour relations: Bangladesh experience*, paper presented at the ILO National Tripartite Seminar on Globalization and its Impact on Industrial Relations in Bangladesh, Dhaka, 13–16 July.

Akkas, A.M. 1999. "Politicization of trade unions in Bangladesh: Causes and consequences", in *Dhaka University Journal of Business Studies*, Vol. 20, No. 2, pp. 37–60.

Alavi, H. 1979. "The state in post-colonial societies: Pakistan and Bangladesh", in H. Goulbourne (ed.): *Politics and state in the third world* (London, Macmillan), pp. 38–69.

Bangladesh Garment Manufacturers and Exporters Association (BGMEA). 2012. *BGMEA at a glance.* Available at: http://www.bgmea.com.bd [30 May 2012].

Basu, D. 1993. *The working class in Bengal* (Calcutta, K.P. Bagchi & Co.).

Bhuiyan, S. 1991. "The trade union politics in Bangladesh: A study of textile mills workers union", in *Dhaka University Studies Part C*, Vol. 12, No. 1, pp. 141–57.

Cheng, E. 2006. "Bangladesh: Workers revolt against pay squeeze", in *Green Left Weekly*, 26 July. Available at: http://www.greenleft.org.au/node/34903 [30 May 2012].

Dannecker, P. 2002. *Between conformity and resistance: Women garment workers in Bangladesh* (Dhaka, University Press Ltd).

Das, R.K. 1923. *The labour movement in India* (Berlin and Leipzig, De Gruyter).

Etienne, G. 1979. *Bangladesh: Development in perspective* (Delhi, Macmillan India).

Fair Labor Association. 2005. "Freedom of association in Bangladesh", in *Annual Report 2004*. Available at: http://www.fairlabor.org/sites/default/files/documents/reports/2004_annual_public_report_ part4.pdf [1 July 2012].

Hossain, A. 2005. *Bangladesher sramik andoloner itihash* [The history of labour movements in Bangladesh] (Dhaka, Parua).

International Labour Office (ILO). 1998. *Labour and social issues related to export processing zones*, Report for discussion at the Tripartite Meeting of Export Processing Zones-Operating Countries, Geneva, 28 Sep.–2 Oct.

Kabeer, N. 1991. "Cultural dopes or rational fools? Women and labour supply in the Bangladesh garment industry", in *European Journal of Development Research*, Vol. 3, No. 1, pp. 133–60.

—. 2004. "Globalization, labour standards, and women's rights: Dilemmas of collective (in)action in an interdependent world", in *Feminist Economics*, Vol. 10, No. 1, pp. 3–35.

Kelly, J. 1988. *Trade unions and socialist politics* (London, Verso).

Khan, S. 2008. "Prospects of RMG export to USA under Obama", in *The Financial Express*, 10 Nov. Available at: http://www.thefinancialexpress-bd.com/more.php?news_id=50328&date=2008-11-10 [1 July 2012].

Khan, S.I. 2001. "Gender issues and the ready-made garment industry of Bangladesh: The trade union context", in R. Sobhan and N. Khundker (eds): *Globalisation and gender: Changing patterns of women's employment in Bangladesh* (Dhaka, Centre for Policy Dialogue and University Press Ltd), pp. 167–218.

McCarthy, F.; Feldman, S. 1983. "Rural women discovered: New sources of capital and labour in Bangladesh", in *Development and Change*, Vol. 14, No. 2, pp. 211–36.

Mamoon, M.; Ray, J.K. 1998. *Civil society in Bangladesh: Resilience and retreat* (Dhaka, Subarna).

Mirdah, R. 2010. "Bangladesh ranks fourth in global apparel exports says WTO report", in *Daily Star*, 25 July. Available at http://www.thedailystar.net/newDesign/news-details.php?nid=148118 [30 May 2012].

Rahman, Z.; Langford, T. 2010. "The limitations of global social movement unionism as an emancipatory labour strategy in majority world countries", in *Socialist Studies*, Vol. 6, No. 1, pp. 45–64.

Rashid, M. 2006. "RMG in Bangladesh: Wakeup call and the ground realities", in *Daily Star*, 6 June. Available at http://www.thedailystar.net/2006/06/06/d60606050356.htm [1 July 2012].

Read, M. 1931. *The Indian peasant uprooted* (London, Longmans, Green & Co.).

Rock, M. 2001a. "Globalisation and Bangladesh: The case of export-oriented garment manufacture", in *Journal of South Asian Studies*, Vol. 24, No. 1, pp. 201–26.

—. 2001b. "The rise of the Bangladesh independent garment workers' union (BIGU)", in J. Hatchison and A. Brown (eds): *Organising labour in globalising Asia* (London, Routledge), pp. 27–47.

Saha, P. 1978. *History of the working-class movement in Bengal* (New Delhi, People's Publishing House).

Sharma, G.K. 1963. *Labour movement in India (its past and present)* (Jullundur, University Publishers).

Siddiqi, H.G.A. 2004. *The ready-made garment industry of Bangladesh* (Dhaka, University Press Ltd).

Siddique, S.A.; Akkas, A.M. 2003. "The role of the state in the industrial system in Bangladesh", in *Dhaka University Journal of Business Studies*, Vol. 24, No. 1, pp. 1–15.

Sobhan, R. 2003. *Bourgeoise rasto babosther sankat* [Crisis of the bourgeois state system] (Dhaka, Shahitika).

—; Ahmad, M. 1980. *Public enterprise in an intermediate regime* (Dhaka, Bangladesh Institute of Development Studies).

Taher, M.A. 1998. "Politicization of trade unions: Issues and challenges in Bangladesh perspective", in *Journal of Asiatic Society of Bangladesh (Hum.)*, Vol. 34, No. 2, pp. 68–79.

Talukder, M.A.S. 1997. *Labour and industry* (Dhaka, Nasa Prokashony).

Umar, B. 2004. *The emergence of Bangladesh*, Vol. 1: *Class struggles in East Pakistan (1947–1958)* (Oxford, Oxford University Press).

—. 2006. *The emergence of Bangladesh*, Vol. 2: *The rise of Bengali nationalism (1958–1971)* (Oxford, Oxford University Press).

—; Kabir, S. 1978. *Bangladesh marxbad o sramik andoloner samasya* [Bangladesh Marxism and the problems of labour movements] (Dhaka, Jubo Prakashani).

Zaman, F.; Arefin, K.; Ahmed, M. 2002. "Comparison of trade unions in developed and developing countries: Bangladesh perspectives", in *Journal of Business Administration*, Vol. 2, Nos. 3–4, pp. 21–33.

Ziring, L. 1992. *Bangladesh from Mujib to Ershad: An interpretative study* (Dhaka, University Press Ltd).

PART II

POLITICAL MOVEMENTS AND TRADE UNIONS

BRAZILIAN LABOUR RELATIONS IN LULA'S ERA: TELEMARKETING OPERATORS AND THEIR UNIONS

6

Ruy Braga

The uncommonly high approval ratings of Luiz Inácio Lula da Silva's Government, which guaranteed Dilma Roussef's victory as his successor in the 2010 presidential election, clearly stimulated the Brazilian sociological imagination, prompting the question: what are the bases of the current Lulist hegemony? Undoubtedly, one of the most important contributions to the debate over so-called "Lulism" has been André Singer's famous article of 2009. According to Singer's now well-known argument, beginning in May 2005, during the scandalous "Mensalão" (monthly backhander) period, when members of Parliament bought votes, Lula's Workers' Party (PT) Government would have lost to the opposition Social Democratic Party (PSDB) a significant number of the supporters it had won over in 2002 from the urban middle class. However, low-income Brazilian voters, though traditionally not in favour of Lula, would have been attracted by government-promoted public policies; during the 2006 presidential campaign they would have warmed to the PT programme and, in a movement known in political science as electoral realignment, decided solidly to side with the incumbent candidate, thereby guaranteeing his victory (Singer, 2009).

Comparing electoral research for 2002 and 2006, Singer offered a vast body of evidence for this realignment, and demonstrated that a vote for Lula in 2006 was largely a "popular" vote, whereas the opposing candidate, Geraldo Alckmin, would have been preferred by the middle and upper classes. This identification with Lula and the PT on the part of the unqualified, underpaid, low-status workers known as the "sub-proletarian" class led Singer to identify in Brazil the revival of a phenomenon genealogically associated with the rich history of Latin American populism. Singer understands the "sub-proletariat" to consist of those who receive up to the minimum wage plus half of those paid up to twice the minimum wage. According to this criterion, 63 per cent of the Brazilian proletariat consisted of sub-proletarians. Singer's hypothesis runs as follows: *Lulism is the ideological expression of a class fraction incapable of constructing autonomous forms of organization that looks instead to the State for the optimal path to reducing social inequality.* Our aim here will be to test this hypothesis through an analysis of one of the sub-proletarian groups which has grown most strongly over the past decade: telemarketing operators, or tele-operators.

Characteristics of the Brazilian call centre industry

In Brazil, this sector was formed only very recently. In fact, 96 per cent of the Brazilian tele-activity centres (CTAs) were created after 1990, and 76 per cent after 1998, the year Telebrás was privatized and at the height of neoliberal policies in the country. Between 1998 and 2002, the number of jobs in the sector grew at an annual rate of 15 per cent: figures from the Ministry of Labour indicate that during Lula's time in government this accelerated to 20 per cent per year, representing total growth of 282 per cent between 2003 and 2009 (see figure 6.1).

In fact, the total numbers are even greater, for the Ministry of Labour figures take into account only outsourced tele-operators. When in-house CTAs are included, the Brazilian Association of Teleservices, which represents call centre businesses,

Figure 6.1 Numbers of telemarketing operators in Brazil, 2003–09

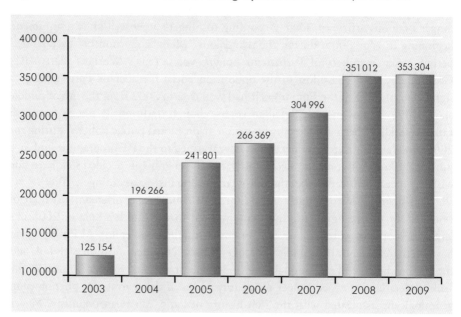

Note: Telemarketing operators defined according to Brazilian occupational classification 4223.

Source: Brazilian Ministry of Labour and Employment/Rais.

Table 6.1   Percentage growth in numbers of telemarketing operators in Brazil, by region, 2004–09

Region	Growth over previous year (%)						Growth 2004–09
	2004	2005	2006	2007	2008	2009	
North	1.20	13.04	36.46	–7.37	–1.66	10.42	57.02
North-east	101.68	21.98	4.02	13.85	19.73	8.11	277.12
South-east	62.22	22.79	11.86	16.61	15.48	–0.02	199.96
South	20.16	29.33	11.89	7.91	4.93	–0.92	95.08
East-central	40.12	21.42	–2.21	6.61	22.01	–0.73	114.83
All Brazil	56.82	23.20	10.16	14.50	15.09	0.65	182.30

Note: Telemarketing operators defined according to Brazilian occupational classification 4223.

Source: Brazilian Ministry of Labour and Employment/Rais.

estimates that in 2010 more than 1.2 million workers were employed in the sector. This increase transformed the call centre sector into the main gateway for young people into the country's formal labour market, in addition to creating the second and third biggest private employers in the country, Contax (78,200 employees) and Atento (76,400 employees). Furthermore, this increase, despite still being concentrated in the south-east of the country (where total employment in the sector, according to the Ministry of Labour, reached 259,108 in 2009), is now extending to the north-east. During Lula's time in government, it was the north-east that showed the greatest growth (277.12 per cent) in the number of tele-operators in the Brazilian call centre industry (see tables 6.1 and 6.2).

It is worth remembering that nearly all these jobs constitute formal employment: that is, they are governed by labour legislation and subject to collective bargaining. Consequently, the recognized trend towards informal employment in the north-east region has transformed telemarketing into an appealing activity for young workers

Table 6.2   Numbers of telemarketing operators in Brazil, by region, 2003–09

Region	2003	2004	2005	2006	2007	2008	2009
North	1 417	1 434	1 621	2 212	2 049	2 015	2 225
North-east	9 253	18 661	22 763	23 678	26 958	32 278	34 895
South-east	86 381	140 125	172 063	192 470	224 431	259 162	259 108
South	16 692	20 057	25 940	29 024	31 319	32 863	32 562
East-central	11 411	15 989	19 414	18 985	20 239	24 694	24 514
All Brazil	125 154	196 266	241 801	266 369	304 996	351 012	353 304

Note: Telemarketing operators defined according to Brazilian occupational classification 4223.

Source: Brazilian Ministry of Labour and Employment/Rais.

with no previous work experience. When, as a result of the development of a new regime of post-Fordist accumulation, supported by entrepreneurial outsourcing, neoliberal privatization and labour financialization, Brazilian call centres spread to the north-east under Lula's Government, they could draw on a vast pool of young, largely female and black, workers in search of their first opportunity in the formal labour market. In encapsulating part of the recent evolution of work relations in the country, the call centre industry has proved to be a privileged place to observe current modifications in the Brazilian post-Fordist sub-proletarian class. To sum up:

- This is a group of young workers.

- The workers are unskilled or semi-skilled.

- The workers are in precarious conditions of employment.

- The workers earn between once and twice the minimum wage.

- The workers are employed in labour relations that inhibit collective organization.

- The call centre industry gathers thousands of workers from the informal sector, without prior experience of unionization.

- The sector provides access to labour rights.

- The sector provides access to some sort of professional qualification.

- The sector condenses salient features of the current peripheral post-Fordist regime of accumulation: business outsourcing, privatization and neoliberal financialization of work.

In following the trajectory of tele-operators, our research emphasizes four key variables: model of labour organization; level of skills; rates of pay; and forms of collective mobilization.[1]

In respect of the general characteristics of tele-operators' work process, our field research in two of the largest Brazilian call centre businesses, one in domestic and the other in international ownership, found that with the automatization of tele-operator work, productivity gains come at the cost of a sharp increase in physical fatigue, fixed posture, part-time work contracts, dizziness from the multiplicity of calls, and illness at work. In fact, throughout our field research, from the questionnaires administered to the selected sample in both businesses and from our contact with tele-operators through in-depth interviews, we came across a reality marked by repetitive strain injury, tendonitis, Ménière's disease (bouts of severe dizziness with ringing in the ears and progressive hearing loss), acute depression, urinary tract infections (because of the limits on bathroom breaks), obesity, uncontrolled hypertension and vocal cord nodules. The answers to our questionnaire revealed a clear link between working hours and the declining health of operators (see Braga and Antunes, 2009).

To a great extent, it seems reasonable to us to assume that workplace illness in the telemarketing sector, as recorded both by academic researchers and in investigations conducted by the Department of Labour Relations, derives from a combination of factors, among which are inadequate training, stress arising from pressure to meet targets, negligence with respect to ergonomics and the ambient temperature of the workplace, insufficient breaks during the day, lack of days off, the strict monitoring of tele-operators and the increased hours of work which accompany the process of technological innovation (see Freire, 2002; also Assunção et al., 2006; Marx, 2000; Pimentel, 2009).

Another salient characteristic of the Brazilian call centre industry is its oligopolistic nature. In 2011 the total number of workers in the two largest companies (154,600) corresponded to 86 per cent of the total number of workers of the 18 next largest companies (180,479). This is a feature that clearly differentiates the Brazilian call centre industry from its counterparts in, for example, France and the United States. This oligopolistic characteristic, in addition to the low-skilled workforce and the relative weakness of the unions acting in this sector, helps us to understand why – even though the large majority of Brazilian tele-operators (70 per cent) are covered by collective bargaining – Brazilian salaries in this sector (averaging US$3,415 a year where covered by collective bargaining, and US$4,484 a year where not covered by collective bargaining) are among the lowest in the world in this sector, surpassing only those of Indian workers. For the sake of comparison, a US tele-operator earns a yearly salary of US$35,000 and a tele-operator in South Africa US$11,200: ten and three times, respectively, the salary of a Brazilian tele-operator. The low wages correspond to the low skill level of the workforce: among the 17 countries sampled by David Holman, Rosemary Batt and Ursula Holtgrewe, Brazilian tele-operators had the lowest level of education (see Holman, Batt and Holtgrewe, 2007).

With the rate of female participation in the workforce approaching 70 per cent, and a high proportion of Afro-Brazilians, it is possible to say that Brazilian tele-operators are mainly black women – in other words, they belong to precisely that sub-proletarian group that has historically occupied the worst positions in the labour market, as well as heading 80 per cent of the single-parent families in the country. In addition, as we will see, our field research, both in the businesses and in the unions, showed that, as well as large majorities of women and black people, there are among the Brazilian tele-operators countless workers with special needs, in addition to a significant proportion of lesbian, gay, bisexual, transvestite, transsexual and transgendered people (LGBTs). Again, we find ourselves among the groups most discriminated against in the Brazilian labour market.

It was no surprise, therefore, that we identified in our field research the presence of a significant minority of tele-operators who were prepared to adapt to the working hours demanded and who felt, to some extent, satisfied with this type of work. As revealed in the interviews, this was a group formed mainly of black women around 20 years old and dealing with urgent family responsibilities. We noted that it was often those female workers who stated that their husbands were unemployed who were inclined to adapt to the work flow and to associate the work with positive values. On the basis of the interviews, we realized, as was to be expected, that being the breadwinner produced a very strong disciplinary effect, particularly in cases where – a well-known and frequently adopted business recruitment strategy to keep wages low – the worker declared herself to be a single mother. This same tendency towards adaptation was found in interviews with gay tele-operators. During the research, we realized that the call centre industry had become a type of "refuge" for those sub-proletarian groups in the Brazilian labour market suffering the highest levels of discrimination.

Infotaylorism: Dissatisfaction and difficulties for collective organization

Notwithstanding these factors conducive to accommodation with the demands of the work, many tele-operators did become critical of the working conditions and of the businesses that employ them, provoked by their encounter with infotaylorism and the constant turnover of workers on short-term contracts.[2] We frequently encountered acute dissatisfaction with pay and with the ever-increasing pressure from the business to meet targets. On the one hand, according to our interviewees, the operations coordinators and human resources (HR) managers are constantly trying to impress on the tele-operators that they are involved in a cut-throat economic competition, thereby attempting to dissuade them from any collective action of a trade union or political-organizational nature. On the other hand, workers are selected on the basis of behavioural qualities such as availability, flexibility and readiness to accept new rules, all of which tend to go with a certain inclination to subordinate oneself to the system. It should also be borne in mind that tele-operators are recruited on temporary, short-term contracts, which are renewed or not on the basis of one's behaviour in the job, notably one's availability and loyalty towards the business.

Obviously, these characteristics, associated with the high rate of staff turnover, impose structural difficulties for collective organization (Rosenfield, 2009). And indeed, when we began our field research during the second quarter of 2004, reports of collective mobilizations or strikes were extremely rare among the tele-operators spoken to. The only exception was the mention of a defensive strike that took place in the Quatro A company on 4 February 2000, regarding the quality of the food provided in the works canteen. The interviews with trade union directors and trade unionists inevitably began highlighting the huge obstacles that unionism confronted in this industry: as soon as a tele-operator approached a union and began to develop some sort of organizational activity, he or she was harassed by the company or simply dismissed at the end of the fixed-term contract, forcing the union to restart the work all over again, without being able to consolidate and expand.

Another frequent observation linked to the trade-union diagnosis of the organizational challenges posed by the telemarketing sector referred to the lack of political experience among the tele-operators. Because most were young people new to the labour market, we often heard opinions from trade unionists such as "They're very depoliticized", "They don't understand the importance of unions" and "It's difficult to communicate with them". In the case of one union, the Professionals in Telecommunication Union in the State of São Paulo (Sintetel-SP), for example, which until 1998 was associated with Telesp, a state-run Fordist company in the São Paulo telecommunications sector, the age gap between trade unionists and tele-operators seemed to impede collective action (Rombaldi, 2007).[3]

Immediately following the privatization cycle, which was marked by the outsourcing of jobs and firing of many workers, the sector's unions ended up focusing primarily on maintaining and creating jobs. In the case of the former Telesp, for example, the Sintetel union substituted long-term demands for short-term, and adopted a more defensive stance. This happened during a period in which many of the benefits won through previous collective bargaining agreements (such as extra pay for extra hours, fines for dismissal without cause, and aid in cases of illness or injury) were steadily reduced by the companies to the minimum levels allowed by law. In addition, the diversification of businesses and activities stemming from the privatization of Telesp in 1998 gave rise to intense disputes between trade unionists over the representation of their rank-and-file members. Sintetel's right to represent tele-operators in the city and metropolitan region of São Paulo was challenged by another union, launched in 1992: Sintratel (Professionals in Telecommunication Union of São Paulo) – a dispute eventually won by Sintetel.[4]

Call centre unions and their demands

In the period prior to the privatization of Telesp, the main union demands concerned wage adjustments and length-of-service bonuses. After privatization, because of the rise in unemployment and job insecurity, the priorities shifted from higher wages to safeguarding jobs, and from length-of-service bonuses to the negotiation of wage subsidies, with (largely unsuccessful) attempts to include profit-sharing and some social benefits, such as health plans and arrangements with private universities. Furthermore, in the period prior to privatization, the very low staff turnover and the relative homogeneity within the Fordist business environment allowed relatively stable ties of solidarity to form among workers, which facilitated trade union action. In other words, a certain symbolic structure that focused on validating the identity of the "Telesp worker" promoted collective mobilization.

Maintaining this symbolic structure for a long period allowed workers and trade union leaders to share a reference system, even though the latter, as part of union management, maintained a distance from the daily practices of the workers they represented. Owing in large part to the rise in unemployment that followed privatization, Sintetel's defensive approach led to the reinforcement of a model of trade union action characterized by pragmatism and refinement of strategies for making demands: bargaining with companies completely replaced any open confrontation whatsoever.

As a response to Sintetel's model, Sintratel charted a new course. Through greater integration in the non-union social movements, in particular the black and LGBT movements, the Sintratel leadership sought to strengthen alternative forms of class solidarity by encouraging collectives geared towards the discussion of questions of race, gender and sexual orientation, thus bringing tele-operators closer to the everyday life of the union. In addition, the union has been acting with the LGBT Pride Parade Association of São Paulo, establishing itself as one of the few trade unions or professional associations of São Paulo to organize, year after year, a separate float during the parade. This link between Sintratel and LGBT Pride has encouraged transvestites and transsexuals to participate in the trade union movement as rank-and-file delegates, which is unusual in the history of the Brazilian labour movement (Braga et al., 2011).

Nonetheless, despite these differences, it is also possible to observe some important convergences between Sintetel and Sintratel's lines of action. Both, for example, have been investing in the organization of professional courses through partnerships with businesses in the sector, in addition to taking part in the "Brazilian Programme of Self-Regulation of the Customer Relations Sector" created by employers running call centres. Similarly, both Sintetel and Sintratel have been following a model known as "citizen unionism", by which the union offers its associates a variety of services formerly provided by the State, such as health-care plans and vocational training, in addition to supporting employment agencies funded by the Workers Relief Fund.[5]

Lula's election as President in 2002 represented a genuine watershed in the relationship between Brazilian trade unionism and the state apparatus. In the first place, Lula's Government filled nearly half of its key steering and advising positions – about 1,305 in all – with trade unionists, who were thereby placed in control of an annual budget of over 200 billion real (BRL). Furthermore, some trade union leaders took up highly prestigious roles in state-run businesses such as Petrobrás and Furnas Centrais Elétricas, including positions relating to their pension funds, while others joined the administrative board of the Brazilian Development Bank (BNDES). Lula's Government also promoted reform of trade union law, legalizing Brazilian trade union federations, raising union dues and transferring nearly BRL100 million annually to these federations. All in all, Brazilian trade unionism rose to the role of a strategic actor with regard to capitalist investment in the country.

This new reality, as was to be expected, modified the relationship between the call centre industry's trade union and the state apparatus in the country. Throughout our interviews with trade union leaders and rank-and-file activists of both unions, a favourable opinion of Lula's Government clearly predominated. In order to justify their adherence to the PT programme, trade unionists made repeated comparisons with the "FHC era" of Fernando Henrique Cardoso, Lula's predecessor. Moreover, professional development projects – not to mention agreements with private universities – implemented by trade unions, depend on resources from the Workers Relief Fund and the support of federal initiatives such as the University for All Programme, which distributes full or partial study grants to low-income students to finance private university education. It is not surprising, therefore, that the main initiative taken by Lula's Government in relation to the telemarketing sector, the Telemarketing Law passed on 1 December 2008, provoked nothing more than routine protest from trade unionists, despite its being limited exclusively to the rights of consumers and doing nothing to improve the working conditions of the tele-operators (Peres et al., 2006).[6]

The cycle of strikes and the experience of trade unionism in the city of São Paulo

In the absence of direct union pressure on government, with regard to strike action Sintratel has shown itself to be more active than Sintetel. At this point it is worth noting that, despite the structural obstacles to collective mobilization in the sector, there have been a fair number of strikes in the call centre industry in São Paulo. As noted above, when we began our research we noted very few references to strikes in telemarketing. This scenario, however, changed after the famous strike of August 2005 in the Atento unit in São Bernardo. This was a crucial episode in Sintratel's history, because the strike broke out in the same city that, 30 years earlier, had seen the eruption of the great cycle of strikes which, under the leadership of Lula, gave rise to the "new unionism".

The workers' dissatisfaction stemmed from the absence of any wage increases for the two previous years, shortfalls in meal vouchers, the "banking" of overtime working hours, precarious working conditions and psychological harassment. When lower transportation allowances were introduced various demonstrations were organized, with the backing of Sintratel (and the opposition of Sintetel), culminating in a day-long work stoppage of approximately 150 tele-operators – enough to provoke the police to imprison trade unionists and the company to fire about 30 tele-operators who went on strike. Then about half of the 900 tele-operators in the unit decided to join the movement, which went on for nine days and demanded, in addition to a 17.74 per cent pay rise, an increase in the value of meal vouchers from BRL2.74 to BRL6, wage equality across all tele-operators in the unit and profit-sharing. Although the dismissals were not reversed, the strike was considered a victory by both the union and the tele-operators, almost all of whose demands were met. Thereafter shorter strikes began to happen every year, with the same list of demands: profit-sharing, child care, wage increases, shorter working hours, higher-value meal vouchers and so on.

During our interviews with tele-operators and rank-and-file trade unionists in early 2006, we recorded references to the Atento strike. However, having been overly influenced by the prevailing defensive trend in the unions at the beginning of 2005 we incorrectly interpreted this movement as part of the struggles more or less related to the recognition of an individual's dignity – against psychological harassment and for the right to bathroom breaks, longer rest breaks, an improvement in the snacks provided and so on. In reality, however, more offensive shutdown movements began emerging at that time.[7] Since we were not focused on the close analysis of trade union movements, we did not grasp the importance of certain key factors relating to the work process in the CTAs in the formation of class solidarity among the tele-operators.[8]

In the first place, while it is true that the characteristics of a first job in telemarketing, along with the high turnover of employees in call centres, tend to impede class-based political action, and while it is also true that in a labour market where for every three jobs created in non-agricultural private enterprise, two are in companies with up to ten workers who earn on average BRL633.03 per month, the call centre industry came to be regarded by many as a more or less inescapable occupational horizon. Despite the intense job turnover in this sector (42 per cent per year) (DIEESE, 2010), we managed to interview tele-operators with as much as ten years' experience in telemarketing. This means that the union bonds are not simply lost, but frequently taken from one company to another. Second, the progressive monopolization of the Brazilian call centre industry led to ever tougher working conditions, feeding a diffuse dissatisfaction among the rank-and-file workers. Finally, it is worth pointing out two aspects of the working process that foster solidarity: the emphasis on the need to reach goals through cooperative teamwork, which tends to nurture ties between tele-operators who demonstrate during occasions of conflict with the company; and the shared experience of discrimination on the basis of gender, sexual orientation and race, which often further reinforces these ties of solidarity, thereby creating a certain inclination towards collective mobilization.

This is not to imply a simplistic conclusion that tele-operators form a group mobilized by unions. Rather, what we have are workers who, despite the difficulties placed by the industry in the way of collective mobilization, *have started to form an embryo of collective consciousness strong enough to guarantee some important steps on the path to union self-organization*. In fact, the rapid and concentrated growth in the call centre industry in Brazil, added to the accumulation of experience in the sector on the part of the tele-operators, has tended to favour the emergence of certain more assertive demands. This may not seem much, in the historical context of the Brazilian union movement; but if we take into account the model of labour organization predominant in the industry, as well as the very recent formation of this group of workers, it becomes apparent that *any image that associates tele-operators with the absence of the basic conditions for participation in the class struggle must be immediately rejected.*

In fact, observing this post-Fordist sub-proletarian group has allowed us to test the "passive Brazilian revolution" hypothesis outlined by the present author with Alvaro Bianchi after Lula's first election (Braga and Bianchi, 2005). At that time, we posited two scenarios. First, we argued that Lula's Government would not simply be another example of neoliberalism, along the lines of those headed by Fernando Collor or Fernando Henrique Cardoso, precisely because, in order to achieve the necessary margin of popular consent, he would have to respond to certain demands pent up in the social movements. We used the – admittedly rather weak – notion of "social liberalism" in an attempt to address the emphasis on income distribution policies, even if they are shaped by the reproduction of the rentier orthodoxy. Second, we argued that the "transformist" direct relationship of the high-level union bureaucracy with its pension funds might not be sufficient to generate a "new class", as Oliveira (2003) contended, but would certainly pave the one-way street of the "new trade-unionism" towards the globalized financial system of concentrated economic power/accumulation. We argued that this path would completely destroy any possibility of this bureaucracy once again defending the historical interests of Brazilian subaltern classes. We called this process the "financialization of the trade union bureaucracy".

The experience of the city of São Paulo's trade unions within the telemarketing sector allowed us to test this hypothesis. In fact, we found both tendencies in action. On the one hand, we noted, in particular, a resolute initiative on Sintratel's part to narrow the gap between the union's demands and those formulated by the social movements in the country throughout the 1980s and 1990s: struggles for equality across differences of gender, race and sexual orientation, access to university education, social protection and so on. Furthermore, Sintratel sought not only to associate with other unions in countries where Atento maintains operations, but also to coordinate with the Human Rights Secretary of the President of the Republic in order to develop projects to combat psychological harassment and discrimination based on sexual orientation. Thus the union, in its own way, helped to increase the margin of popular consent among the tele-operators, bringing them closer to certain historical demands of the country's social movements.

On the other hand, Sintratel supported the reform of union legislation undertaken by Lula's Government, in an attempt to take advantage of the situation: during our research, we were able to follow the outbreak of a series of conflicts within the union – with reports of physical aggression between leaders – motivated in large part by the process of disaffiliation from the CUT federation and the building of a new federation (the CTB), created by the Communist Party of Brazil exclusively to receive a larger portion of the tax revenue destined for the trade union associations. In one way or another, the result of the encounter between the demands pent up in the social movements and "trade union transformism" undoubtedly represented an increase in the control of the trade union movement by the state apparatus.

Conclusion

Our research into these post-Fordist sub-proletarians and their unions certainly does *not* generate an image of a class fraction incapable of constructing autonomous forms of organization that would turn to the State for the optimal path to reducing social inequality. In fact, the tele-operators constitute a remarkably ambiguous phenomenon in ideological terms. While it is true that they possess very little political experience, they have already started organizing their own strikes; although they are not interested in parties, they do know how to manifest their dissatisfaction within and outside the companies where they work; they associate the rise in popular consumption with the continuity of Lulism, but do not delude themselves with the "miracle" of credit subsidized by the Government.

With regard to the cycle of economic growth and the distribution of wealth among those who make a living wage, this group drew lessons that foster not an attitude dependent on the State so much as a more or less permanent state of *social unrest*. They momentarily adhered to Lulism, but let us not fool ourselves: this indication of passivity does not adequately characterize them. On the contrary, it is more likely a type of diffuse popular pressure, all too familiar to the trade unionists who work in the sector, that criticizes the present and looks beyond it into the future. This project might spill over the boundaries of the trade union movement and further reduce popular support for the Government, if the standard of living of those who make a living wage were to be undermined. If we consider the historical characteristics of semi-peripheral capitalism, it should come as no surprise that Dilma Roussef's Government has already announced substantial cuts to the federal budget and forced Congress to approve a rise in the minimum wage far lower than the trade unions had expected.

Returning to the history of Brazilian populism, we should remember that exaggeration of the virtues of non-manual jobs by newcomers in the workforce was a phenomenon widely documented in the ethnographies that dealt with the formation of the new Brazilian working class between 1930 and 1960. Unfamiliar with this type of work amid their initial contacts with factory despotism in semi-peripheral conditions, the workers envied desk jobs and wished that their daughters could study, abandon their housekeeping jobs and occupy such positions in the future. The rising sociology of Brazilian professional labour interpreted this as a clear indication of the individualism that, supposedly characteristic of this social group, dissolved the workers' identification with their social environment; the aspiration to find freedom from the furious work pace of the assembly line and take refuge in office work was mistaken for a feeling of helplessness in the face of the large Fordist company.

The history of the emergence of a new trade unionism, with Lula at its head, at the end of the 1970s showed that the sociological imagination simply was not capable of correctly capturing the aspirations of Brazilian workers. On the contrary, what arose from the strikes of the late 1970s was the trade union leadership. Currently, the daughters – and grand-daughters – of those workers attend a private night college, abandon their housekeeping jobs and settle into desk jobs. As we have seen, there is no shortage of positions in the post-Fordist call centre industry, especially in the north-east of the country. Whether or not they will keep quiet faced with low wages, high turnover, long and pressurized working hours, racial discrimination, psychological harassment and illness, all of which are prevalent in the sector, remains to be seen. Perhaps they will decide to follow in the footsteps of their fathers and grandfathers some 30 years ago.

Acknowledgements

The author thanks Mariana Riscali, Fábio Pimentel, David Flores and Vitor Vaneti for their comments and contributions. Any remaining errors are the author's responsibility.

Appendix: Methodological note

The field research that led to this chapter was guided by the extended case method. To this end, we combined over a period of approximately five years research techniques based on a questionnaire with qualitative methods of ethnographic observation. Concerning the pre-tests, sample definition and systematization of data collected through the directive questionnaire, I received invaluable help from Natália Padovani and Gabriel Casoni. Mariana Riscali helped me with the research at the database of the Ministério do Trabalho e Emprego (Ministry of Labour and Employment). Regarding the in-depth interviews, I benefited from a formidable trio of students: David Flores, Fábio Pimentel and Vitor Vaneti. In addition, the work made use of interviews conducted by another student, Maurício Rombaldi, in his dissertation on Sintetel.

After an exploratory phase that lasted about three months and covered the first group of non-directive interviews with tele-operators, the classification of responses and the elaboration of a structured questionnaire, the field research itself began in the first half of 2004, lasting until the first half of 2006 and including the in-depth interviews.

The programme of research was as follows. (1) Visits to two companies were undertaken in order to observe the organization of work and the industrial production process of the service relationship. (2) Interviews were conducted with the main agents (managers, coordinators, quality monitors, supervisors, union leaders and tele-operators) involved in the process and in the organization of work. (3) A questionnaire was distributed among tele-operators aiming to collect information about the pace of work, career prospects, duration of operations, cooperation, supervising activities, corporate goals policy and duration of rest breaks. (4) In-depth interviews were conducted with tele-operators.

We chose to conduct our research in the two most important companies of the Brazilian call centre market, here called "Company A" and "Company B". Between them they have cornered the Brazilian market. To illustrate, in 2005 these two companies employed a total of 75,926 people (Company A: 38,000; Company B: 37,926). Company A had 14,500 available operators (AOs), and Company B 17,507. All other thirteen largest companies together had a total of 59,721 employees and 35,353 AOs. This means that Companies A and B together represented 56 per cent of the sector in terms of total number of employees and 47.5 per cent of the market in terms of the number of AOs. As expected, both companies operate with the latest technology in the sector, as well as having a diverse array of institutional clients from different economic sectors – especially telecommunications, banks, internet businesses, government, public administration, medical services, energy companies and industry. The services offered to clients were mostly focused on research, scheduling, billing and sales (active telemarketing); phone banking, customer service, scheduling, helpdesks, research and sales (receptive telemarketing); and services connected to the internet, such as email, chat, co-browsing and video conferencing. Database, consulting and subscription services were also offered to a smaller extent.

We understand that because these two companies even today define the para-meters in the sector, all other Brazilian call centres are guided in their competitive initiatives by the two leading companies. This tends to equalize the working condi-tions and, to a large extent, the remuneration of tele-operators. Thus, these companies offer a privileged field for the study of the behaviour of workers in this sector. Moreover, it is noteworthy that our field observations were made in what were considered "reference" sites by the companies themselves. This is to say that, either because of their size – about 2,400 tele-operators each – or because of the diversity of operations, they offered at that time a representative sample of the reality of the working processes of both companies.

The visits occurred during the months of March, April and May 2004 (Company B) and May 2004 (Company A). Interviews were conducted with an HR manager (Company B), with operation coordinators (Companies A and B) and with supervisors (Companies A and B), in addition, of course, to informal – untaped – conversations with tele-operators during snack breaks. In all, there were five visits to Company B and three to Company A.

Unfortunately, the interviews with tele-operators could not be conducted in reserved spaces – well away from the supervision of managers – on the grounds that this was contrary to "company policy" and would constitute "work interference". Given these limitations, access to tele-operators was made possible by the trade unions active in the sector, Sintetel and Sintratel. The contact with tele-operators was made through two main instruments: a questionnaire with eleven closed questions and in-depth structured interviews with open questions based on preliminary interpretation of data from the questionnaires. The questionnaire was administered over three different weekends in April and May 2004, during the presentation of union (Sintetel) activities to tele-operators from Companies A and B, on a farm beside Rodovia dos

Imigrantes in the city of Santo André. The in-depth interviews were conducted in July 2004, June–July 2005, and January and June 2006 in the course of activities organized by Sintetel and Sintratel and held in the offices of the unions in the city of São Paulo.

The second stage of our field research, conducted with unionists from Sintetel and Sintratel, two of the major unions that operate in the city of São Paulo, was undertaken over three months of participant observation in 2009. Eighteen in-depth interviews were conducted with union officers and grass-roots activists. In addition, we conducted 24 interviews with tele-operators during their work breaks and during their approaches to the unions in order to submit labour demands. In this stage we sought, through systematic observation, to distinguish the external forces (the relationships between local unions and central unions, as well as with the state apparatus) from the internal processes (the relationships between unionists and tele-operators, unionization campaigns and mobilization of workers) that shape collective action in the sector. By this means it was possible to reflexively understand the scope and limits of union activity in relation to the expectations, especially wage expectations, of tele-operators. Moreover, the interviews offered key information for our analysis of the intimate connection between the despotic factory regime – high employee turnover rate, lack of domestic markets, strong job placement rate, autocratic management model, and so on – and the strike mobilization observed after 2006 in the São Paulo call centre industry.

Notes

[1] For details of the research personnel and process, see the appendix to this chapter.

[2] "Infotaylorism" is a mechanism for controlling the workforce based on the use of information technologies to consolidate the power of management and eliminate any autonomous initiative of the employee during the workday.

[3] Sintetel is a union affiliated to the Union Force federation, the chief representative of Brazilian business unionism.

[4] Sintratel was originally affiliated to the CUT federation, but during the union reform negotiations of the Lula Government it decided to join the new federation created by the Communists, the CTB federation.

[5] Despite the strong competition for the right to represent the same rank and file, both Sintratel and Sintetel support Lula's Government. Naturally, the main reason for this lies in the great financial and material advantages provided by the federal Government to those unions that support their policies.

[6] The Telemarketing Law was an attempt by Lula's Government to regulate the telemarketing sector by the formation of a national registry of those who did not accept phone calls from companies.

[7] The demands of these more aggressive movements include salary increases above inflation, the right to share in company profits and the establishment of crèches for the children of workers.

[8] At that time, we were trying to identify the importance of labour process organization for the achievement of workers' consent to the rules of the two companies in which the research was conducted.

References

Assunção, A.; Marinho-Silva, A.; Vasconcelos de Oliveira Vilela, L.; Guthier, M.H. 2006. "Abordar o trabalho para compreender e transformar as condições de adoecimento na categoria dos teleatendentes no Brasil" [Looking at work practices to understand and change labour conditions in call centres in Brazil], in *Revista Brasileira de Saúde Ocupacional*, Vol. 31, No. 114, pp. 47–62.

Braga, R.; Antunes, R. (eds). 2009. *Infoproletários: Degradação rea do trabalho virtual* [Infoworkers: Real degradation of virtual work] (São Paulo, Boitempo).

—; Bianchi, A. 2005. "Brazil: The Lula Government and financial globalization", in *Social Forces*, Vol. 83, No. 4, pp. 1745–62.

—; Flores, F.; Pimentel, F.; Vaneti, V. 2011. "Social movement unionism and neoliberalism in São Paulo, Brazil: Shifting logics of collective action in telemarketing labor unions", in *Societies without Borders*, Vol. 6, No. 1, pp. 73–101.

DIEESE. 2010. *Movimentação contratual no mercado de trabalho formal e rotatividade no Brasil* [Handling contract in the formal labour market and turnover in Brazil] (São Paulo, Inter-Union Department of Statistics and Socioeconomic Studies).

Freire, O. 2002. *"Ser atendente a vida toda é humanamente impossível": Serviço de teleatendimento e custo humano do trabalho* ["Being a lifelong attendant is humanly impossible": Telephone service and human cost of work], Master's thesis, Institute of Psychology, University of Brasília.

Holman, D.; Batt, R.; Holtgrewe, U. 2007. "The global call center report: International perspectives on management and employment", in *Report of the Global Call Center Network* (Ithaca, NY, Cornell University), pp. 13–72.

Marx, R. 2000. "LER e organização do trabalho no setor de serviços: O caso de call centers em atendimento de serviços financeiros" [RSI and work organization in the service sector: The case of call centres in financial services], in Laerte Idal Sznelwar and Leila Nadim Zidan (eds): *O trabalho humano com sistemas informatizados no setor de serviços* [Human work with computerized systems in the service sector] (São Paulo, Plêiade).

Oliveira, F. 2003. *Crítica à razão dualista: O ornitorrinco* [Criticism of dualistic reason: The platypus] (São Paulo, Boitempo).

Peres, C.C.; Marinho-Silva, A.; Cavalcante-Fernandez, E.; Rocha, L.E. 2006. "Uma construção social: O anexo da norma brasileira de ergonomia para o trabalho dos operadores de telemarketing" [A social construction: The attachment of the Brazilian standard of ergonomics at the work of telemarketers], in *Revista Brasileira de Saúde Ocupacional*, Vol. 31, No. 114, pp. 35–46.

Pimentel, F. 2009. *Trabalho e emprego no setor de telemarketing* [Labour and employment in the telemarketing industry], Master's thesis, Faculty of Philosophy, Letters and Humanities, University of São Paulo.

Rombaldi, M. 2007. *Os sindicalistas nas entrelinhas: O caso do Sintetel pós-privatizações* [The unionists between the lines: The case of post-privatization Sintetel], Master's thesis, Faculty of Philosophy, Letters and Humanities, University of São Paulo.

Rosenfield, C. 2009. "A identidade no trabalho em call centers: A identidade provisória" [Identity at work in call centres: A precarious identity], in R. Braga and R. Antunes (eds), 2009, pp. 173–85.

Singer, A. 2009. "Raízes sociais e ideológicas do lulismo" [Social and ideological roots of Lulism], in *Novos Estudos CEBRAP*, No. 85, pp. 83–102.

LABOUR RELATIONS IN URUGUAY UNDER THE FRENTE AMPLIO GOVERNMENT, 2005–09: FROM NEOLIBERALISM TO NEOCORPORATIVISM?

7

Jana Silverman

Introduction

The small Latin American country of Uruguay has long been considered a bastion of progressive labour policy in the region, owing in large part to the early political incorporation of the working class led from above by the reformist President José Batlle y Ordoñez during the first decade of the twentieth century. During the eight years he served in office, Batlle y Ordoñez established fundamental labour rights such as the eight-hour day, union freedoms, unemployment insurance and social security coverage for workers, as well as expanding suffrage and creating a public education system. On the other hand, the Uruguayan union movement never became a fundamental part of the electoral base of Batlle y Ordoñez's political vehicle, the Colorado Party, and subsequent governments never attempted to limit union actions either through the imposition of corporatist structures or through the introduction of a detailed judicial code to regulate labour. These factors, combined with a stable democratic system and relative economic prosperity which lasted until the last quarter of the century, allowed the union movement in Uruguay to develop in favourable socio-economic conditions while preserving its autonomy in relation to the State and the traditional political parties.

After an intensification of social conflict and the installation of an authoritarian regime in 1973, the labour movement and its nascent political ally, the centre-left Frente Amplio (FA) party, were viciously repressed and forced to act clandestinely. When redemocratization of the country began in 1985, this did not lead to a full restoration of the political and organizational capacity of the unions, this time owing to the implementation of neoliberal policies which, in addition to liberalizing trade policies and opening capital markets, truncated the role of the State in promoting union freedoms and collective bargaining in favour of a "voluntary", bilateral system of labour relations that did not take into account the inherent power inequalities between workers and employers.

This type of labour relations system prevailed in Uruguay for over a decade until the historic landslide victory in the October 2004 presidential and congressional elections by the FA, which continued to share ideological, organizational and personal ties with the labour movement. Beginning in 2005, the FA Government led by President Tabaré Vázquez legislated a wide-ranging set of changes to the Uruguayan labour relations framework, through the convening of mandatory sector-wide tripartite wage negotiations known as the *consejos de salarios*, the granting of further guarantees for union leaders and activists through the Ley del Fuero Sindical (Law of Special Union Protections), and the expansion and institutionalization of collective bargaining processes to previously excluded categories of workers, such as teachers, domestic workers and rural labourers. This chapter will attempt to analyse these transformations, investigating how this new activist role of the State in the promotion of union freedoms and collective bargaining has affected unions and their strategies to defend workers' rights, as well as examining the impact of this neocorporativist approach to labour relations in the context of a country still in the process of economic development on the labour market and the political arena as a whole.

In order to understand the political incorporation process of Uruguayan workers during the first part of the twentieth century, we turn to the conceptual framework offered by Collier and Collier (2002), who analyse the changes produced by the entrance of the working class into the national polis – changes that depend upon the initial configuration of classes, the crystallization of the relationship between the union movement and the political party or parties that represent it, and the establishment of institutional mechanisms to regulate conflicts between labour and capital. These changes do not occur in a linear fashion, but only at certain defined moments denominated as "critical junctures", when variations in factors such as the economic and productive structure, geopolitical dynamics and the organizational strength of the union movement combine to generate a radical rearrangement of the links between the working class and the political system, which in turn has an impact on all the players operating within that system. Adopting the concept of path dependency, Collier and Collier (2002, pp. 27–29) argue that the institutionalization of the configuration of power structures in the period following a critical juncture delimits the future strategic choices available to the actors in the national polis, until a new critical juncture arises out of another situation of political uncertainty and transforms the political arena once again. For this reason, in order to understand how the reconfiguration of political opportunities under the FA Government led to changes in the political insertion of Uruguayan workers during the first decade of the twenty-first century, it is necessary to analyse past trajectories that shaped the relationships between unions, employers and the State.

A historical framework of the political insertion of the Uruguayan working class: From premature political incorporation to neoliberal exclusion

Using this theoretical frame of reference, we can characterize the process which integrated the Uruguayan working class into the political arena as one of "premature political incorporation", as it occurred when industrial capitalism was just beginning to be installed and before the union movement was able to establish a truly national presence. The origins of Uruguayan unionism lie in the late nineteenth century, when a wave of immigrants from Italy and Spain brought their anarcho-syndicalist political tradition to the country. Unions with a fixed organizational structure began to appear in 1895, and in the wake of the historic strike of Montevideo municipal workers, the first national labour confederation (the Uruguayan Regional Workers' Federation, known by its Spanish acronym FORU) was formed by anarchist labour activists in 1905. In these early years, the workers' movement was principally characterized by its concentration in urban areas, its organizational fragmentation and its political outlook, dubbed "oppositional unionism" by Supervielle and Pucci (2008, p. 78), which favoured direct action instead of collective bargaining as the preferred strategy to mitigate labour exploitation. Owing to these factors, the initial political incorporation process which began during this period was led not by the relatively weak anarcho-syndicalist forces that rejected the use of state instruments to promote labour rights, but by a traditional "catch-all" political party – the Colorado Party, under the leadership of Batlle y Ordoñez. With the goal of releasing Uruguay from the grips of endemic partisan violence, Batlle y Ordoñez conceived of a far-reaching set of social reforms aimed at creating a democratic, secular and economically stable nation free from foreign intervention. To do this, he saw the need to modernize working conditions and expand democratic institutions, leading to the codification of the country's first set of labour laws, as well as the extension of the right to vote and the creation of public education and social security systems with broad coverage. In the opinion of Cavarozzi (2001), these social reforms, combined with the existence of a strong bipartisan system, allowed Uruguay to gain the distinction of being the most stable democratic regime in all of Latin America during the first half of the twentieth century. However, because of the nascent stage of trade union organization, its anti-partisan political bent, and the large numbers of unionized workers without voting rights (because of their status as migrants), the Uruguayan union movement never integrated itself into the political and electoral base of the Colorado Party, thus opening up the opportunity for it to later become one of the principal social allies of the FA.

The next critical juncture that redefined the historical relationship between the Uruguayan political system and the union movement corresponds to the phase of union consolidation and radicalization, political polarization and economic stagnation

127

which characterized the period 1966–73 and which terminated tragically in the coup d'état of 1973 and the ensuing installation of an authoritarian regime. In the decades that preceded this moment, governments inspired by Batlle y Ordoñez introduced further reformist labour legislation, such as that which created the minimum wage, prohibited child labour and installed obligatory tripartite national wage bargaining processes, known as the *consejos de salarios* (CS). However, in order to combat the economic crisis which began to affect the country in the 1960s, owing to failures in the import-substitution model of industrial development and stagnation in the agricultural sector, subsequent governments began to repeal some of these pro-worker measures, as well as to devalue the currency and freeze prices and salaries (Collier and Collier, 2002, pp. 657–58). This caused a growing tension between the union movement, the recently formed FA party and the Guevarist Tupamaro guerrilla movement on one side, and the Uruguayan Government and armed forces on the other, leading eventually to a rupture in the democratic system. In June 1973, President Juan María Bordaberry declared the suspension of the Congress, prohibited the functioning of all political parties and unions, and curtailed the freedom of the press, thus installing a military–civilian dictatorship which lasted until 1985.

Upon entering the period of redemocratization in the 1980s, there were widespread expectations among the population not only that the dismantled democratic institutions (including unions) would be rebuilt, but also that lost purchasing power would be recovered and decent jobs be created. These hopes were not to be realized: although the first newly democratic government of Julio María Sanguinetti made an effort to reconvene the CS, the arrival of the neoconservative leader of the National Party, Luis Alberto Lacalle, in the presidency in 1989 marked an abandonment of policies to stimulate social dialogue and revalue salaries. Following the predominant ideological current in Latin America at the time, Lacalle decided to apply neoliberal economic policies, including fiscal adjustment, the deregulation of the banking and insurance sectors, the elimination of barriers to international trade and investment, the flexibilization of labour contracts and the imposition of new restrictions on the right to strike. The effects of these policies on Uruguayan workers included an average decline in real salaries of 24 per cent between 1998 and 2003 (Olesker, 2009, p. 13), the loss of jobs in the industrial sector (whose contribution to national GDP dropped from 25 per cent to 16 per cent during the period 1990–94) and an increase in the levels of unemployment and underemployment. The Uruguayan labour confederation PIT-CNT adopted a position of resistance to Lacalle's reforms, but although it was able to block the proposed privatization of several important public utilities companies, it could not stop the haemorrhaging of individual affiliated members that it experienced during this period, especially in the private sector. According to Méndez, Senatore and Traversa (2009, p. 13), the unionization rate fell from 35 per cent of the economically active population in 1987 to only 15 per cent in 2000, with less than 8 per cent of private sector workers registered as unionized that year.

These labour market and macroeconomic tendencies worsened after the 2002 banking crisis, which affected over half of Uruguay's banking establishments and was provoked by a run on deposits by Argentine account holders who were trying anxiously to preserve their own patrimony after the collapse of the financial system in their country one year earlier. In the first quarter of 2002, Uruguayan banks lost over 40 per cent of their reserves and deposits. This in turn led to an increase in the country's sovereign debt and fiscal deficit owing to the massive bailout efforts that were undertaken as well as the rapid devaluation of the currency. The country's real economy was also gravely affected: in 2002 GDP plummeted by 11 per cent, unemployment surged to the record level of 19.8 per cent, and over 58,000 workers left the country in search of jobs overseas (Ladra, 2008).

Thus the social and labour panorama in Uruguay before the arrival of the FA Government in 2005 can be characterized as very precarious, marked by the flexibilization of the labour market, the absence of social dialogue processes, and the persistence of high levels of unemployment, underemployment and informal work. Although the Uruguayan union movement was able to preserve its unitary structure, with a single confederation, the abovementioned PIT-CNT, its rolls were reduced to a mere 115,000 affiliates, of which 68 per cent were employed in the public sector (Zurbriggen, Doglio and Senatore, 2003). In the private sector, the violation of norms that protected union leaders against arbitrary dismissal, and the failure to convene the CS, made the practice of collective bargaining processes extremely difficult. Bargaining was possible only in those economic sectors with a historically strong union presence, such as banking and transportation; and even in these cases, sector-wide agreements could not be reached. In addition, according to Pucci et al. (2010, pp. 41–42), the issues being negotiated were transformed, as unions began to make more defensive claims related to topics such as job stability, productivity and the role of the union in industrial restructuring processes, with less emphasis on wage demands.

The framework of Uruguayan labour law during this period preceding the formation of the FA Government was described by the ILO (1995) as "non-systematic and non-detailed". Unlike countries such as Brazil and France, with highly complex labour codes, Uruguay had not codified its labour laws, which led to a plethora of divergent interpretations and contradictory judicial rulings. Before 2005, little legislation existed regarding labour relations. For example, the only guarantees of union freedoms in Uruguayan law were enshrined in the constitution of 1967 and in three relevant ILO Conventions ratified by the Uruguayan State.[1] Regarding collective bargaining, Law 13.556 of 1966 regulated the negotiation process and stipulated the requirements for the registration of agreements, but in many cases this law was ignored in practice by both employers and unions, leaving the agreements themselves as the only legal framework respected by all actors. As a result, two distinct labour relations regimes existed in Uruguay: one which corresponded to the era when the CS were convened on a regular basis and unions effectively participated in the processes that defined work conditions and salary levels, and one in which the CS were not convened and social dialogue practices and union activity as a whole were hindered. Thus the conversion of the CS into obligatory mechanisms for sector-wide wage negotiation was essential in order for the Uruguayan union movement to overcome the organizational weakness that plagued it after the implementation of neoliberal economic policies in the 1990s and the blowback from the financial crisis of 2002.

Cambia, todo cambia: The transformation of the Uruguayan labour policy agenda under the Frente Amplio Government

The possibility of restructuring the Uruguayan labour relations system became reality in October 2004, when Tabaré Vázquez, the former Mayor of Montevideo standing as presidential candidate for the Frente Amplio/Encuentro Progresista/Nueva Mayoria coalition, obtained 50.5 per cent of the total vote, thus securing a historic victory for the united forces of the left in a single round of balloting (Natanson, 2008, p. 66). In addition to this triumph, the FA also won an absolute majority in both houses of the national Congress, with the election of 16 senators and 53 members of Congress. This allowed the FA to create a "government of the party", excluding all other political groupings from leadership posts in both the executive and legislative branches, giving it greater freedom to construct new public policies in accordance with its political platform, with minimal interference from the opposition.

It is important to note that the triumph of the FA in 2004 was not unexpected, as the vote count for the party's presidential candidates had jumped from only 21 per cent in 1989 to 30.6 per cent in 1994, increasing further to 40.1 per cent in 1999 – victory in this last case being lost in the second round of balloting owing to a pact that consolidated the support of both traditional political parties for the Colorado Party candidate, Jorge Batlle. According to Chavez (2008, p. 104), the key factors that explain the growth and consolidation of the left as the predominant political force in the urban areas of Uruguay include the demographic changes that gave more importance to the youth vote, the widespread popular dissatisfaction with social and economic policy after the banking crisis of 2002, and the innovative and efficient management of the city of Montevideo by the FA since its capture of the mayoralty in 1990. Owing to these factors, in 2004 the FA was able to capture a substantial number of votes from social sectors beyond its traditional electoral base of unionized workers, students and intellectuals.

The electoral platform of the FA, which later formed the base for its policy proposals regarding labour issues, contained the following points:

*   the reactivation of the CS;

*   the restoration of the purchasing power lost by workers during the Batlle Government of 2000–04;

- an even greater upwards revaluation of the minimum wage and of the salaries of teachers and public health-care sector workers;

- a reduction in the levels of structural unemployment, especially for groups of workers with more precarious positions in the Uruguayan labour market (such as youth, women, minorities and unskilled workers);

- a reduction in informal work.

In order to construct the final version of its labour policy agenda, Vázquez and other leaders of the FA entered into dialogue with business and union leaders, in order to ensure that their interests were reflected. Employers' organizations, such as the Uruguayan Chamber of Commerce and Services, doubted the FA's intentions at first but then signalled their relief when Danilo Astori, a centrist leader of the party committed to maintaining economically orthodox policies founded on open markets and inflation targeting, was named as Finance Minister. Under Astori's watch, the Ministry of Economy and Finances (MEF) repeatedly vetoed certain wage and social spending policies proposed by other governmental and legislative actors that contradicted its priority of maintaining price stability and a primary fiscal surplus. In addition, Astori ensured that capital gains were protected from higher levels of taxation in the fiscal reform bill passed by the FA Government in 2006 (Reygadas and Filgueira, 2010, p. 181).

With regard to the union movement represented by the PIT-CNT, the FA's programme incorporated the great majority of its aspirations, owing to the historical and ideological links that the two organizations have shared since the founding of the FA in 1971. For that reason, it has been argued that the PIT-CNT places more endogenous constraints on the ruling leftist party than any other workers' movement operating within the context of the "new left" that has surged to the fore in Latin America during the past decade (Luna, 2010, p. 37). Thus the key issues advocated by the PIT-CNT, such as the reactivation of the CS and the reduction of informal work, were highlighted in the FA's platform, and other policies of interest to the unions, such as greater protections for union negotiators in the CS and a widening of the right to strike, were also included in the FA's policy agenda.

It is important to mention that the capacity of the FA Government to transform the Uruguayan labour relations system after coming to power in 2005 was linked not only to its auspicious position as majority party, but also to the decidedly favourable economic context arising from high international prices for its export commodities, such as beef, soy, rice and forestry products, and from the reactivation of demand for services such as tourism and computer programming in both the national and the regional market. These factors, combined with a boom in FDI estimated at US$6.6 billion during the years 2005–09, help to explain the dramatic growth in GDP during this period, calculated at 35.4 per cent (Olesker, 2009, p. 94). Although most

FDI was concentrated in sectors with low levels of incorporation of technology, such as food and beverages, cellulose and paper pulp, and cattle raising (Red de Economistas de Izquierda del Uruguay, 2010), industrial production was favoured by the increase in internal consumer demand for perishable goods and by the first government industrial promotion policies put into place since the 1950s. The reduction in unemployment since 2005 is consequently due principally to the creation of new jobs responding to this amplified demand and not to the exit of workers from the labour market (ILO, 2012, p. 24).

The social and economic impacts of the reregulation of labour relations in Uruguay

As noted above, one of the highest priorities of the FA after Tabaré Vázquez's inauguration in March 2005 was the reactivation of the CS, a move that did not require new legislation as the regulatory framework created by Law 10449 of 1943 was still technically in force. However, in order to ensure the success of the new round of negotiations in the CS, several new structures were created. The Consejo Superior Tripartito and Consejo Superior Rural were formed to classify all economic sectors and subsectors into groups to facilitate the bargaining process, and to propose provisions to modernize Law 10449. The Consejo Bipartito was also created as a space for social dialogue with public employees. With this new institutional structure in place, the first round of tripartite bargaining processes were convened in 2005, divided into three levels of negotiations. The "macro" level, represented by the Consejo Superior Tripartito, brought national leaders of the PIT-CNT and employers' organizations together with representatives of the Ministry of Labour and Social Security (MTSS): this body defined general parameters for all negotiations and also determined the level of the national minimum wage. The "meso" level involved negotiations between union leaders and employers of individual economic sectors, accompanied by representatives of the MTSS, divided into 20 groups and approximately 190 subgroups defined by the Consejo Superior Tripartito. At the "micro" level negotiations took place at the level of individual companies in order to address issues not covered at the "meso" level. It should be mentioned that the role of the State (embodied by the representatives of the MTSS) is not that of a mere observer whose principal role is to guarantee that the labour legislation is respected, but is actually quite proactive, especially in the negotiations at the "meso" level, where it presents its own proposals for clauses to be negotiated in cases when employers' and workers' representatives cannot arrive at a consensus.

This process, defined as "amplified social dialogue" by Méndez, Senatore and Traversa (2009), in order to differentiate it from the more restricted negotiations which were held during the Sanguinetti Government in the 1980s, culminated in the conclusion of 181, 213, 226 and 205 agreements in 2005, 2006, 2008 and 2010 respectively, incorporating topics related not only to salaries but also to gender equality in the workplace, vocational training, occupational health and safety, and working hours (MTSS, 2011). Out of the total number of collective bargaining agreements signed in these years, 96 per cent (2005), 86 per cent (2006), 84 per cent (2008) and 84 per cent (2010) were resolved by consensus, thus confirming the capacity of this mechanism to mediate and pacifically resolve labour conflicts. These agreements covered a total of 440,000 private sector workers, 150,000 public sector workers, 80,000 rural workers and 95,000 domestic workers (this last category only beginning in 2008), encompassing over 50 per cent of the economically active population of Uruguay. It is also accepted that the agreements reached in the CS helped revalue workers' salaries, which lost an average of 16 per cent of their real purchasing power after the banking crisis of 2002. Furthermore, the fact that over 200,000 new jobs were produced during the period 2005–08 is clear evidence that the improved levels of remuneration for workers agreed upon in the CS did not "crowd out" the creation of new employment opportunities (Olesker, 2009, p. 39).

In addition to the reactivation of the CS, new legislation to strengthen labour rights and social dialogue processes was also approved during the Government of Tabaré Vázquez. In order to protect the activity of union leaders involved in the negotiations taking place in the CS, the Law of Special Union Protections (Ley del Fuero Sindical) was passed in 2005. In accordance with the ILO Freedom of Association and Protection of the Right to Organise Convention, 1948 (No. 87), already ratified by Uruguay, this law explicitly stipulates that the creation of new unions and the activities of existing organizations must take place in a context free of employer influence, and that any worker fired from their job as a result of their union activity must be promptly and automatically reinstated (Ermida, 2006, p. 6). The law also guarantees that union leaders be given paid leave to exercise their functions. It is important to note that this law initially met with stiff resistance from the Uruguayan Chamber of Commerce and Services, but the active support of the PIT-CNT and strict party discipline observed by the members of the FA in the Congress permitted its approval with only minor amendments.

In 2009, towards the end of Tabaré Vázquez's period in office, the Congress worked to pass two new legislative proposals in order to keep up the momentum towards the institutionalization of a new labour relations system based on social dialogue processes, in both the public and the private sector. Law 18508 addresses collective bargaining in the public sector, extending this right to all public employees; previously it was denied to important segments of this workforce, such as certain functionaries in the executive branch and public school teachers, despite the previous ratification of the ILO's Collective Bargaining Convention, 1981 (No. 154), which allows the exclusion only of members of the police and armed forces from collective bargaining processes (Bajac, 2010, p. 8). Specifically, this law states that all workers in the legislative, executive and judicial branches of government, state-owned enterprises, autonomous state entities and local governments are allowed to conclude collective bargaining agreements covering the following issues:

• working conditions and occupational health and safety;

• the design and implementation of vocational training programmes;

• the structure of civil service careers;

• proposals for reform of the public sector;

• relations between employers and employees. (Méndez, Senatore and Traversa, 2009, p. 31)

The general framework of the negotiations between the State and its employees is set by the Consejo Superior de Negociación Publica del Sector Publico, while individual agreements in each state entity are negotiated directly in bipartite processes involving equal numbers of union and state representatives (in their capacity as employers). The responsibility to guarantee compliance with the agreements rests with the MTSS.

In September 2009, after two years of debate, the controversial collective bargaining law for the private sector was passed by the Uruguayan Congress, owing in large part to the partisan discipline of the FA members of Congress and to the intense pressure campaign launched in 2009 by the PIT-CNT. This law enshrines tripartite social dialogue as one of the pillars of the Uruguayan labour relations system, through the regulation of the functions and structure of the Consejo Superior Tripartito. This institution, composed of nine representatives of the MTSS, six representatives of employers' organizations and six representatives of the PIT-CNT, has the authority to establish and modify the legal minimum wage, classify groups of economic activities in order to facilitate the tripartite wage bargaining processes that take place in the CS, indicate the labour and employers' organizations that will participate in the CS, deliberate on questions pertaining to labour and employer issues to be resolved bilaterally and trilaterally, and develop initiatives to advance labour relations in the country.

It should be noted that this law allows any of the three parties represented in the Consejo Superior Tripartito to convene the CS, thus effectively eliminating the ability of the executive branch of the Government to unilaterally block the realization of these sector-wide social dialogue processes, as it did during the reinstallation of a "voluntarist" labour relations system during the years 1990–2004. In addition, the law stipulates that the agreements reached in the CS are legally binding and that compliance for all the actors involved is mandatory, even if the employers refuse to participate in the negotiations. This occurred, for example, in 2008, in the negotiations in the CS for domestic workers, when no representative of an employers' organization took part in the talks. Likewise, according to this new law, all wage agreements remain in force until new agreements are signed, thus giving a greater level of stability and continuity to the labour relations system.

Owing to pressure from employers' groups, a "peace clause" was introduced in the days before the signing of the law, which stipulates that the actors involved in the negotiations in the CS shall not take actions in detriment to the spirit of the agreements. Despite the last-minute inclusion of this clause, the business sector maintained its opposition to the implementation of this law, even taking it to the point where the Uruguayan Chamber of Commerce and Services sent a complaint regarding its contents to the Committee on Freedom of Association of the ILO, and was vindicated when in 2010 this committee recommended to the Uruguayan Government that modifications be made in order to further demarcate the role of the MTSS representatives in the collective bargaining processes that take place in the CS (ILO, 2010). To comply with this recommendation, the Government established a new tripartite commission in October 2011 to formulate the suggested modifications; its work is still in progress.

Besides these laws regarding collective bargaining and protections for union leaders, over 35 other legislative proposals regarding labour issues were made by the FA Government and approved by the Uruguayan Congress during the years 2005–10, giving this period the distinction of having produced more labour legislation than any other in the history of the country. Although a detailed description of these other laws is beyond the scope of this chapter, we may briefly note here some of the issues dealt with in this legislation: they include the limitation of the working day for domestic and rural workers, the inclusion of domestic workers in the national social security system, the establishment of a new public institute for vocational training, and the prohibition of outsourcing labour in cases where this practice is principally used to reduce costs and disguise a de facto employer–employee relationship. In the light of this proliferation of legislative activity, it is reasonable to conclude that the Uruguayan labour relations system has been transformed from one in which negotiated norms prevail, such as in the United Kingdom and the United States, into one in which labour norms are explicitly codified through national law rather than bilateral agreements, following the French and German tradition.

The implementation of these new norms has had significant impacts on the Uruguayan labour market, especially in relation to the creation and formalization of employment and to the strengthening of union actors in the labour relations system. Olesker (2009, p. 31) shows that the unemployment rate declined from over 13 per cent to 7 per cent, the real value of the minimum wage increased by 135 per cent and wages in all economic sectors were revalued during the period 2005–08. Olesker also estimates that informal employment was reduced by 3 per cent; however, further action in this sphere is still necessary, as the Instituto Cuesta Duarte (2009) estimates that approximately 33 per cent of all employment in the country can still be classified as informal. With regard to the strengthening of the social actors in the labour market, it is evident that the union movement (traditionally the weakest actor) has taken advantage of this new labour relations framework: over 200,000 new members joined unions affiliated to the PIT-CNT during the years 2005–10, thus raising the unionization rate in this period from 14.4 per cent to over 25 per cent (Confederación Sindical de Trabajadores de las Américas, 2010). During the Tabaré Vázquez Government, the representativeness of the union movement also increased qualitatively, as new unions were created in formerly under-represented sectors such as domestic work, retail sales and private security services.

Latin American neocorporativism: The reconfiguration of interest representation in post-neoliberal Uruguay

Taking into consideration factors such as the increased promotion of tripartite social dialogue, the united action of unions and employers' organizations, and the redefinition of the role of the State in the new labour relations system installed by the FA Government, it is possible to pose the question whether the type of political representation of Uruguayan social actors now prevailing can be classified as "neocorporativist" or "societal corporatist". Utilizing the concept proposed by Schmitter, corporatism can be defined as a

> system of interest representation in which the constituent units are organized into a limited number of singular, compulsory, noncompetitive, hierarchically ordered and functionally differentiated categories, recognized ... by the state and granted a deliberate representational monopoly within their respective categories in exchange for observing certain controls on their selection of leaders and articulation of demands and supports. (Schmitter, 1974, pp. 93–94)

"Social corporatism" refers to a political system with open and competitive electoral processes and coalition-based executive powers, which also exhibits processes of rationalization of state policy-making that serve to incorporate subordinate social groups more closely within the political process, in this way corresponding to social democratic systems such as that which operate in the north European countries.

On the basis of these definitions it can be deduced that there is an approximation between the neocorporativist or social corporatist model and the current system of interest representation in Uruguay. This can be confirmed in structural terms. The representation of workers' interests is carried out by the unitary labour confederation PIT-CNT, which has a hierarchical framework (being composed of federations, which in turn are made up of individual unions), is recognized by the State as the sole legitimate actor representing labour interests in the CS, and – even if its selection of leaders is completely autonomous of the State – accepts the rules of the game implicit in its participation in the CS, including the "peace clause" mentioned above. Although

Uruguayan employers' interests are represented by a plurality of organizations without a defined hierarchy, it is important to note that these groups do not dispute the spheres of participation in which they operate and strictly coordinate their actions within the CS. The identification can also be affirmed in historical terms. Schmitter (1974, p. 126) states that the transition to social corporatism depends on past liberalism, involving a history of autonomous organizational development, distinctive class self-images and loyalties, the presence of a competitive electoral arena in which wider appeals can be launched, and a gradual expansion of the role of the State occurring in response to the needs and pressures of organized private interest groups. The autonomy and distinct cultural identity of the Uruguayan union movement, the country's traditional egalitarian values stemming from the social welfare regime constructed by Batlle y Ordoñez, the strong levels of party identification, and the historic role of the unions in stimulating state involvement in labour relations through the use of their influence on FA leaders all concur with this definition. Finally, the Uruguayan labour relations system follows the neocorporativist model on a procedural level. The tripartite social dialogue that takes place in the CS is now convened on a permanent basis, leading to comprehensive, legally binding agreements. Also, tripartite dialogue processes are now being developed in other institutions related to the world of work, such as the national social security institute (Banco de Previsión Social) and the national vocational training institute (Instituto Nacional de Empleo y Formación Profesional).

Despite these indications, the installation of neocorporativism on an institutional, political and cultural level in Uruguay is not yet complete. According to Offe (1985), the development and stability of corporatist political structures depend on the traditions and specific national configurations that labour movements assume, the suppression of other forms of interest expression, and continuous economic prosperity. In the case of Uruguay, the unitary structure of the union movement and its strategic decision to prioritize tripartite collective bargaining over other types of conflict resolution favour a deepening of corporatist practices. However, it is possible that alternative interest groupings could emerge, as the process of incorporation in the leadership of the PIT-CNT and in the bargaining committees of the CS of workers representing non-traditional union constituencies, such as women, youth and informal sector workers, has been quite slow. In addition, the premise of continued economic growth is also in doubt: despite the fact that Uruguay registered an impressive increase in GDP in 2010 (8.5 per cent), aftershocks from the 2008 world financial crisis still threaten to reduce demand for its principal exports to European and North American markets and thus weaken the national economy. Another worry stems from recent protectionist measures being implemented by Argentina, which threaten to restrict Uruguay's capacity to export products from important industrial sectors, such as textiles, auto parts and paper, to its larger southern neighbour (Cámara Nacional de Comercio y Servicios del Uruguay, 2012).

Offe also cautions that social corporatist structures could be threatened by the internalization and sharpening of class conflict, which would damage the capacity of the State to direct the institutional mechanisms put into place to ameliorate the tensions between labour and capital. Taking this into account, in the Uruguayan context, Senatore and Méndez (2010, p. 28) warn of the possibility of a regression in the consolidation of a neocorporativist labour relations system, if conflict between employers, unions and the State begins to escalate, particularly in relation to the distribution of public resources, macroeconomic policy-making and the redefinition of the new collective bargaining law for the private sector. On the other hand, the maintenance of the political hegemony of the FA in the executive and legislative branches of the national Government, the sustained quantitative and qualitative growth of the Uruguayan union movement, continued macroeconomic stability, and the widening of policy space on a regional level with the consolidation of centre-left political tendencies in the Southern Cone all contribute positively to the deepening of a social democratic political system based on social dialogue and a more equitable distribution of resources in this Latin American nation. Only with the passage of more time will it be possible to discern with greater clarity if this moment truly marks a new critical juncture in the history of the political development of the Uruguayan labour movement and a clear shift towards a neocorporativist system of interest representation; nevertheless, so far short-term indicators do show that the structural changes implemented to date by the FA Government have been able to benefit both Uruguayan workers and their organizations in a way that has not been seen since the introduction of Batlle y Ordoñez's labour reforms over a century ago.

Note

[1] These were the Freedom of Association and Protection of the Right to Organise Convention, 1948 (No. 87); the Right to Organise and Collective Bargaining Convention, 1949 (No. 98); and the Labour Relations (Public Service) Convention, 1978 (No. 151).

References

Bajac, L.C. 2010. *La negociación colectiva en el sector publico en la Republica Oriental del Uruguay*, paper presented at the Fifth Congress of the Latin American Center for Development Administration (CLAD), Santo Domingo, Dominican Republic, 9–12 Nov.

Cámara Nacional de Comercio y Servicios del Uruguay. 2012. *Ventas a Argentina en rubros clave 70 por ciento.* Available at: http://www.cncs.com.uy/softis/0/nv/8582 [30 May 2012].

Cavarozzi, M. 2001. "Transitions: Argentina, Bolivia, Chile, Uruguay", in M.A. Garreton and E. Newman (eds): *Democracy in Latin America: Reconstructing political society* (Tokyo, United Nations University Press).

Chavez, D. 2008. "The left in government: Between continuity and change", in P. Barrett, D. Chavez and C. Rodríguez-Garavito (eds): *The new Latin American left: Utopia reborn* (London, Pluto Press).

Collier, R.B.; Collier, D. 2002. *Shaping the political arena*, 2nd ed. (Notre Dame, IN, University of Notre Dame Press).

Confederación Sindical de Trabajadores de las Américas. 2010. *Sindicalización y densidad sindical en las Américas*. Available at: http://white.oit.org.pe/spanish/260ameri/oitreg/activid/proyectos/actrav/proyectos/proyecto_ssos/act_regionales/mexico_nov2010/documentos/3erdia_cancun1.pdf [30 May 2012].

Ermida, O. 2006. "La nueva legislación laboral Uruguaya", in *IUSLabor*, No. 4 (Barcelona, Universitat Pompeu Fabra).

Instituto Cuesta Duarte. 2009. *Informe de Coyuntura Junio 2009* (Montevideo, Instituto Cuesta Duarte).

International Labour Office (ILO). 1995. *Las relaciones laborales en Uruguay* (Madrid, Ministry of Labour and Social Security).

—. 2010. *Informe número 356 del Comité de Libertad Sindical.* http://www.ilo.org/wcmsp5/groups/public/@ed_norm/@relconf/documents/meetingdocument/wcms_124974.pdf [24 August 2012].

—. 2012. "Uruguay: Continúa la disminución del desempleo y el incremento de los salarios", in *Trabajo y Utopía*, No. 115 (Montevideo, PIT-CNT).

Ladra, A. 2008. *La crisis del 2002*. Available at: http://www.elacontecer.com.uy/954-la-crisis-del-2002.html [30 May 2012].

Luna, J.P. 2010. "The left turns: Why they happened and how they compare", in M. Cameron and E. Hershberg (eds): *Latin America's left turns* (London, Lynne Rienner).

Méndez, G.; Senatore, L.; Traversa, F. 2009. *La política laboral de un proyecto socialdemócrata periférico: Un análisis de los cambios institucionales en Uruguay 2005–2009* (Montevideo, Friedrich Ebert Foundation in Uruguay (FESUR)).

Ministry of Labour and Social Security (MTSS). 2011. *Negociación Colectiva: Junio 2011* (Montevideo).

Natanson, J. 2008. *La nueva izquierda* (Buenos Aires, Editorial Sudamericana).

Offe, C. 1985. *Capitalismo desorganizado* (São Paulo, Editora Brasiliense).

Olesker, D. 2009. *Crecimiento e inclusión: Logros del gobierno frenteamplista* (Montevideo, Ediciones Trilce).

Pucci, F.; Nion, S.; Ciapessoni, F.; Rojido, E. 2010. "Viejos y nuevos temas en la negociación colectiva uruguaya", in F. Pucci (ed.): *El Uruguay desde la Sociología VIII* (Montevideo, Faculty of Social Sciences, University of the Republic).

Red de Economistas de Izquierda del Uruguay. 2010. *La torta y las migajas: El gobierno progresista 2005–2010* (Montevideo, Ediciones Trilce).

Reygadas, L.; Filgueira, F. 2010. "Inequality and the incorporation crisis: The left's social policy toolkit", in M. Cameron and F. Hershberg (eds): *Latin America's left turns* (London, Lynne Rienner).

Schmitter, P. 1974. "Still the century of corporatism?", *Review of Politics*, Vol. 36, No. 1, pp. 85–131.

Senatore, L.A.; Méndez, G. 2010. *Las relaciones laborales en el Uruguay: Entre el neocorporativismo y la concertación salarial* (Montevideo, FESUR).

Supervielle, M.; Pucci, F. 2008. "El trabajo y las relaciones laborales en el siglo XX", in B. Nahum (ed.): *El Uruguay del SIGLO XX: La sociedad* (Montevideo, Ediciones de la Banda Oriental).

Zurbriggen, C.; Doglio, N.; Senatore, L. 2003. *Notas a propósito de los desafíos del movimiento sindical uruguayo* (Montevideo, FESUR).

Interviews

Peloche, Jorge, Secretary of Education, Federación de Empleados de Comercio y Servicios (FUECYS), Montevideo, Uruguay, 3 June 2011.

Pereyra, Martin, Director of Youth Department, PIT-CNT, Montevideo, Uruguay, 2 June 2011.

Picco, Alejandra, Research Director, Instituto Cuesta Duarte, Montevideo, Uruguay, 3 June 2011.

CAN A LABOUR-FRIENDLY GOVERNMENT BE FRIENDLY TO LABOUR? A HEGEMONIC ANALYSIS OF BRAZILIAN, GERMAN AND SOUTH AFRICAN EXPERIENCES

8

Christoph Scherrer and Luciana Hachmann

Introduction

A labour movement is bound to become involved in politics, because so many aspects of its own conditions of action as well as of its members' lives are shaped by the prevailing laws and balance of forces in the political arena. In many countries, therefore, organized labour operates with two "arms": one a trade union, the other a political party. However, the relationship between the two arms is seldom without tension, especially once the party rises to power (Howell, 2001; Webster, 2007).

The common explanation for the inevitability of the disappointment of trade unions in these circumstances refers to economic constraints. It is argued that external and domestic economic pressures limit governments' room for manoeuvre (Hunter, 2007). However, this explanation assumes that economic constraints are indisputably fixed, and not open to contestation. It also rests on the idea that trade unions always and inevitably reject the economic constraints – which is not always the case, as certain limitations on government action may be acknowledged by trade unions. Thus, economic conditions cannot be held solely responsible for the tensions between a left-leaning government and trade unions.

Another common interpretation of the move of a leftist party to the political middle ground refers to the median voter model. It states that competing politicians will adopt policies which reflect the preferences of the median voters, because their vote is decisive (Congleton, 2002). This focus on elections, which take place only once in a while, seems to be too narrow to fully capture the dynamics of the political process.

Our theoretical approach takes into account societal power relations. It is inspired by Antonio Gramsci's conception of hegemony, which includes both coercive and consensual elements. We argue that the extent of neoliberal hegemony has had a decisive influence on the relationship between trade unions and left-leaning parties in government in the past two decades. In an attempt to explore the explanatory powers of the various theoretical approaches by way of comparison, we have selected three cases which are similar only in respect of the fact that parties came to power which have traditionally enjoyed good relations with the respective countries' main trade unions: Brazil 2003–10, Germany 1998–2005 and South Africa 1999–2008. Such a comparison of countries which differ along many dimensions is expected to yield a good assessment of the various factors influencing the relationship between trade unions and a labour-friendly party in government.

In Brazil and South Africa, the trade union federations – Central Única dos Trabalhadores (CUT) and the Congress of South African Trade Unions (COSATU) – provided the top leadership for the Partido dos Trabalhadores (PT) and the African National Congress (ANC), respectively. In Germany, by contrast, the leadership of the Deutscher Gewerkschaftsbund (DGB) emerged distinct from that of the Sozialdemokratische Partei Deutschlands (SPD) in Germany and did not share such decisive experiences, being a generation apart from the common opposition to Nazism.

Despite these differences in originary relationships, all three left-leaning parties in government disappointed their labour constituencies in terms of macroeconomic policies in the early part of the twenty-first century. The alienation of labour was greater in Germany and South Africa than in Brazil, as in the former two countries it extended beyond macroeconomics into labour market and social policies. In Germany it led to a switch of loyalty among a significant part of organized labour from the Social Democrats to the newly formed party Die Linke (The Left) and to the eventual electoral defeat of the Social Democrats under Chancellor Schröder in 2005. In South Africa, President Mbeki's centralized style of ruling marginalized COSATU in the triple alliance between the ANC, COSATU and the South African Communist Party (SACP). When it became obvious that his neoliberal macroeconomic policies had not delivered employment growth, COSATU members rallied together with left-leaning ANC members against Mbeki, who had to step down from the party leadership and the presidency in 2008. In Brazil, while the trade unions were disappointed on macroeconomic policies, the relationship between the PT and CUT remained generally cordial, most visibly during President Lula's second term.

These broadly similar, yet in detail distinct, experiences in the relationship between party and trade unions provide the basis for deeper insights into the factors that influence the relationship of a labour-friendly party in government to trade unions.

Our analysis begins with a brief description of the three governments' macroeconomic and labour market policies. Then we explore to what degree economic and electoral constraints explain the experience of the trade union–government relationship in each of the three countries. Since economic and electoral constraints cannot explain these experiences sufficiently, we introduce the Gramscian concepts of hegemony and *transformismo* and apply them to the three cases. We conclude with a summary of our main findings.

The trade union–government relationship

Chancellor Schröder (1998–2005)

While the predominant German trade union confederation, the DGB, and its member organizations are not explicitly aligned with any party, they always had a social democratic identity.[1] Many trade unionists were also active in the SPD. They contributed substantially to the electoral victory of the coalition of the Green Party and the SPD in September 1998, which ended 16 years of a conservative–liberal government under Chancellor Helmut Kohl (the Greens obtained 6.7 per cent and the Social Democrats 40.9 per cent of the electoral vote). The DGB unions' relationship with the new Government under the Social Democrat Gerhard Schröder started out as a "honeymoon", but ended in a "war of roses". We have identified three phases of the Red–Green reform agenda. (The phases have been named after their leading policy entrepreneurs: see in more detail Beck and Scherrer, 2005.)

The "Lafontaine phase", from September 1998 to March 1999 (Lafontaine, 1999), saw repeals of previous cuts in the social security safety net, the promulgation of neo-Keynesian macroeconomic policies and the initiation of an "Alliance for Jobs" on the suggestion of the metalworkers' union IG Metall. Oskar Lafontaine's progressive economic policies were met with particularly stiff resistance from industry, which threatened to move jobs and operations out of Germany. His resignation from the Treasury came unexpectedly and is still clouded in mystery. With it, the progressive phase came to an end.

The "Eichel–Riester phase", from April 1999 to February 2002, brought a cautious reversal of the previous policy stance, with more restrictive macroeconomic policies, substantial tax relief for corporate Germany (under Hans Eichel, the new Secretary of the Treasury) and the introduction of a supplementary private pension system (the so-called *Riester Rente*, named after the Minister of Labour, Walter Riester, a former trade unionist). All in all, despite some improvements for labour, for example, in the case of co-determination through the reform of the Works Constitution Act (*Betriebsverfassungsgesetz*), this phase was marked by a clear redirection of economic policies towards improving supply-side conditions and competitiveness.

In preparing for the general election of September 2002, a third policy phase was inaugurated in March 2002 with the appointment of Peter Hartz, Volkswagen's personnel manager, to chair a commission on labour market reforms. After its very narrow re-election in September 2002, the Red–Green Government hastened to implement the Hartz reforms under the slogan "Agenda 2010". For this purpose, Chancellor Schröder replaced Riester with Wolfgang Clement, the most neoliberal of the Social Democratic heads of state governments, and united the ministries of economics and labour under Clement's leadership.

The "Hartz–Clement phase", from March 2002 to March 2004, opened the door to temporary work agencies, tightened the eligibility criteria for unemployment benefits, gave tax incentives for low-wage employment and massively reduced long-term unemployment benefits. Popular discontent with these policies, including within the SPD, proved to be enduring, even increasing as one reform after another was enacted. Schröder was forced to quit as party leader, and in a desperate move to regain momentum called for early elections, which his Red–Green coalition narrowly lost in September 2005 (Seeleib-Kaiser and Fleckenstein, 2007).

President Mbeki (1999–2008)

Even before Thabo Mbeki had assumed the presidency of South Africa, tensions between him and COSATU had arisen. In his capacity as Deputy President, Mbeki had initiated the Growth, Employment and Redistribution (GEAR) programme in 1996. In pursuing macroeconomic austerity, external liberalization and domestic privatizations, GEAR broke with the social democratic goals of the Reconstruction and Development Programme (RDP), the ANC's election manifesto of 1994. While the RDP ("the anti-apartheid alliance's consensus": UNDP, 2003, p. 60) called for bottom-up consultations, GEAR represented a non-negotiable macroeconomic policy imposed from the top down (Gevisser, 2007, p. 666). Mbeki had launched GEAR without regard for either the ANC's political allies, above all COSATU, or public opinion (Gumede, 2007, p. 76).

Mbeki's tenure as President increased the strain between COSATU and his ANC Government. His term came to be characterized as "elitist" (Mathekga, 2008, p. 132). Indeed, Mbeki had long believed that the ANC would have to end the alliance with the SACP in post-apartheid South Africa. He had envisioned the ANC as a centre-left party, loosely connected to trade unions and the SACP (Gumede, 2007, p. 43).

This belief translated into a top-down approach to government which undermined the ANC's internal democracy and marginalized grass-roots members and activists (Gumede, 2009, pp. 35–45). Similarly, institutional forms of social dialogue such as the National Economic Development and Labour Council lost their significance for the Government. At the same time, key financial and mining conglomerates gained influence in the Government and among the ANC elite (Butler, 2007, p. 41).

Mbeki's "modernization agenda" gave priority to "capital reform", that is, to the deracialization of economic power. Thus an "implicit bargain" took shape. On the one hand, the ANC pledged to foster macroeconomic stability and international openness; on the other hand, business agreed to the principles behind "black economic empowerment", that is, increasing the ownership of assets by black South Africans (Gelb, 2005, p. 369).

Since GEAR did not deliver in terms of employment (official unemployment rates for 1997 and 2009 were 22.7 per cent and 24 per cent, respectively: Statistics South Africa, 1998, 2009), COSATU remained committed to the RDP. Despite its increasing frustration with Mbeki's neglect of working-class interests, however,

COSATU recognized (as it continues to do) that the ANC remains the only political party capable of representing those interests. Therefore, COSATU tried to advance working-class interests within the ANC (COSATU, 2006).

In 2008 COSATU, together with the left wing of the ANC, forced Mbeki to resign. With the support of COSATU he was replaced by Jacob Zuma, a former Deputy President under Mbeki, first as the leader of the ANC, and in 2009 also as President of South Africa.

President Lula (2003–10)

The historical ties between the PT and CUT in Brazil are well documented (Sluyter-Beltrão, 2010; Secco, 2011). Indeed, the PT owes its foundation in 1980 to the desire of the trade union movement for an autonomous political party. Many leaders in this process were responsible for founding the CUT later in 1983.

The relationship between the CUT and PT has remained cordial during Lula's five presidential campaigns. Once in government, Lula broke with the leadership style of his predecessor and became very accessible for trade unionists and civil society groups. He also established an institutional channel, the Economic and Social Development Council (CDES) – a plural consultative body which for the first time in Brazil put the trade unions on an equal footing with employers in the field of economic policy formulation (Costa, 2010a). Initially, the media and the opposition parties in Parliament accused the President of trying to use the CDES to bypass the democratic processes of Parliament itself (Costa, 2010b); however, the benefits of the new arrangements were later widely recognized across the different sectors of society. The CUT considered the CDES particularly important for elaborating a common agenda to face the consequences of the 2008 global crisis (CDES, 2010).

In addition, the Lula Government passed a law which finally recognized trade union confederations de jure (and not only de facto, as it was the case until 2007) as representative bodies of workers. This act provided the CUT and other federations with legal guarantees of their participation in forums and councils. It also had financial repercussions, stipulating an increase in the federations' share of the compulsory tax equivalent to one day's work a year for all formal employees. In 2007, the CUT received approximately US$9.5 million from this tax (Portal Vermelho, 2008).

On the macroeconomic front, however, Lula maintained his predecessor's market-oriented policies. This was considered unacceptable by a significant number of PT and CUT members who wanted to see a more radical leftist approach. As a result, they left both organizations to build new trade union federations and new left-wing political parties (Costa, 2010b).

However, the Government's social policies (in respect of, for example, the minimum wage and efforts to reduce poverty) were in line with the expectations of the trade unions in Brazil and acted to neutralize its controversial orthodox macroeconomic policies. For example, the minimum wage increased by 53.67 per cent in real terms between 2003 and 2010, and the booming economy brought down unemployment from 12.4 per cent in 2003 to 6.7 per cent in 2010, creating 15.3 million formal jobs and reducing the poverty rate by 50.6 per cent (Zimmerman and Spitz, 2005; DIEESE, 2012; FGV, 2011; MTE, 2011). In the light of these positive economic developments, especially in the labour market, the majority of CUT members welcomed the CUT's support of the Lula Government.

Comparison of the three administrations

In all three countries, the trade union federations had supported the electoral campaigns of their allied political parties. Nevertheless, the relationship between labour and party varied, characterized in each case by differing degrees of dissatisfaction. Lula was most active in pursuing a pro-worker policy, while at the same time placating conservative forces with a restrictive macroeconomic policy. While Mbeki pushed forward a neoliberal economic agenda in technocratic fashion, he neither cut social security provisions nor reduced protection for workers in the formal labour market. It was Schröder who not only pursued restrictive macroeconomic policies but also made cuts in the welfare state and promoted the flexibilization of labour.

The three heads of state also differed in their leadership styles. While Lula adopted an inclusive style of governance and conducted an open dialogue with civil society, Mbeki opted for a technocratic style with little dialogue with social groups or even with the ANC itself. Schröder became famous for his *Basta-Politik* – the term used to indicate his brusque way of ending policy debates.

One of the surprising observations arising from the comparison is that the PT met some of the demands of trade unions despite being in coalition with conservative parties, while the ANC, which did not have to fear any electoral challenge and thus theoretically was under less pressure to compromise with conservative forces, made fewer concessions to the unions.

The explanatory power of economic and electoral constraints

As noted in the introduction to this chapter, trade unions' disappointment with allied parties in government is commonly explained with reference to economic constraints and the median voter model. In the countries examined, we find that the labour-friendly government of the country facing the least external economic constraints, the export champion Germany, alienated organized labour the most. Under pressure to fulfil his campaign promise of 1998 to lower unemployment significantly, Chancellor Schröder could have attempted to reflate the economy instead of opting for labour market reforms to the detriment of workers. Brazil and South Africa faced much more severe domestic and external economic constraints. In spite of such constraints, Brazil was able to implement some social policies with significant reach which were well received by labour; Mbeki, however, did not test the limits of progressive economic policies. Therefore, while economic constraints should not be underestimated, they are not sufficient to explain the governments' macroeconomic, social and labour market policies.

Might the behaviour of the three governments be better understood with recourse to the median voter model? While this model has been developed for majoritarian electoral systems, it has been adapted to systems of proportional representation where coalition governments are the rule. Here coalitions fight for the middle ground of the political spectrum and the coalition partner closest to the middle may become decisive for the simple reason that the party in the middle can easily switch sides and join the other coalition (Mayer and Meier-Walser, 2002). Applying this analysis to the trade union question, it would explain labour's disappointment with the need of the left-leaning party to accommodate a more centrist coalition partner and to appeal to voters to the right of the trade unions. Even so, plausible as this argument sounds, it does not quite capture the three cases at hand.

First, the policies of these three governments which disappointed or even alienated labour were neither the manifestation of an election-day mandate nor the realization of long-held beliefs of the parties in government (Samuels, 2004; Gumede, 2007). In fact, the SPD would not have had majority support for these laws before coming to power (Heinrich, Lübker and Biehl, 2002, p. 39).

Second, the coalition dynamics were not in line with the model's predictions. Unlike the social democratic Schmidt Government of the 1970s, which had to reach compromises with an economically liberal coalition partner (the Free Democrats), Schröder was not forced to the right by the Green Party. The same is true for Mbeki's ANC alliance, which held a comfortable lead in the elections, but not for Lula, who headed a coalition with conservative parties and without a clear majority of parliamentary seats in the first term – and yet the Lula Government implemented policies supported by trade unions.

While the electoral dynamics should not be ignored, politics cannot be reduced to elections, which take place only every so often. Politics are made every day. The victory at the election booth allows the winning coalition to occupy the top government positions, but it does not guarantee the implementation of its policies (if it has any). The case of Lafontaine, who attempted a progressive macroeconomic policy shift, is very instructive.

Lafontaine's agenda depended on the cooperation of the central bank, the Bundesbank, in lowering interest rates, and on the finance ministries of other OECD countries in coordinating their fiscal policies as well as preventing tax evasion. However, the cooperation of these partners was not forthcoming: indeed, the US Treasury did not hide its dislike for Lafontaine's neo-Keynesianism and the German business community railed relentlessly against him (Hippler, 1999).

147

Learning from the defeat of Lula in the previous presidential election, the PT leadership had recognized the need to placate business interests even before Lula came to power in 2003. This recognition is reflected in the change of campaign rhetoric from 1989 to 2002 in a shift which opened the way to a coalition with conservative parties. Once in power, Lula accommodated the right-wing party, the PSDB, by appointing individuals close to it to head the Ministry of Agriculture, the Ministry of Development, Industry and Foreign Trade and the Central Bank (Borges Neto, 2003, p. 10).

By itself, pressure from the business community and the conservative media was not so much to be feared if it did not affect electoral competition. However, this was a real threat for both Schröder and Lula. While the activation of the SPD core constituency contributed to Schröder's initial victory, the bulk of the party's new supporters in that election had previously voted for the centre-right party, the Christian Democrats (Infratest dimap, 1998). These voters were more receptive to the arguments of the conservative opposition. This latter point was fully confirmed in the first state elections following the federal elections that brought the Red–Green coalition to power. Running on a platform against the Greens' pet project of dual citizenship for immigrants, the Christian Democrats under Roland Koch pushed the Red–Green coalition out of office in the state of Hessia (Hofrichter and Westle, 2000). Hence there are good reasons for a left-of-centre government in a competitive electoral system to listen to the voters to their right and to those who might have influence over them.

The alternative would be to mobilize one's own forces, to exhaust the reservoir of support within one's own camp. Left-of-centre governments have seldom resorted to such a strategy (Burnham, 1980). Why have they hesitated to pursue this alternative? They might have wanted to avoid risking a profound alienation of the powers that be and a right-wing populist counter-mobilization.

Instead of turning to the party, could not the trade unions mobilize their members and other workers in support of a progressive agenda? All three trade union movements had a good record in mobilizing against the conservative governments that had previously held office, but the coming to power of "their" parties confronted them with a strategic dilemma: namely, the risk that their mobilization would alienate those non-core voters for the left-leaning parties and thus contribute to these parties' failure in government. In Germany, the SPD leadership was not shy about pointing out this risk. So the unions were caught in a dilemma: the Red–Green Government was moving against them on important issues, but opposing these moves would make it even more likely that these detrimental laws would be enacted by the next conservative government (Zeuner, 2000).

The CUT faced a similar quandary. As the media in Brazil are largely conservative, open dispute is always a concern for left-of-centre forces. In 2005, the PT faced one of its major crises when a corruption scandal took over the political agenda in the country. This episode was widely covered by the conservative media and opened up a prospective challenge to Lula's re-election in 2006.

In contrast, the ANC did not face serious electoral competition. COSATU did not have to fear that its opposition to GEAR would topple the Government. However, COSATU, in alliance with the SACP, continued for a long time to try to uphold the ideal of the unity of the alliance. By 2008 the situation had changed and COSATU campaigned for a change in the presidency.

To sum up, there are plenty of incentives for a left-of-centre coalition to listen to the centre and the powerful players in society. In addition, the trade unions did not want to be blamed for bringing down a former friend and ending up with a current enemy in government. Yet, in the light of variations in the three governments' policy stances, the economic and political constraints do not quite explain the dynamic of the relationship between trade unions and left-of-centre parties. In the German case the adoption of the unpopular "Agenda 2010" remains particularly puzzling, especially in hindsight. Why would a government turn against its core constituency at the risk of getting voted out of office? A Gramscian perspective might shed some more light on the trade union–party relationship by contextualizing it in a broader frame of power relations in capitalist societies.

A Gramscian perspective on the hegemony of capital

The point of departure of Antonio Gramsci's analysis of power relations is that capitalist society cannot ensure its own reproduction. The "dull compulsion of the production relations", based on the separation of producers from their means of production, is insufficient to keep the working class in its dependent position for ever. But even the use of coercion is not adequate for this purpose; other, "non-coercive" strategies are required. To analyse these strategies, which aim at creating active consent among the subordinate classes, Gramsci developed several concepts, of which we will use here those of *hegemony* and *transformism*. Hegemony refers to an entrenched form of rule that resorts to coercion only in exceptional cases. A ruling class is hegemonic and not just dominant if it succeeds in winning approval for its authority among the members of other societal classes. The more this authority is not merely passively tolerated but actively supported, the more secure the hegemony is. Whenever hegemony essentially relies on cunning and coercion, as Gramsci believed the ruling middle class did after successfully removing the yoke of feudal power, it lacks ethical legitimacy. One particularly effective form of hegemony by deception, Gramsci argued, is the co-option of the leadership of subordinate classes: this is what he called transformism. The ethical side of hegemony – leading other groups to the pinnacle of knowledge, technology and culture – pertains only to allied classes, not to rival, "ruled" classes (Gramsci, 1991–96, Notebook 7 §19, Notebook 8 §§173 and 179, Notebook 10 §44).

The task at hand here is first to analyse the impact of the then prevailing neoliberal hegemony on the behaviour of the left-leaning parties and the trade unions in the three countries. The next step explores the extent of co-optation of the left-leaning party leadership in favour of existing property relations.

The extent of neoliberal hegemony

The electoral victories of Lula, Mbeki and Schröder came at a time when in many other countries progressive leaders like New Democrat Bill Clinton in the United States and New Labour's Tony Blair in Britain had embraced markets as solutions for social and economic problems. Hence their emphasis on the epithet "new" in relation to their parties' traditional role as stalwart defenders of the welfare state.

The embracing of markets, and thus of private capital, by left-of-centre parties reflected not only the reassertion of private business interests in Western societies but also the intellectual hegemony of market proponents. The appeal of markets, that is, private property holders in competition against each other, went far beyond the economic profession, especially in Germany. It extended to public policy advisers and the media. The impressive job performance of the "New Economy" in the United States seemed to provide the empirical evidence for the theoretical assertion of neoclassical economists: namely, that deregulated markets were superior to the (allegedly) oversized welfare state (cf. Sturm, 2003, p. 90). Despite many well-founded alternative perspectives on the factors driving job growth in both countries (cf. Palley, 1998), the public debate focused almost solely on labour market flexibility (Beck, 2005).

At the same time, proponents of corporatist, statist solutions to globalization in general and unemployment in particular remained on the defensive. Although most of them had not supported Soviet policies, the collapse of the Soviet Union severely discredited state intervention in the economy and took away a point of reference for arguing in favour of state planning. In addition, the West's answer to the communist challenge, Keynesian policies, had been discredited by the inflation of the 1970s and their unsuccessful revival under the early Mitterrand Government in France. It all added up to a lack of a unifying vision beyond the defence of the status quo (Zeuner, 1998).

Brazil had already gone through a period of explicit neoliberalism by the time Lula came to power, while the 16 years of the conservative Chancellor Kohl had brought only a small dose of neoliberalism to Germany. Therefore, the PT was much more conscious of the negative aspects of neoliberalism. Together with a mixed group of political and economic experts, especially at Instituto Cidadania, the PT had developed a body of alternative economic expertise (Instituto Cidadania, 2012). Nevertheless, the PT faced a broad elite consensus inside and outside Brazil on the need to pursue conservative monetary and fiscal policies, with pressure from, for example, the Instituto Liberal, Liberty Fund and Cato Foundation. (See in more detail Gros, 2004.) The leadership, therefore, had decided not to challenge this elite policy stance. By Lula's second term, criticism of conservative macroeconomics had lost strength within the PT. One reason for this was that, despite restrictive policies, the Brazilian economy had been growing; the other reason was that PT members and voters also opted for moderation (Samuels, 2008).

The economic legacy of the apartheid regime in South Africa does not fit the Keynesian/developmental versus neoliberal categorization. The apartheid governments pursued import substitution first by choice and later by necessity because of economic sanctions. The primary characteristic of the apartheid economy, however, was the exclusion of the black majority from holding property or gaining access to well-paid jobs. Therefore, the main issue confronting the post-apartheid regime was opening up opportunities for black citizens. The original idea of the ANC was to achieve this objective by a mixture of socialist and Keynesian policies. As noted above, this approach was quickly superseded by the neoliberal GEAR programme favoured by Mbeki and the white power elite. While COSATU remained in opposition to GEAR, much of the impetus towards building a convincing and strong alternative strategy evaporated as many key leaders and experienced researchers left the trade unions to work for the Government or in business.

Transformism: Co-optation of leadership

The SPD had already made peace with capitalism in the late 1950s. By the 1990s, its leadership at the lower and middle ranks consisted mainly of government employees; few representatives had been workers. The top leadership consisted of professional politicians, in some areas with close ties to the energy sector (Clement was a case in point). In a break with the past, by the 1990s many party officials expected to land jobs in the private sector after leaving public office. Chancellor Schröder himself became chairman of the supervisory board of Nord Stream AG, a subsidiary of the Russian energy behemoth Gazprom, immediately after he left office (Lütgert, 2011).

The Brazilian press frequently reports on illicit strategies for enrichment adopted by the PT leadership. It is not illegal for parliamentarians to run private consulting firms while in office;[2] some of them make use of this option (Istoé Dinheiro, 2011). A problem of legality does arise, however, when political influence is used to expand personal wealth.

The opposition has also criticized the Lula Government for filling government positions not on merit but to serve political considerations. Praça, Freitas and Hoepers (2011) suggest, however, that such political appointments were necessary to maintain the government coalition. Moreover, political appointments are not used exclusively for patronage ends as many positions are held by career civil servants.

In South Africa, political engagement is a major avenue of upward mobility. Salary levels for government employees are a legacy of the apartheid era, when these jobs were reserved for whites. Political connections also help to break into the white business world. It is very important, however, to note Mbeki's non-partisan commitment in relation to appointing his administration. The appointment of some individuals as public officials without prior consultation with the ANC has widened the gap between the party's leaders and the Government (Mathekga, 2008).

Career expectations similar to those of Social Democratic politicians can also be found among high-ranking German trade unionists, many of whom move on to positions in government (as noted above), or on the boards of public enterprises, or as heads of personnel departments of co-determined companies.[3] This may in part explain the lack of resistance initially mounted by German trade unions to "Agenda 2010". Only when core organizational interests were threatened and many lower-ranking officials voiced their dissatisfaction did they distance themselves from Chancellor Schröder openly (Weßels, 2007).

During Lula's term in office, many CUT leaders began to work for the Government. Among the political appointees were many leaders of trade unions for public employees, which had gained many members in the 1990s and most of which were affiliated to the CUT (D'Araújo, 2009).

The issue of "brain drain" also affected the trade unions in South Africa as some important COSATU leaders took political office with the ANC or important positions in the corporate sector (Buhlungu, 1999). COSATU's loss of key leading personnel seriously diminished its pool of skilled and experienced leaders. This "brain drain" led to a decline in the quality both of services provided to members and of democratic processes (Webster, 2001, pp. 267–68). The union activists who became part of the corporate sector through the policy of black economic empowerment were, according to a study by Prevost (2006, p. 175), often less sympathetic to union demands than the previous board members.

The extent of intellectual co-optation is also related to the question of independent expertise. While German trade unions own many training institutions for their members, invest much in the training of work council members and fund research through their foundations, they found themselves on the intellectual defensive in the field of macro and labour market economics. They commanded little in-house expertise on these issues and their network of friendly economists at universities had become a severely marginalized group. In fact, Chancellor Schröder had installed a neoclassical economist as president of the only trade union-friendly government-sponsored economic think-tank (Lieb, 2005).

Similarly, the intellectual base for progressive economic policies was rather small in South Africa (Webster and Adler, 1999, p. 370). In contrast, the CUT could draw on economic expertise from its own Inter-Union Department of Statistics and Socioeconomic Studies (DIEESE) and from institutions such as the University of UNICAMP. The trade unions' own training schools, the *escola sindical*, also provide assistance for trade unionists.

The three political leaders' treatment of trade unions reflects their respective political backgrounds. Lula, as a former trade unionist, had the closest ties; Schröder, as a trained lawyer and professional politician, and Mbeki, as the representative of the ANC in exile, had both made their careers at a distance from the trade unions.

The three parties also differ in terms of their identity. While the PT has a pronounced working-class identity, not only in name (Secco, 2011), the German SPD sees itself as a people's party (Lösche, 1992) and the ANC's self-image is still that of a liberation movement (ANC, 2007). These different identities mirror the parties' relationships with the trade unions: the ties are closest in Brazil and loosest in Germany. In the case of South Africa, the formal tripartite alliance between the ANC, COSATU and SACP did not translate into much influence for labour on key economic policy decisions during Mbeki's term. The ANC did not pick up on working-class demands in a "consistent" and "strong" form (Williams, 2008, p. 132), despite the fact that the black working class predominantly supported the ANC (García-Rivero, 2006).

Conclusion

Disappointment of trade unions with a labour-friendly party in government is a quite common phenomenon. To different degrees we found this disappointment among trade unions in three major countries, Brazil, Germany and South Africa, in recent years. The experiences of these countries under government by representatives of left-of-centre parties, respectively the PT, SPD and ANC, only partially fit the standard explanations for the estrangement of trade unions and labour-friendly parties in government. The Government subject to fewest economic constraints moved most strongly against trade union interests (Schröder's in Germany). The Government with the most complex coalition, including conservative parties, and therefore most vulnerable to coalitional defection, was most friendly to labour (Lula's in Brazil). The Government with the lowest threat of electoral defeat was least willing to engage with labour (Mbeki's in South Africa). While these standard explanations should not be discarded, the different experiences of the three countries call for a complementary look at overall societal power relations.

The extent to which market-friendly policy ideas became hegemonic explains the behaviour of the German SPD and the Brazilian PT fairly well. The societal penetration of neoliberalism went deeper in Germany than in Brazil, which had already gone through a period of explicit neoliberalism, so that the PT was much more aware of its negative aspects. In line with these differences on neoliberalism, the PT and SPD differed with respect to the level of co-optation and the identity of the party in relation to workers. The SPD has for many decades called itself a people's party, while the PT is still explicit about its working-class heritage.

The behaviour of the ANC under Mbeki represents a departure from this pattern. Despite the fact that a large number of party activists opposed neoliberalism and most ANC voters were living a life far removed from neoliberal conceptions of individual entrepreneurship, a neoliberal agenda was pursued in the macroeconomic realm and in relation to civil society representation. This theoretically unexpected behaviour can be explained by Mbeki's exclusive leadership style, even towards the ANC, and the use of public office to co-opt many activists into a lifestyle formerly reserved for the white population.

Finally, the lower level of acceptance of neoliberalism in Brazil was accompanied by a broader base of alternative policy expertise than existed in either Germany or South Africa. The same holds true for the mobilization capacities of the trade unions in the comparison between Brazil and Germany. Here again, South Africa stands apart. There, mobilization capacity is high, but was long hampered by the belief in "unity". COSATU's outstanding ability to mobilize its members, however, explains the downfall of Mbeki in 2008, brought about through a revolt within the ANC and not through general elections as in the case of Schröder.

To sum up, a labour-friendly party faces a difficult task in the attempt to stay friendly towards labour when it attains power. However, it does not inevitably have to become unfriendly towards labour. If, on the one hand, the party and labour can develop their own vision of society and buttress this vision with policy expertise and the capacity to mobilize their constituency in the face of the business agenda and power, and if, on the other hand, the trade unions recognize the policy constraints on a party in government and do not evaluate the Government's performance against the background of unrealistic expectations, party and unions can stay on friendly terms, although they might disagree from time to time.

Notes

[1] Christian Democrats were usually represented on the executive board of the DGB trade unions, but always in a minority position; Communists were present in some of the trade unions at lower ranks.

[2] These consulting firms may be in various sectors, including engineering, construction or taxation.

[3] Authors' observation.

References

African National Congress (ANC). 2007. *African National Congress constitution as amended and adopted at the 52nd national conference, Polokwane.* Available at: http://www.anc.org.za/show. php?id=207 [31 May 2012].

Beck, S. 2005. "After the miracle: The exhaustion of the German model?", in S. Beck, F. Klobes and C. Scherrer (eds): *Surviving globalization? Perspectives for the German economic model* (Berlin, Springer), pp. 33–68.

—; Scherrer, C. 2005. "Explaining the dynamics of Red–Green economic reforms", in S. Beck, F. Klobes and C. Scherrer (eds): *Surviving globalization? Perspectives for the German economic model* (Berlin, Springer), pp. 201–24.

Borges Neto, J.J. 2003. "Um governo contraditório", in *Revista da Sociedade Basileira de Economia Política*, Vol. 6, No. 12, pp. 7–27.

Buhlungu, S. 1999. "Generational transition in union employment: The organisational implications of staff turnover in COSATU unions", in *Transformation*, No. 39, pp. 47–71.

Burnham, W.D. 1980. "The appearance and disappearance of the American voter", in R. Rose (ed.): *Electoral participation* (Beverly Hills and London, Sage), pp. 33–73.

Butler, A. 2007. "The state of the African National Congress", in S.S. Buhlungu, J. Daniel, R. Southall and J. Lutchman (eds): *State of the nation: South Africa 2007* (Cape Town, Human Science Research Council (HSRC)), pp. 35–52.

Confederation of South African Trade Unions (COSATU). 2006. *Political resolutions of the 9th National Congress*. Available at: http://www.cosatu.org.za/show.php?ID=1247 [27 June 2012].

Congleton, R. 2002. "The median voter model", in R.K. Rowley and F. Schneider (eds): *The encyclopedia of public choice* (Berlin, Springer).

Conselho de Desenvolvimento Econômico e Social (CDES). 2010. *4.º Pleno do CDES: Discurso do conselheiro Artur Henrique*. Available at: http://www.cdes.gov.br/noticia/14931/34-pleno-do-cdes-discurso-do-conselheiro-artur-henrique.html [31 May 2012].

Costa, V.M. 2010a. *Apreensão e temor: Repercussões da criação do CDES na imprensa*. Available from Conselho de Desenvolvimento Economico e Social (CDES) at: http://www.cdes.gov.br/estudo.html [31 May 2012].

—, 2010b. *CDES e a Agenda nacional de desenvolvimento: Um modelo de diálogo social*. Available from Conselho de Desenvolvimento Economico e Social (CDES) at: http://www.cdes.gov.br/estudo.html [31 May 2012].

D'Araújo, M.C. 2009. *A elite dirigente do Governo Lula* (Rio de Janeiro, Fundação Getulio Vargas).

Departamento Intersindical de Estatística e Estudos Socioeconômicos (DIEESE). 2012. *Política de valorização do salário mínimo: Considerações sobre o valor a vigorar*, Technical Note No. 106. Available at: http://www.dieese.org.br/notatecnica/notatec106PoliticaSalarioMinimo.pdf [27 June 2012].

Fundação Getulio Vargas (FGV). 2011. *A Evolução dos Indicadores Sociais Baseados em Renda. Desigualdade de Renda da Decada* (Rio de Janeiro, FGV).

García-Rivero, C. 2006. "Race, class and underlying trends in party support in South Africa", in *Party Politics*, Vol. 12, No. 1, Jan., pp. 57–75.

Gelb, S. 2005. "An overview of the South African economy", in R. Southall and J. Lutchmann (eds): *State of the nation: South Africa 2004–2005* (Cape Town, HSRC), pp. 367–400.

Gevisser, M. 2007. *The dream referred: Thabo Mbeki* (Jeppestown, Jonathan Ball).

Gramsci, A. 1991–96. *Gefängnishefte 1–15*, 7 vols, ed. K. von Bochmann and W.F. Haug (Hamburg and Berlin, Argument Verlag).

Gros, D. 2004. "Institutos liberais, neoliberalismo e políticas públicas na nova república", in *Revista Brasileira de Ciencias Sociais*, Vol. 19, No. 54, pp. 143–59.

Gumede, W.M. 2007. *Thabo Mbeki and the battle for the soul of the ANC* (Cape Town, Zebra Press).

—. 2009. "Modernizing the African National Congress: The legacy of Thabo Mbeki", in P. Kagwanja and K. Kondlo (eds): *State of the nation: South Africa 2008* (Cape Town, HSRC), pp. 35–58.

Heinrich, R.; Lübker, M.; Biehl, H. 2002. *Parteimitglieder im Vergleich: Partizipation und Repräsentation – Kurzfassung des Abschlussbericht zum gleichnamigen DFG-Projekt* (Potsdam, Faculty of Economic and Social Sciences, University of Potsdam).

Hippler, J. 1999. "Die Siege der Lobbyisten", *Freitag: Die Ost-West-Wochenzeitung*, 13 Aug. Available at: http://www.freitag.de/1999/33/99330501.htm [31 May 2012].

Hofrichter, J.; Westle, B. 2000. "Wahlkampf wirkt. Eine Analyse der hessischen Landtagswahl 1999", in P.P.P. Mohler (ed.): *Querschnitt. Festschrift für Max Kaase* (Mannheim, Zentrum für Umfragen, Methoden und Analysen (ZUMA)), pp. 149–76.

Howell, C. 2001. "The end of the relationship between social democratic parties and trade unions?", in *Studies in Political Economy*, No. 65, pp. 7–34.

Hunter, W. 2007. "The normalization of an anomaly: The workers' party in Brazil", in *World Politics*, Vol. 59, No. 3, Apr., pp. 440–75.

Infratest dimap. 1998. *Deutschland hat gewählt – Infratest dimap Wahlreport. Wahl zum 14 Deutschen Bundestag* (Berlin, Infratest dimap).

Instituto Cidadania. 2012. *História*. Available at: http://www.institutolula.org/historia/ [31 May 2012].

Istoé Dinheiro. 2011. *Dez parlamentares têm empresas de consultoria*, 25 June. Available at: http://www.istoedinheiro.com.br/noticias/60202_dez+parlamentares+tem+empresas+de+consultoria [31 May 2012].

Lafontaine, O. 1999. *Das Herz schlägt links* (Munich, Econ).

Lieb, W. 2005. "Über Methoden, mit denen Neoliberale die Säuberung des DIW von nachfrageorientierten Ökonomen rechtfertigen", in *NachDenkSeiten: Die kritische Website*, 4 May. Available at: http://www.nachdenkseiten.de/wp-print.php?p=549 [31 May 2012].

Lösche, P. 1992. *Die SPD: Klassenpartei, Volkspartei, Quotenpartei* (Wiesbaden, Wissenschaftliche Buchgesellschaft).

Lütgert, C. 2011. "Rot–Grün macht Kasse", ARD-Dokumentation (Norddeutscher Rundfunk). Available at: http://www.ardmediathek.de/das-erste/reportage-dokumentation/ard-exclusiv-rot-gruen-macht-kasse?documentId=7943466 [27 June 2012].

Mathekga, R. 2008. "The ANC 'leadership crisis' and the age of populism in post-apartheid South Africa", in J. Pretorius (ed.): *African politics: Beyond the third wave of democratization* (Cape Town, Juta), pp. 131–49.

Mayer, T.; Meier-Walser, R. 2002. *Der Kampf um die politische Mitte. Politische Kultur und Parteiensystem seit 1998* (Munich, Olzog).

Ministério do Trabalho e Emprego (MTE). 2011. *Balanço Anual*. Available at: http://www. mte.gov.br/caged_mensal/2010_12/default.asp [31 May 2012].

Palley, T. 1998. *Plenty of nothing: The downsizing of the American dream and the case for structural Keynesianism* (Princeton, NJ, Princeton University Press).

Portal Vermelho. 2008. *Legalização dará às seis centrais sindicais cerca de R$ 56 mi*, 6 Aug. Available at: http://www.vermelho.org.br/noticia.php?id_noticia=38984&id_secao=8 [31 May 2012].

Praça, S.; Freitas, S.; Hoepers, B. 2011. "Political appointments and coalition management in Brazil, 2007–2010", in *Journal of Politics in Latin America*, Vol. 3, No. 2, pp. 141–72.

Prevost, G. 2006. "The evolution of the African National Congress in power: From revolutionaries to social democrats?", in *Politikon*, Vol. 33, No. 2, pp. 163–81.

Samuels, D. 2004. "From socialism to social democracy: Party organization and the transformation of the workers' party in Brazil", in *Comparative Political Studies*, Vol. 37, No. 9, pp. 999–1024.

—. 2008. "A evolução do petismo (2002–2008)", in *Opinião Pública*, Vol. 12, No. 2, pp. 302–18.

Secco, L. 2011. *História do PT* (Cotia, São Paulo, Atelie Editorial).

Seeleib-Kaiser, M.; Fleckenstein, T. 2007. "Discourse, learning and welfare state change: The case of German labour market reforms", in *Social Policy and Administration*, Vol. 41, No. 5, pp. 427–48.

Sluyter-Beltrão, J. 2010. *Rise and decline of Brazil's new unionism: The politics of the Central Única dos Trabalhadores* (Oxford, Peter Lang).

Statistics South Africa. 1998. *Unemployment and employment in South Africa* (Pretoria, Government of South Africa).

—. 2009. *Labour market dynamics in South Africa 2009* (Pretoria, Government of South Africa).

Sturm, R. 2003. "Wettbewerbs- und Industriepolitik: Zur unterschätzten Ordnungsdimension der Wirtschaftspolitik", in M. Seeleib-Kaiser and A. Gohr (eds): *Sozial- und Wirtschaftspolitik unter Rot–Grün* (Wiesbaden, Westdeutscher Verlag), pp. 87–102.

United Nations Development Programme (UNDP). 2003. *South Africa Human Development Report. The challenge of sustainable development in South Africa: Unlocking people's creativity* (Geneva, Oxford University Press).

Webster, E. 2001. "Alliance under stress: Governing in a globalizing world", in *Democratization*, Vol. 8, No. 1, pp. 255–74.

—. 2007. *Trade unions and political parties in Africa: New alliances, strategies and partnerships*, Briefing Paper No. 3/200, Friedrich-Ebert-Stiftung, Bonn.

—; Adler, G. 1999. "Towards a class compromise in SA's 'double transition'", in *Politics and Society*, Vol. 27, No. 3, pp. 347–85.

Weßels, B. 2007. "Organisierte Interessen und Rot–Grün: Temporäre Beziehungsschwäche oder zunehmende Entkoppelung zwischen Verbänden und Parteien?", in C. Egle and R. Zohlnhöfer (eds): *Ende des rot–grünen Projektes* (Paderborn, VS Verlag für Sozialwissenschaften), pp. 151–67.

Williams, M. 2008. *The roots of participatory democracy: Democratic communists in South Africa and Kerala, India* (London and Sandton, SA, Palgrave and SG Distributors).

Zeuner, B. 1998. "Das politische wird immer privater. Zu neoliberaler Privatisierung und linker Hilflosigkeit", in M. Heinrich and D. Messner (eds): *Globalisierung und Perspektiven linker Politik* (Münster, Verlag Westfälisches Dampfboot), pp. 284–300.

—. 2000. "Gewerkschaften 2000 – politisch auf sich gestellt? Sechs Beziehungsmuster zur SPD", in *Gewerkschaftliche Monatshefte*, No. 1, pp. 40–46.

Zimmerman, P.; Spitz, C. 2005. *Brasil é oitavo país em desigualdade social, diz pesquisa*, Folha Online, 9 July. Available at: http://www1.folha.uol.com.br/folha/cotidiano/ult95u112798.shtml [31 May 2012].

PART III

WORKER ALTERNATIVES

THE RECOVERED FACTORIES AND THE ARGENTINE LABOUR MOVEMENT: A GREY ZONE IN A "NEW" SOCIAL MOVEMENT

9

Bruno Dobrusin

Introduction

This chapter attempts to connect the recovered factories movement in Argentina both with historical Peronism and with current Peronism in its different forms, centred on the Peronist trade unions. The recovered factories movement is considered one of the most relevant contemporary political phenomena in Argentina, a by-product of the socio-economic crisis of 2001, when workers began occupying and taking control of factories and companies throughout the country. These recovered factories became a symbol of Argentina's crisis and social responses to it. The main connection between the recovered factories movement and Peronism in its functional and structural aspects is made through an analysis of the Peronist Government of Carlos Menem in the 1990s. The analysis covers the reconfiguration of traditional Peronist ideas and the reshaping of policies towards a neoliberal model. Analysis of the effects of these changes on labour politics, workers' unions and the Peronist movement itself will contribute to an understanding of the recovered factories movement in relation to historic workers' movements as opposed to the perspective that looks at the factories movement as a process alienated from historical roots (Heller, 2004; Rebón, 2004; Fernández, 2006; Rebón and Saavedra, 2006).

The sociologist Javier Auyero identifies a "grey zone" in the context of the lootings that occurred in Argentina during the popular protests of December 2001. He argues that the activities of the looters were not independent of party politics and the police, and specifically that they were connected with informal Peronist party networks. In this framework, the "grey zone" is a zone in which "activities of those perpetrating the violence and those who presumably seek to control them coalesce" (Auyero, 2007, p. 32). It is therefore a "murky area where normative boundaries dissolve, where state actors and political elites promote and/or actively tolerate and/or participate in damage-making" (Auyero, 2007, p. 32). In this chapter, this idea is reinterpreted and adapted in the context of the relationship between the recovered factories movement and Peronist culture and ideology as represented in the form of the union movement. Analyses of the formation of "new" social movements in Argentina tend to apply a rigid dichotomy in defining the new movements as either Peronist or non-Peronist. This dichotomy is based on both an interpretation and a simplification of Peronism, which at this period (between 1999 and 2004) is strictly associated with Menemist Peronism. The argument presented in this chapter is that in the case of Peronism and new social movements, particularly the recovered factories movement, there is a "grey zone" in which a blurred combination of different aspects of Peronism affected and influenced the movement.

The formation of the "grey zone" surrounding Peronism and the recovered factories movement is explained by analysing the dynamics within Peronism during the Menem years. This analysis includes the divisions and confrontations within the Peronist movement, mainly concerning conflicting understandings of the Peronist doctrine and the reinterpretation attempted, and finally applied, by the Menem Government. These divisions sparked a debate between "traditional/true" Peronism and "new/Menemist" Peronism (Galasso, 1990; Levitsky, 2003; Levitsky and Murillo, 2005), which is essential in explaining the diverse forms by which Peronism is connected to the recovered factories movement. Taking into consideration the influence of labour policies and the positioning of unions on the recovered factories movement, this chapter carefully addresses the effects of Menem's policies in creating the split inside the General Labour Confederation (CGT). The confrontations within the union confederation over whether or not to support the liberalization process led to the creation of the Workers' Confederation of Argentina (CTA), challenging the monopoly on workers' organization and also defying the CGT's claim to be the sole representative of Peronist ideals. The CTA erupted onto the labour scene with banners based on Peronist conceptions of social justice and the role of the working class in the Argentine political and economic sphere. This splitting apart of the union movement confirmed lasting divisions inside Peronism between those who defended a leftist tendency – represented by figures like John William Cook and the Resistencia in the 1970s – and those who preferred to negotiate in order to maintain relative positions of power. Both the CGT and the CTA played a critical role in the development of the recovered factories movement, and are accordingly central to the thesis of this chapter.

Although the recovered factories movement is a recent phenomenon, beginning in 2001, with the greatest numbers of companies being recovered in 2002 and 2003 (Lavaca Collective, 2007), it has already received attention from several scholars in Argentina and in North America. These studies tend to focus directly on the process of recovery, on the forms of organization of the workers inside the factories, and on the various challenges that the movements faced at the outset, as well as those that confront them now and are likely to do so in the future (Magnani, 2003; Almeyra, 2004; Heller, 2004; Rebón, 2004; Fernández, 2006; Rebón and Saavedra, 2006). This approach to the movement contributes to an understanding largely on a practical level, deriving from a problem-solving orientation. The explanation provided focuses on the movement as a consequence mainly of the application of neoliberal policies under the Menem Government (Rebón, 2004; Fernández, 2006). Some might go even further to include the "deperonization" of Peronism under Menem as part of the liberalization package (Rebón and Saavedra, 2006, p. 25). In spite of this connection, the analyses generally emphasize the working-class nature of the movement (Heller, 2004), but do not connect it to historical working-class movements in Argentina, among which Peronism is the most influential. The analyses narrow down the Peronist movement to Menem's Government and the CGT (Rebón and Saavedra, 2006, p. 27), misunderstanding the differences within the movement as well as the fluidity and hybridization that characterize the movement, allowing it to adapt into different forms and structures. It is through these informal structures, as well as the formal "true Peronist" ones mentioned above, that most of the historical connections can be made. The prevalent isolation of the recovered factories movement from informal and formal connections to wider political movements creates a superficial understanding of the conditions from which it arises and in which it persists. In an attempt to reshape the understanding of the nature of the recovered factories movement, this chapter analyses these intrinsic connections to the Peronist movement. The movement is presented as a reflection of a grey zone of politics (Auyero, 2007), incorporating traditional union politics along with traditional Peronist cultural norms and ideologies.

As Auyero (2007) points out, in every socio-political process there is a grey zone, in which factors not obvious at first sight appear (p. 32). The analysis of this zone provides a "conceptual tool that warns us against too rigid – and misleading – dichotomies" (p. 32). It is in this zone that exchanges take place between actors that do not normally feature in standard accounts, but that nevertheless represent a key element in the process. This concept of the "grey zone" is essential in arguing for the connection between Peronism and the recovered factories movement. In this instance, this grey zone links the recovered factories movement to the Peronist movement through the roles played by the CGT and the CTA. The role of both unions is relevant in understanding that the process initiated in 2001 took place not in a vacuum, but in a politicized context in which unions – and especially the union leadership – were influential in either supporting or confronting the process of recovery. The two cases analysed later in this chapter illustrate this context.

This chapter links the internal transitions within Peronism, both ideological and institutional, with their effects on Argentine politics and particularly with the recovered factories movement that began in 2001. By concentrating the analysis on the union movement, the intention is to focus on one of the most influential elements of the broad movement that is Peronism – labour – and view the transition through that lens. Coincidentally, the labour movement is the sector of mainstream politics most actively involved with the recovered factories phenomenon.

Peronism in brief

Peronism began under the figure of General Juan Domingo Perón in the early 1940s. Initially appointed Minister of Labour in a military government, Perón increasingly gained decision-making power within the group that had staged the coup d'état of 1943, leading to his appointment in 1945 as Minister of War and Vice President. Perón achieved his greatest success at the Ministry of Labour, where he managed to build working-class support and unify the largest sector of the union movement under the CGT leadership (Levitsky and Murillo, 2005, p. 25). From 1945 onwards, with Perón elected as President the following year, Peronism established itself as the leading movement in Argentine politics and went on to promote some of the most profound socio-economic reforms the country had witnessed.

During the Peronist decade (1945–55) hundreds of schools were built at both elementary and secondary levels. The Government built more schools and classrooms in these first two terms of Peronist rule than in all the previous periods of Argentine history added together (Galasso, 2005, p. 514). The numbers of students increased dramatically, principally in the first Peronist government, rising from 143,000 in 1940 to 446,000 in 1954 (Galasso, 2005, p. 516). The schools and classrooms became a useful channel for expanding the ideology and culture being created by Peronism, but also for promoting various government measures through propaganda in school texts. The universities in particular became a main source of new cadres and militants for the Peronist movement, and tertiary education became an important sector during the years of "Peronist Resistance" after 1955. The immersion of the State in both the economy, through nationalization and regulation, and in the field of social benefits, through education, health care and housing, contributed largely to the concept of the "organized community" in which the State was the main organizer. Perón asserted that "we seek to surpass the class struggle, replacing it by a just agreement between the workers and the employers, based on a justice that springs from the state" (James, 1988, p. 34).

Peronism was predominantly a working-class movement and a working-class culture. This identity is rooted in the prominent position that organized workers gained in Perón's Government. To them, he was the leading figure in their struggle; the workers became the main pillar of the "organized community", and the workforce was, in Perón's own words, "one of the main determinant powers, as long as it was organized under a strong union movement" (Eloy Martínez, 1996, p. 60). This strong organization was provided by the CGT, which was given priority over other national unions and became the leading organization influencing both governments and workers' claims throughout the years of Peronist rule and also the opposition to military juntas and non-Peronist regimes. To this day, the CGT is still the organ-ization that most clearly identifies itself with traditional Peronist values. In many aspects this consideration of Peronism as a working-class movement is still present today, and the appropriation of working-class identity has spread to other social and political movements that are not directly identified with Peronism, such as the recovered factories movement.

The fall of Perón's Government through a military coup in September 1955 signified the beginning of a period known as la Resistencia Peronista – the Peronist Resistance (James, 1988; Horowitz, 1990; Brennan, 1998). With Perón himself in exile, and therefore directing events from a distance rather than being present as a unique and charismatic leader, this period saw the reconfiguration of the mass-based movements. The power vacuum in the movement left by Perón's absence led to disputes between prominent rank-and-file delegates, union leaders and some figures of the Peronist business sector. The predominance of rank-and-file delegates with strong allegiance to the leftist ideals of Peronism led to a shift in parts of the Peronist cultural identity towards a more revolutionary and confrontational tone.

The revolutionary identification of many Peronist rank-and-file delegates, combined with the co-optation and inertia of the main CGT leaders, reconfigured Peronism towards a leftist revolutionary movement and ideology. The Peronist command coordinated the various actions of the Resistance in several places, two of the main locations being the factories and the prisons. However, this command did not have full control over the remaining resources of the movement, nor did it have the explicit confirmation of Perón himself that it was supposed to lead the Resistance. Nevertheless, despite the lack of formal organization, the Resistance had support in the barrios, in the factories and wherever the cultural identity of Peronism was still alive (Galasso, 2005, p. 797). Old rank-and-file cadres did the organizing work in the factories, since the main union leaders were not completely supportive of the Resistance. The primary reason for the Resistance in the factories was the defence of the gains workers had achieved throughout the Perón years, which were now being challenged by the military regime. However, the Resistance was divided even among the workers' organizations. One sector was radically opposed to the military regime and to any negotiations with the generals in power. This was the sector in which the nature of Peronism was most strongly reshaped into a revolutionary movement, away from an "organized community", but still strongly associated with the ideals of social justice propagated under Perón's Government.

The other main sector of the Peronist Resistance was led by some new union leaders who had not abandoned the movement, but had taken up a different and less extreme position with regard to the military Government. Many of its members were still officially recognized union leaders, and therefore still had the legal power vested in the union to deal with the Government over policy. The main institutional manifestations of this group were the Intersindical and the 62 Organizations (James,

1988, p. 74; Horowitz, 1990, p. 219). They engaged in legal activities such as strikes and mobilizations, focusing on regaining workers' benefits rather than on the return of Perón.

On Perón's death in 1974 power of the presidency passed to his wife, Isabel Perón, but in reality the Government was in the hands of right-wing Peronists led by José López Rega. The transitional Government of Isabel Perón then led to the 1976 coup that began one of the bloodiest episodes of Argentine history. The years that followed the ending of dictatorship in 1983 were a challenge for Peronism – as for every other political movement in Argentina – since many cadres had been lost and the divisions initiated in the period of the Resistance had deepened. This disunity was aggravated by the election of Menem in 1989 and the ensuing application of some of the most radical neoliberal reforms ever witnessed by a single administration. As the following section shows, Menem's Government exacerbated the existing confrontations within Peronism and led to the break-up of one of its most fundamental elements: the union movement.

Menem's candidacy and Government

Carlos Menem represented a new face for Peronism in the transition and trans-formation through which the movement passed between electoral defeat in 1983 and the selection of the Peronist candidate for the presidential election in 1989. Menem was one of the first main critics of organized union leadership inside Peronism. However, a surprising shift in Menem's political ideas came about in the primary elections to select the party's presidential candidate in July 1988 (Levitsky, 2003, p. 121). Here Menem based his opposition to the other candidate, Antonio Cafiero, on the proposition of a populist platform drawing its main organized support from the union movement (Galasso, 1990; Levitsky, 2003; Levitsky and Murillo, 2005). Accordingly, the CGT and a newly formed labour coalition supported Menem and provided the main financial resources for his campaign (Levitsky, 2003, p. 121). In contrast, Cafiero represented the party apparatus and the old-style leadership that favoured negotiations rather than confrontation. In this particular contest, Menem used traditional ideas regarding the leader, social justice and the "organized community", expressed in terms of Peronist cultural identity and ideology, to gain substantial support from the lower classes and from the union movement. Menem's campaign was based on recreating these values of social justice and the "organized community" in the particular context of Argentina at that time. The country was in the middle of a serious economic crisis, with massive unemployment, and the Peronist movement needed to put forward a populist figure who could bring back the memories of Perón's first two governments, and also bring back people's ideas of Perón himself. Menem reinvigorated the "organized community" by asserting the importance of the organized union movement, as well as the need to bring the State back into decision-making. Moreover, Menem portrayed himself as the leader who could take the country out of economic crisis by restoring some of the old values embodied in Perón.

Menem won the presidential primaries against Antonio Cafiero, and in the national presidential poll of 1989 took close to a majority of the popular vote, 47.3 per cent, which provided him with control of the Congress. From that point onwards, Menem's Government was to commit one of the most controversial betrayals by any Argentine leader of the majority that had elected him into government (Levitsky, 2003; Galasso, 2005). The Menem Government proposed a strictly neoliberal economic policy, contrary to his electoral promises, and made space in the ruling elite for the right-wing elements in Peronist cadres. Nevertheless, Menem gained the support of some sectors of the union movement, despite the reforms opposing traditional claims made by labour organizations. The period of economic liberalization and state retrenchment ushered in by the Menem Government was made possible not only through political negotiations, but also, and primarily, through a reconfiguration of the Peronist movement, its ideologies and its cultural identities, within the working class as well as in the leadership of the movement at the time.

The "organized community" underwent its greatest changes in Menem's period, opposing the ideas presented in the Peronist governments between 1945 and 1955. Peronism was reoriented towards a neoliberal programme. Moreover, at this time Peronism incorporated the massive informal framework of territorial-clientelistic power (Auyero, 2001, 2007).

Under Menem, the State was redirected towards "regulating" the liberalization and privatization of the economy. If under Perón's Government the State acted as main regulator through the use of state-led enterprises, under Menem most of those enterprises were privatized at low prices, justified by the assertion that they were inefficient in providing services. The privatizations included almost every national-level organization, from the most deficit-ridden sectors (e.g. the railways) to the most profitable (e.g. the energy concern YPF), and from those most closely linked to national security (e.g. a few nuclear power plants) to the most inconsequential in national security terms (e.g. sanitation services) (Corrales, 1998). In addition to the privatizations, the State eliminated a variety of regulations, price controls, industrial subsidies and restrictions on foreign investment, and lowered tariff barriers.

Another main player in this period was the business class, which during the Menem years presented itself as one of the closest allies and benefactors of the reforms that the Government was undertaking. The promotion of Structural Adjustment Programmes, beginning during the presidency of Raúl Alfonsín and reinforced under Menem, led to the consolidation of large (private) companies and so-called *grupos económicos* (economic groups) (Teubal, 2004, p. 174). One of the main policies that led to the strengthening of economic groups was the Convertibility Plan of 1991, which managed to bring down inflation and the inflationary expectations that characterized the period of hyperinflation at the end of Alfonsín's Government

(Teubal, 2004, p. 181). This plan was implemented alongside the liberalization of markets and the reform of labour laws, which made it easier for companies to hire and lay off workers. These measures benefited many transnational economic groups (Teubal, 2004, p. 183), but also many members of the national bourgeoisie, which was now supporting Menem as in the past it had supported Perón.

The role of the CGT under Menem and the formation of the CTA

During the 1990s, unions preserved a large share of the power gained during Perón's governments and through the Resistance period. The most striking aspect of the workers' union activities at this time, especially those of the CGT, was their backing of Menem's structural reforms. The support given by the dominant Peronist union leadership to the reforms led to a split in the union movement and the formation of the CTA. This group became a key player in challenging official and corrupt union politics. In addition, the CTA reshaped the ideas around Peronism and Peronist identity. The so-called "betrayal of Menem", in abandoning both his campaign promises and Peronist historical claims (Galasso, 1990, p. 128), led to a division generally characterized as that between Peronist–Menemist, often considered non-Peronist, and Peronist of Perón, identified as true Peronist (Auyero, 2001). As Galasso expresses it, the opposition of "true" Peronists to the Menem Government and its supporters "attempted to continue the same old struggle for workers' rights, by ratifying the 'best' Peronist history and excluding the current leadership of the movement as part of that history" (Galasso, 1990, pp. 136–37).

The dominant union movement, the CGT, seemed to have a clear goal in the process of liberalization: to preserve a non-competitive corporatist institutional order (Etchemendy, 2005, p. 64). Peronist union support for government initiatives was secured by benefiting certain unions and their leaders through the following mechanisms: maintaining a corporatist labour structure; preserving the role of unions in administering the health-care system; granting unions a privileged position in the private pension funds market; and granting unions a share of the proceeds of privatization (Etchemendy, 2005, p. 74). These measures ensured compliance in supporting the reforms on the part of the union leadership and also some rank-and-file delegates. The administration of the benefits provided by the Government, such as the pension plans and the health-care system, was in the hands of the union leaders, who enjoyed increasing bargaining power with regard to the Government, within the union and in the workplace. Decisions taken at top level in the unions were hardly ever challenged by shop-floor workers owing to the leaders' increasing control over resources (Etchemendy, 2005, p. 79).

The split in the union movement occurred on the same lines as that which had divided the unions at the time of the Resistance, based on conflicting conceptions of Peronism held by activists (Martucelli and Svampa, 1997, p. 163). While some argued in favour of a welfare-oriented state, others were inclined towards a pragmatic understanding, and therefore supported Menem's changes. Among the latter was the faction that dominated the CGT and enjoyed the benefits proffered by Menem. The former constituted the core of the CTA. Based on the leadership of the State Workers Association (ATE), the CTA was created in 1991 not solely to confront the policies undertaken by the Government, but also to lead a new way of "political construction" (Martucelli and Svampa, 1997, p. 282). The CTA modelled itself on the experience of Solidarity in Poland and the CUT in Brazil, these being examples of workers' confederations that integrated unions with other sectors of society such as the Church and the unemployed.

The CTA can still be considered within the framework of a Peronist movement. The majority of its leadership is drawn from the Peronist Resistance and integrated in the Peronist Party (Martucelli and Svampa, 1997, p. 295). Peronism in this alternative to the CGT is less explicit, limited to the private sphere, but is present nonetheless.

The CTA and the CGT represent different strands of Peronism, the former more strongly linked to the Resistance and figures from that period, the latter associated with an institutional tendency, inclining towards negotiation rather than confrontation. Despite its growing presence, CTA does not have the mobilization capacity that the CGT enjoys: in negotiating with governments and business, the CGT is still the more powerful of the two, being able to paralyse strategic industries by strike action. The CTA, committed to a genuine model of community trade unionism, was determined to expand its sphere of influence by incorporating social movements of the unemployed and other sectors of civil society. However, while this imperative was strongly felt at the outset, over time the CTA has also become a large and influential union, recognized as such in practice albeit not officially by the Government. The CTA is present alongside the Government at the negotiating table when the minimum wage is discussed, and has an increased potential for mobilization and the application of pressure.

When economic crisis hit Argentina in 2001 as a result of Menem's neoliberal reforms, the CTA was involved in sectors of the newly created social movements, providing mainly institutional support and legal defence. This grey zone of politics that ran through the union movement also affected the recovered factories movement. In some cases the CTA played a substantial role in promoting and consolidating the struggle of the newly created cooperatives, while the CGT was a dominant player on the opposite side, its bureaucratized union leaders participating actively in boycotting the processes of retaking the factories. These connections will be explained in the next section of the chapter.

The factories are running again

The period of Menem's Government led to one of the most significant crises in Argentine history. By 1998, the country's economy was stagnating, with no increase in gross national product, leading to a situation of protest and crisis. Mass unemployment, high poverty levels and the lack of state intervention created a swelling discontent with the policies of the Government (Teubal, 2004, p. 185). The 1999 elections offered an opportunity for change in the country, as represented by the popularity of a coalition of former members of the Peronist Party, "true" Peronist, left-wing parties, and the historical opposition to Peronism, the Radical Civic Union (Unión Cívica Radical; UCR). The coalition won the elections, defeating the Peronist–Menemist candidate Eduardo Duhalde. The hopes for change initially created with the change in government and the victory of a centre-left coalition were nearly dashed immediately by the growing economic crisis the new Government faced. The economics minister appointed by De la Rúa (the new President) attempted to get the country out of stagnation by taking loans from foreign banks and financial institutions, called the *blindaje financiero* (financial bailout), while also pursuing even deeper structural adjustment programmes and cuts in state expenditure (Teubal, 2004, p. 185). The overall situation of macroeconomic instability, together with the increasing numbers of poor and unemployed, led to a national collapse in December 2001.

In this context, Argentina's shantytowns and neighbourhoods were immersed in "political hyperactivity" (Magnani, 2003, p. 38). This enabled the new social movements that had been taking shape in the country since the beginning of the structural crisis in 1998 to gain relevance and support among the wider Argentine population. The case of the recovered factories movement was one example of how a new actor came to participate in the political and social life of the country. At its centre were the factories that had been locked up in the crisis at the end of Menem's mandate, when many companies declared bankruptcy and laid off their workers. Most of these factories were left abandoned, with most of the machinery inside. Slowly, laid-off workers began organizing and reoccupying – "recovering" – the factories, both as a solution to their current unemployment and as a claim on the former ownership that had fired them (Magnani, 2003; Almeyra, 2004; Heller, 2004; Fernández, 2006; Lavaca Collective, 2007). The workers' main motivation was to become the new owners of the factories, therefore being their own bosses in the production process (Heller, 2004, p. 43).

The moment at which the recovered factories movement began has not been exactly pinpointed, but most studies place it in the mid- to late 1990s, at the end of the Menem mandate (Magnani, 2003, p. 43). However, it is clear that it did not become relevant as a social movement until the 2001 crisis (Magnani, 2003, p. 46; Heller, 2004, p. 11; Lavaca Collective, 2007). The actions undertaken by the movement are based on two national laws: the Ley de Expropiación (Expropriation Law) and the Ley de Quiebras (Law of Bankruptcies) (Heller, 2004, p. 145). These laws established that the workers were not the owners of the factories or companies, but rather that they were "momentarily occupying" the sites (Heller, 2004, pp. 145–46). This meant that the workers could organize the production and functioning of a factory, as long as the judge in charge of the bankruptcy of the company had not made a final decision with regard to its assets. Basing themselves on the combination of these two laws, workers began retaking their old sources of employment, and founded several new operations and companies in a wide range of sectors. No precise number of recovered factories has been established, but an estimate provided by one of the main leaders of the movement, Eduardo Murúa, is around 170 by mid-August 2003 (Magnani, 2003, p. 43), when the process was at its peak. The sectors in which factories and companies have been recovered by the workers include food, construction, cosmetics, leather, education, electrical products, restaurants, graphic arts, gasoline, hotels, lumber, automobiles, manufacturing, communications, plastics, chemicals, health, textiles and transport (Lavaca Collective, 2007, pp. 229–36).

In order to illustrate the situation of the recovered factories and their relations with the unions, the cases of two companies are considered below: Cerámica Zanón and the ADOS medical clinic, both situated in the province of Neuquén.

Zanón and FASINPAT

Cerámica Zanón has been the subject of many studies (see Ranis, 2005; Aiziczon, 2009). It is symbolically the most significant example of the recovered factories movement, both economically (accounting for just over 10 per cent of overall countrywide ceramics production) and also politically (since the workers' initiative was pursued against opposition from both the owner and the provincial administration).

Long before it gained notoriety as the site of conflict between the workers and the bosses after 2001, Cerámica Zanón was a quality workplace. As Aiziczon has explained (2009, pp. 118–19), working for Cerámica Zanón was seen as "a dream" for most workers in the area, since the salaries were high and the benefits and working atmosphere were good. The changes began in the 1990s, with the restructuring of Argentine industries and labour laws under the Menem Government. Zanón grew in size, which meant also a restructuring of workers' relations, especially those between the managers and the floor workers. Managerial pressure for higher productivity and greater efficiency altered the existing patterns of relationships, leading to increasing competition among the workers themselves (Aiziczon, 2009, p. 123). Moreover, in this period, Zanón opened a third sector of production, in porcellanato. The opening of this highly sophisticated new operation involved several different dynamics in the factory, which were later to influence the progress of the conflict. Through a process that is unclear, the provincial and national Governments (Menem himself even visited the factory in 1994 for the opening of the new sector) credited Zanón with a sum of just over US$19 million (Aiziczon, 2009, p. 122) as part of a Provincial Development Fund programme. This connection between the owner and the factory and the provincial and national political class played a critical role in the process of recovery and conflict with the workers.

The second key factor in the evolution of the conflict over recovery was the union. The Sindicato de Obreros y Empleados Ceramistas de Neuquén (SOECN), a member of the CGT at national and provincial level, was a key ally of the owner in promoting the changes. The union made no attempt to defend the workers in their struggle against the changes in the labour laws or in the restructuring of the factory itself (Aiziczon, 2009, p. 127). Inside the union, traditional Peronist cadres took over the leadership in the mid-1980s and were to remain in place until 2000, when the majority of the workers voted for a change in leadership and their removal from the union. These leaders represented the most institutionalized and bureaucratized sector of the union movement in Argentina at the time, closely linked to the main heads of the CGT and supporters of the Menem Government's reform process.

The conflict in Zanón began around 1997, as the country entered an increasingly difficult economic situation. As noted above, the process of change in the factory had two key components: the owner's initiative, with the support of provincial and national Government; and the support given by the CGT-dominated union to this process. It should therefore come as no surprise that the main conflicts were on these two fronts: against the owner and Government, but also against the union. The first conflict, which arose before the process of recovery even began, came inside the union itself, when floor workers (headed by Sergio Godoy) declared their opposition to the main union leaders, the Montes brothers (Aiziczon, 2009, p. 139). The assemblies inside the union saw increasingly heated debates regarding compliance with the owner by the existing leadership of the union. After years of discussions and confrontations (for a detailed description, see Aiziczon, 2009, pp. 139–80), the workers headed by Godoy finally won control of the union in December 2000 (Aiziczon, 2009, p. 168). In order to win such a dispute, the floor workers had to mobilize all their efforts in getting people to support them in the assembly. This victory, and the "recovery" (as they call it) of the union by the workers, stayed in the workers' consciousness for years to come, and was one of the pillars in the later move to recover the factory itself.

The second conflict was economic. Towards the end of the Menem period Argentina entered a period of economic downturn, and Zanón was no exception to its effects. Zanón began to suspend workers' duties and to cut back on production; slowly the workers witnessed a process of "emptying" (*vaciamiento*) of the factory. Owing to poor administration, Zanón ceased to pay its dues to either its workers or its creditors (Aiziczon, 2009, p. 173). The economic downturn extended beyond the factory to all sectors of society, creating an atmosphere of protest across the country expressed in constant demonstrations and strikes. The workers of Zanón, and especially the SOECN, now under their control, became a representative and combative element in the collective actions taken by a broad sector of society, including unions, social movements and political parties.

The crucial clash came when Zanón decided to close the doors of the factory and send telegrams of dismissal to all its workers. The company justified this action by claiming that it owed over US$75 million in debts to public and private creditors and that the running of the factory was unsustainable. At this point, the workers decided to camp in the factory, arguing that it could still operate productively (Aiziczon, 2009, p. 186). In October, the workers proved that the factory still had enough material to work with, and that two days of production would generate enough to pay the salaries of all the workers. In addition to paying salaries, the workers occupied the factory to prevent the owner from emptying it completely. The owner did not stand idly by as this was happening but went to the courts in order to get back what he claimed was his. There were a few attempts by the police to expel the workers from the factory, but these failed in the face of the workers' organization and resistance, and also the strong support given by large segments of Neuquén society, which came out in defence of Zanón's workers (Aiziczon, 2009, p. 197). In addition to resisting this pressure from the owner and police, the Zanón workers had to resist campaigns in the media against them, mainly organized by the Montes brothers and their followers (Aiziczon, 2009, p. 197).

By March 2002 the available stock of materials had run out, and at this point the workers decided to start up production without bosses, with the entire process under worker control. The factory was up and running again; however, the organization went on for four years without any legal standing whatsoever. It was not until October 2005, after several petitions to provincial and national authorities, that the workers were allowed to form a cooperative with the right to run the factory for one year. This cooperative was, and still is today, named FASINPAT, *fábrica sin patrones* ("factory without bosses"). In the first year following this decision, FASINPAT won a hard battle in the courts to gain permission to run the factory for three more years, when the decision would come up for review. The main claim by the workers, now organized in FASINPAT, throughout these years has been that the State should expropriate the factory, pay off the old debts (acquired in the times of Luiggi Zanón) and declare the factory "under workers' control", *bajo control obrero*. In August 2009, in a historic decision made by Neuquén's provincial legislature, the provincial Government expropriated Zanón and committed itself to cancelling those of its debts held by public institutions. The other issue that will come up for debate is whether the workers are to keep functioning under the banner of the cooperative FASINPAT, or whether they manage to get the provincial Government to agree with their proposal of a "state-led company under workers' management", a model with no precedent in Argentina.

ADOS

The case of the medical clinic ADOS has not received much attention in the main studies on the recovered factories movement, possibly because it is not a "factory" but rather a clinic that has been retaken and run by the workers. For the purpose of this chapter, however, ADOS represents a key example of the recovered factories movement and its links with Peronism. In order to understand the process by which the clinic was retaken, it is useful to see it in connection with the process of liberalization undertaken in the early years of the Menem Government. As explained above, crucial support for Menem's neoliberal reforms was provided by the main branch of the CGT, which in exchange for this support was given control over areas of the health-care system and also benefits in the private pension plan market. Moreover, these reforms included the move towards self-financed and administered hospitals, of which ADOS (Asociación de Obras Sociales: Association of Health Care Organizations) would be the most common form.

ADOS in Neuquén was created in 1958, and for the following 30 years its administration fell under the aegis of the Superintendencia de Servicios de Salud (Health Services Secretariat), an agency belonging to the Ministry of Health (Favoro and Iuorno, 2008, pp. 13–14). This secretariat has been historically administered by the CGT, both at the national and at the provincial level. In Neuquén, throughout the years of Menem's Government, ADOS was administered by representatives of the most pragmatic sector of the CGT in the province, drawn mainly from the Healthcare Union and the Union of Commercial Employees (Favoro and Iuorno, 2008, p. 16).

Together with all other government-controlled institutions, as government funding diminished, ADOS witnessed a downward spiral in its capacity to provide coverage and plunged into serious financial and fiscal crisis. This in turn led to a political crisis and criticism of the administration, which was accused of corruption and maladministration. Towards the end of the 1990s a combination of factors led to the recovery of the clinic under workers' control. The administration of the clinic called an assembly of creditors and declared the organization bankrupt, unable to pay salaries to its workers and with high debts to the national pension plans and to the national tax agency (Favoro and Iuorno, 2008, p. 15). In the process leading to bankruptcy, many of the clinic's workers ended up unemployed and with unpaid salaries. In the initial years of this episode, the role of the CTA was critical in organizing the workers and providing institutional support for the creation of a cooperative that could administer the clinic once it was recovered. This role will be discussed below, in conjunction with the other cases covered in this chapter.

Towards the end of 2000 the workers at the clinic organized themselves into a new union, called the Sindicato de Salud Privada del Neuquén (SUTRASPRIN). This union included all the workers in the clinic, irrespective of their professions, with the exception of the administrators, who were blamed for the crisis into which the clinic had fallen. Through this unionized move, the workers put pressure on the Government to finally declare ADOS bankrupt and give its administration to a newly created cooperative, under workers' control. The process of dispute continued for two years, during which the clinic kept functioning at a minimal level under the administration of a tripartite (*triunvirato*) body consisting of representatives of the CTA, the Doctors'

Association of Neuquén and the workers (Favoro and Iuorno, 2008, p. 16). The judge in charge of the case investigated the situation, and at the end of 2003 decided to approve the bankruptcy and give the administration of the clinic to the newly created Cooperativa de Trabajo ADOS Ltda. This cooperative is still in charge of the administration of the clinic today, and has amply proved its capacity to administer the clinic, increase its coverage and improve the livelihoods of its workers.

Union engagement in Zanón and ADOS

The interaction between the CTA and the CGT in the conflicts surrounding Zanón and ADOS was rather similar, although manifested at different times. The CGT represented the opposing side in both the conflicts. In the words of Godoy, the leading figure in the Zanón recovery process, victory over the union was a major blow against the "bureaucracy of the UOCRA [Construction Workers' Union]" (Aiziczon, 2009, p. 78). The CGT, embodied in the persons of the Montes brothers, was a living illustration of the changes that the mainstream Peronist leaders had undergone in supporting Menem's policies. The Montes stood firmly side by side with the owner and the status quo of the factory as this was more convenient for the strength of their own political position, even though this led to the rebellion of several other workers. The CGT leadership in the city and the province of Neuquén aligned itself with Menem and the local Peronist Government, run by the neo-Peronist MPN. This alliance was a direct reflection of the alliance arrived at nationally between the CGT and Menem. In Neuquén, the Ceramist Union was among the leading provincial unions controlled by the CGT.

In the case of ADOS, too, the CGT represented the enemy, the face of the former fraudulent administration that had presided over the ruin of the clinic. Being identified with the target of the outrage, the CGT had lost any legitimacy to represent the workers. Furthermore, not only was the CGT directly responsible for the administration of ADOS prior to the recovery, it was backed up by the provincial authorities. In contrast with Zanón, where the bosses of the CGT were excluded from any intervention in the working of the cooperative, in ADOS the CGT is trying to strike back and regain control of the clinic, because there is potential for economic gains. However, the rejection of the CGT by the leadership of the cooperative shows that the image of the former administration and the struggle they had to go through to recover the clinic is still very fresh in the mind. In addition, the provincial Government, still in the hands of the MPN, has also shown an interest in promoting a rapprochement between the cooperative and the former administration. This only further tarnishes the image of the CGT in the eyes of the workers.

The CTA had a different impact in both these processes of recovery. The Neuquén affiliate of the CTA is led mainly by ATE, which includes among its leading cadres an important proportion of former Peronist youth associated with the Peronist

Resistance of the 1960s and 1970s. Neuquén has a history of migration into the province of many leftist Peronist cadres, who arrived there in a form of internal exile during the military dictatorship (Aiziczon, 2009, p. 69). Many of these cadres became integrated in, and still belong to, the ranks of ATE, since the state bureaucracy was a leading sector in the economic and social life of the province. Since the CTA was created and established throughout the country in the mid-1990s, it has gained an importance in the provincial sphere, possibly even in excess of its importance at national level. Neuquén was one province in which it had particular relevance, leading the struggle against Menem's neoliberalization programme and its application in the province. This confrontation, added to the high levels of social discontent towards the end of the 1990s, placed the CTA at the centre of the struggles under way and as a key player within the politics of the province. The CTA also played a part in the specific processes of recovery at Zanón and ADOS, to a greater extent at ADOS than at Zanón.

The CTA in Neuquén has been engaged in the most important political moments of the last decade in the province. Its capacity to mobilize and to confront the MPN governing elite make it a pillar of Neuquén's political and social movements. As emphasized earlier in this chapter, the CTA has a traditional Peronist identity linked to a national–popular model of political participation, with the State as an active player in providing social justice. This identity is also present in Neuquén, where the CTA, mainly through ATE, progressively attained a leading role in confronting the reforms of MPN governments throughout the 1990s (Aiziczon, 2009, p. 71). The challenge to liberalization came from the belief in the need for a government presence in the economy, but also in the need for a fairer distribution of the province's immense resources – especially oil.

Despite the progressive role of the CTA in Neuquén, it is debatable whether it represents a new style of unionism. Zanón has managed to maintain a certain autonomy from larger political movements; however, this autonomy has been more rhetorical than real. The main influence, at least in its leadership, comes from leftist tendencies similar to those characteristic of the Peronist youth and the Peronist Resistance in the 1970s. This influence leads to a firm belief in the process of consensus and assemblies, which is not shared by the more vertical unionism espoused by the CTA, based on delegates participating in daily debates rather than incorporating the entire membership in the decision process. The modes of decision-making are crucial for Zanón: the assembly as a decision-making body is defended at all times. Nevertheless, this difference over the definitive form of determining the outcome of debate has not impeded the collaboration between the CTA and the cooperative in Zanón. And the CTA was one of the most important groups in defending the recovery of the factory.

In the case of ADOS, the CTA played a major role in the process of recovery of the clinic (Favoro and Iuorno, 2008, p. 21), heading up the initial struggle and providing the legal defence for the workers and the institutional support needed to undertake the recovery. This leading role was recognized later by granting the CTA a presence on the governing tripartite council. However, ADOS has different dynamics from Zanón, arising from the different composition of the cooperative. In ADOS there are doctors, nurses, administrators and cleaning staff: the class composition is therefore more complex, which leads to the cooperative being less politically active. The general line of decisions is maintained throughout the different mandates, but political activity varies according to whether the director of the cooperative is a doctor, a nurse or an administrator. The CTA's greatest influence is definitely exercised through the nursing and administrative groups in the cooperative.

In spite of these internal differences in ADOS, the cooperative is one of the cornerstones of ANTA (the Self-administered Workers' Association). ANTA is an autonomous group, but operates inside the CTA and has gained support from its leadership, at both national and provincial levels. ANTA is a conglomeration of different workers' cooperatives, recovered companies and cooperatives originally formed as such. It operates under the umbrella of the CTA and since 2004 it has broken through the antagonism between the two main national union groups that dominated the recovered factories movement. ANTA gained relevance in the context of the CTA through its great symbolic significance for workers' organization. None of the cooperatives is particularly significant in terms of economic importance or in numbers of members. However, the recovered factories everywhere, including the ones in ANTA, have had a profound impact on other movements as examples of successful working-class struggle against hegemonic movements (including the CGT and Peronism) and the business sector.

Conclusion

The focus throughout this chapter has been on the structural connection between the recovered factories movement and the union movement in Argentina. Following an analysis of Peronism's historical roots, and its transformations and development into different political forms, an outline of Menem's period in government was presented, with an especial focus on the split in the union movement. It was in this sector that a "grey zone" was identified. The argument is that despite the confrontation between the CGT and the CTA, at the core of both unions there is an undeniable Peronist identity and mode of action. The participation of these unions, whether through opposition or support, was critical in the process of retaking factories in the period after 2001. The roles played by the unions were not only institutional, but also influenced issues of identity of the newly created movement.

Analysis of the cases of Zanón (FASINPAT) and ADOS in Neuquén offers important evidence in understanding the struggles in the recovered factories movement and its relationship with older forms of political participation, mainly the unions. Zanón and ADOS were in the midst of a fight not only between the workers and the bosses, but also between the CGT and the CTA. In both these cases, the CGT represented the opposing side of the struggle, and also the main face of the enemy. Its role represented that of the union at the national level during Menem's years, siding with the *patronal* (bosses), supported by the governing authorities and becoming instrumental in delegitimizing the struggle of the workers. On the other side, the CTA took the part of the workers trying to retake their sources of labour. In their claim to strive for social justice and for broader participation of the working class in the economic and political spheres, the CTA represented a strand of Peronism that identifies with leftist politics, following a line established by Cook in the 1950s and 1960s. This was reflected in its involvement with the cases of both Zanón and ADOS, where the CTA has maintained firm support of the workers. This combined influence of the CGT and the CTA creates a "grey zone" in the factories movement, in which the old forms of political participation and political identity mix with more recent forms.

The recovered factories movement has elsewhere been presented as a novel social, economic and political movement that confronts old forms of organization and participation. This chapter has addressed and refuted that claim. It has shown that there is a zone in which old and new forms are intertwined with each other, and that there is not a clear separation between the one and the other. Peronism has played a leading role in the history of Argentina throughout the second half of the twentieth century and continues to do so in the present. This is not to say that all new movements are Peronist; it is, rather, to assert a link with historical roots and with other pre-existing organizations that can in turn help in understanding current phenomena. The recovered factories movement has also to face this dilemma, caught as it is between old and new identities, between autonomy and the need to articulate its struggle with other existing institutions, notably the unions.

The development of the recovered factories movement is a clear representation of the need for labour to relate to other social movements, and to integrate historic political currents. The majority of the factories recovered in 2001–02 are today (mid-2012) still running under workers' control, among them Zanón and ADOS. However, one relevant aspect of the environment has changed, and that is the intransigence towards collaborating with the Government. The arrival of the Kirchner administrations (beginning in 2003 and continuing at the time of writing) not only heralded the economic recovery of Argentina, but also opened the doors for a pro-worker administration. The factories have benefited from this change, especially in terms of receiving financial support and subsidies for maintaining their production.

Raymond Williams, in his book *Marxism and literature* (1977), discussed the different interpretations of the idea of "culture", its uses and development. He asserted: "The complexity of a culture is to be found not only in its variable processes and their social definitions – traditions, institutions, and formations – but also in the dynamic interrelations, at every point in the process, of historically varied and variable elements" (Williams, 1977, p. 121). Peronism as a culture and political formation has profoundly influenced the Argentine working class. As Williams illustrates, culture and politics have a dynamic interrelationship, constantly being reinterpreted according to contextual situations. Peronism is no exception to this principle. Having played a considerable role throughout the last 50 years, it is also a contested movement. Understanding Peronism, interpreting Peronism, requires an exploration of Argentina's history from the early 1940s to the present day. Connecting this history with current struggles such as the recovered factories movement is therefore critical in understanding these novel formations. The "grey zone" idea is a useful tool not only in approaching "new" social movements, but also in understanding present expressions of political mobilization.

References

Aiziczon, F. 2009. *Zanón, una experiencia de lucha obrera* (Buenos Aires, Herramienta).

Almeyra, G. 2004. *La protesta social en la Argentina (1990–2004)* (Buenos Aires, Ediciones Continentes).

Auyero, J. 2001. *Poor people's politics: Peronist survival networks and the legacy of Evita* (Durham, NC, and London, Duke University Press).

—. 2007. *Routine politics and violence in Argentina: The gray zone of state power* (New York, Cambridge University Press).

Brennan, J. (ed.). 1998. *Peronism and Argentina* (Wilmington, SR Books).

Corrales, J. 1998. "Do economic crises contribute to economic reform? Argentina and Venezuela in the 1990s", in *Political Science Quarterly*, Vol. 112, No. 4, Winter, pp. 617–44.

Eloy Martínez, T. 1996. *Las memorias del general* (Buenos Aires, Editorial Planeta).

Etchemendy, S. 2005. "Old actors in new markets: Transforming populist/industrial coalition in Argentina, 1989/2001", in S. Levitsky and V. Murillo (eds), 2005, pp. 62–87.

Favoro, O.; Iuorno, G. 2008. "Nuevas formas organizativas en la Argentina de los últimos años. El caso de las cooperativas Ados y Fricader (Neuquén y Río Negro), 1990–2006", in L. Pasquali and O. Videla (eds): *Historia social e historia oral. Experiencias en la historia reciente de Argentina y América Latina* (Rosario, Homo Sapiens Ediciones).

Fernández, A. 2006. *Política y subjectividad. Asambleas barriales y fábricas ocupadas* (Buenos Aires, Tintalimon Ediciones).

Galasso, N. 1990. *De Perón a Menem: el Peronismo en la encrucijada* (Buenos Aires, Ediciones Colihue).

—. 2005. *Perón: formación, ascenso y caida (1893–1955)* (Buenos Aires, Ediciones Colihue).

Heller, P. 2004. *Fábricas ocupadas, Argentina 2000–2004* (Buenos Aires, Ediciones Rumbo).

Horowitz, A. 1990. *Los cuatro Peronismos* (Buenos Aires, Editorial Planeta).

James, D. 1988. *Resistance and integration: Peronism and the Argentine working class, 1946–1976* (New York, Cambridge University Press).

Lavaca Collective. 2007. *Sin patrón: Stories from Argentina's worker-run factories* (Chicago, Haymarket Books).

Levitsky, S. 2003. *Transforming labor-based parties in Latin America: Argentine Peronism in comparative perspective* (New York, Cambridge University Press).

—; Murillo, V. (eds). 2005. *Argentine democracy: The politics of institutional weakness* (University Park, PA, Pennsylvania State University Press).

Magnani, E. 2003. *El cambio silencioso. Empresas y fabricas recuperadas por los trabajadores en la Argentina* (Buenos Aires, Prometeo).

Martucelli, D.; Svampa, M. 1997. *La plaza vacía. Las transformaciones del peronismo* (Buenos Aires, Editorial Losada).

Ranis, P. 2005. "Argentina's worker-occupied factories and enterprises", in *Socialism and Democracy*, Vol. 19, No. 3, pp. 1–23.

Rebón, J. 2004. *Desobedeciendo al desempleo. La experiencia de las fábricas recuperadas* (Buenos Aires, Ediciones PICASO).

—; Saavedra, I. 2006. *Empresas recuperadas la autogestión de los trabajadores* (Buenos Aires, Capital Intelectual).

Teubal, M. 2004. "The rise and collapse of neoliberalism in Argentina: The role of economic groups", in *Journal of Developing Societies*, Vol. 20, Nos. 3–4, pp. 173–88.

Williams, R. 1977. *Marxism and literature* (Oxford, Oxford University Press).

ORGANIZING INFORMAL WOMEN WORKERS FOR GREEN LIVELIHOODS: THE SELF EMPLOYED WOMEN'S ASSOCIATION IN GUJARAT

10

Sarbeswara Sahoo

Climate change, and the threat it poses to human civilization, are among the most widely and urgently discussed subjects in these early years of the twenty-first century. Evidence of its impact is widely reported by both developed and developing economies around the world. It has been calculated that over a period of 140 years the temperature of the earth has increased by 0.6°C. Fighting climate change without compromising the present and future economic needs of the 7 billion or more people of the globe will be a daunting task, requiring joint effort from all the stakeholders likely to be affected, and the issue has already attracted sustained attention from governments, researchers, trade unions and other civil society organizations.

Many economies around the world, seeking to avoid the industrial use of fossil fuels, have devised strategies to supply goods and services with help of "green technology". In this endeavour, trade unions working in both the formal and the informal employment sectors have worked cooperatively with governments and NGOs. For instance, in India the Self Employed Women's Association (SEWA), a trade union of informal workers, has realized that it is poor women workers who are most likely to bear the brunt of climate change. In order to protect the livelihoods of these women, SEWA has developed an innovative concept of "green livelihood", whereby members can earn a sustainable livelihood and in the process contribute positively towards adapting to and mitigating climate change.

This chapter documents the "green livelihood" initiatives of SEWA with reference to a few case studies in both rural and urban areas of Gujarat. In doing so, it sets out to explain the meaning and importance of green livelihoods in the context of climate change; to describe the structure, profile and functions of SEWA and its role in improving the livelihoods and social security of informal women workers; and to outline SEWA's green livelihood initiatives in urban and rural areas. In the urban context, the chapter focuses on a cooperative of waste-pickers; in the rural context, it examines SEWA's initiatives relating to smokeless cooking stoves (*nirdhum chula*), solar lamps, eco-tourism, watershed management and organic farming.

Green livelihood: Its meaning and importance

Scientific studies support the contention that excess emissions from the burning of fossil fuels for industrial and domestic energy production and consumption and transportation are largely responsible for global warming and other manifestations of climate change. This process can be best fought by the adoption of eco-friendly practices using clean and green technology. According to the United Nations Environment Programme, "greening the economy refers to the process of reconfiguring businesses and infrastructure to deliver better returns on natural, human and economic capital investments, while at the same time reducing greenhouse gas emissions, extracting and using less natural resources, creating less waste and reducing social disparities".[1] "Green livelihood" refers to a process whereby the individual earns a livelihood while contributing positively towards this process of greening the economy. This concept echoes the UNEP definition of "green jobs" as work in agriculture, industry, services and administration that contributes to preserving or restoring the quality of the environment (UNEP, ILO, IOE, ITUC, 2008, pp. 35–36), ultimately reducing the environmental impact of enterprises and economic sectors to sustainable levels. Thus green jobs achieve the dual objective of sustainable economic development without compromising the interests of future generation. A summary of the various sources of green jobs is set out in table 10.1.

The sectors that generate green jobs may be formal or informal in nature. For example, much work in recycling, or in agriculture, is informal. SEWA's green livelihoods initiative aims to focus on developing eco-friendly skills, technologies and tools, renewable energy and green rural infrastructure, involving women working in the informal sector across India (SEWA, 2011).

The Self Employed Women's Association

Location and scope

SEWA is a membership-based organization made up of informal women workers. Its head office is located in the Ahmedabad district of Gujarat State. Gujarat, located in western India, is administratively divided into 26 districts and 226 *talukas* (blocks). SEWA is one of the largest trade unions not only in India but across the world in the informal sector, with a membership of more than 1.3 million in 2010.[2] At present it is active in 14 districts of Gujarat, covering 50 per cent of the State's area. SEWA also works in seven other Indian states, and has extended its operations into a few countries outside India, including South Africa, Turkey and Yemen. In the coming decade it aims to increase its membership to 2.5 million.

Table 10.1   Sources of green livelihood, by sector

Economic sector	Activity/source of green jobs
Energy supply	Integrated gasification/carbon sequestration
	Co-generation (combined heat and power)
	Renewables (wind, solar, biofuels, geothermal, small-scale hydro); fuel cells
Transport	More fuel-efficient vehicles
	Hybrid electric, electric and fuel-cell vehicles
	Car sharing
	Public transport
	Non-motorized transport (cycling, walking), and changes in land-use policies and settlement patterns (reducing distances travelled and dependence on motorized transport)
Manufacturing	Pollution control (scrubbers and other tailpipe technologies)
	Energy and materials efficiency
	Clean production techniques (avoiding toxic substances)
	Cradle-to-cradle (closed-loop systems)
Buildings	Lighting, energy-efficient appliances and office equipment
	Solar heating and cooling, solar panels
	Green buildings (energy-efficient windows, insulation, building materials, heating, ventilation and air-conditioning)
	Passive-solar houses, zero-emissions buildings
Materials management	Recycling
	Extended producer responsibility, product take-back and remanufacturing
	Durability and reparability of products
Retail	Promotion of efficient products and use of eco-labels
	Store locations closer to residential areas
	Minimization of shipping distances (from origin of products to store location)
	New service economy (selling services, not products)
Agriculture	Soil conservation
	Water efficiency
	Organic growing methods
	Reducing farm-to-market distance
Forestry	Reforestation and afforestation projects
	Agro-forestry
	Sustainable forestry management and certification schemes
	Halting deforestation

Source: adapted from UNEP, ILO, IOE, ITUC, 2008.

Membership profile

Since the enrolment in 1972 of its first member, Rudiben – without whose contribution the organization would not have reached the position it occupies today – SEWA has expanded continuously, growing from just 1,070 in that first year to 1.3 million in 2010. The distribution of the membership across India is set out in table 10.2. In Gujarat, the State with the highest membership (735,617), around two-thirds of these women live and work in rural areas (see table 10.3).

The members of SEWA represent more than 125 different trades; there are about 3,500 local producer groups and nine economic federations.

The members are broadly divided into four categories, as follows:

* home-based workers;

* vendors or hawkers;

* manual labourers;

* service providers and producers.

Goals, approach and structure

SEWA's main goal is to organize women workers for full employment and self-reliance. Full employment means employment whereby workers obtain work security, income security, food security and social security (at a minimum, health care, childcare and shelter). Self-reliance means that women should be autonomous and self-reliant, individually and collectively, both economically and in terms of their decision-making ability. To promote its goals SEWA pursues a combination of what it calls "struggle" and "development": that is, unionizing activities to address constraints and demand

Table 10.2   SEWA membership across India, by state, 2010

State	No. of members
Gujarat	735 617
Madhya Pradesh	401 080
Uttar Pradesh	82 500
Delhi	37 183
Bihar	35 640
Rajasthan	24 501
West Bengal (Murshidabad)	3 500
Kerala	2 000
Uttarakhand	3 357
Total	1 325 378

Source: http://www.sewa.org/Thirty_third_issue.asp [accessed 25 June 2012].

Table 10.3 Rural–urban distribution of SEWA membership in Gujarat, 2009

Main categories of workers	No. of women	Percentage of total membership
Urban	230 184	36.46
Rural	401 161	63.54
Total	631 345	100.0

Source: http://www.sewa.org/Twenty_Fifth_Issue.asp [accessed 25 June 2012].

change, and development interventions to promote alternative economic opportunities (Chen, Khurana and Nidhi, 2004).

In pursuit of these goals, SEWA has drawn up a list of questions on 11 key themes that together form an eleven-point strategy for assessing progress:

• Employment: have the members obtained more employment?

• Income: has their income increased?

• Ownership: do they have more assets in their name?

• Nutrition: are they and their families better nourished?

• Health care: do they and their families have access to better health care?

• Housing: do they have improved or more secure housing?

• Childcare: do they have access to childcare, if needed?

• Organized strength: has their collective organizational strength increased?

• Leadership: have more and stronger leaders emerged from the membership?

• Self-reliance: have members become more self-reliant, both individually and collectively?

• Education: has their education (and that of their children) improved?

SEWA's approach is demand driven: through discussions with members it identifies their needs and the problems they face, and then suggests programmes to improve their livelihoods and social security that are practicable within existing budget constraints and appropriate to members' skill levels. To quote Reema Nanavati,

> SEWA's approach to organizing is a need based and demand driven approach. It identifies the needs and issues of the communities and links them up with government programmes and schemes rather than creating parallel programmes. This helps in leveraging government resources and also policy action. In addition to this, provision of need based and demand driven services like banking, insurance and health care led to expansion and growth of the organization and new membership. (Nanavati, 2008, p. 3)

To support and direct its work, SEWA has devised a two-tier structure to represent its grass-roots members. This consists of:

- **The Trade Council**, which is elected by the members of each of the trades (for example, saltpan workers, handicraft workers, garment workers, vegetable vendors, dairy workers, and so on) in a ratio of one representative per 100 members. In addition, and in parallel to the general Trade Council, each trade has its own trade committee with between 15 and 50 members, which meets monthly to discuss specific trade-related problems and solutions. All Trade Council members are also members of their respective trade committees.

- **The Executive Committee**, which consists of 25 members elected every three years by the Trade Council. Representation on the Executive Committee is proportional to the membership. The office-holders of the Trade Council are elected from among the members of the Executive Committee. (Verhagen, 2004)

Over a period of four decades SEWA's activities have expanded significantly and it is still working hard to increase its membership base. As a result of globalization, all over the world formal sector employment has been in decline and more and more workers are joining the informal sector. Obtaining a sustainable livelihood and even a minimal level of social security will continue to be a substantial challenge for informal sector workers and their families. In India, as in many other countries, women members traditionally worked in the household; but now, largely as a result of initiatives taken by SEWA, it has been realized that women can contribute significantly towards both improving their own family's quality of life and the country's national production by pursuing their own livelihoods. For 40 years SEWA has struggled hard to assert the rights of poor women workers, and has had some success in persuading state governments as well as central Government to introduce legislation in this area. Among the important achievements of SEWA in this regard are:

- an act that protects the rights of construction workers;

- an act that protects the rights of street vendors;

- an act that protects the rights of *beedi* (cigarette) rolling workers;

- a social security act guaranteeing minimum social security to informal workers across the country;

- the setting up of the unorganized sector welfare board by the Government of Gujarat.

As well as fighting for the rights of informal workers, over the years it has also sought to improve their financial and social security. SEWA found that the main cause of poverty among these workers is dependence on moneylenders for credit, for which they are charged excessive rates of interest. If credit could be provided with little or no transaction cost, most of the workers' financial problems would be solved. SEWA therefore started the Swashrayi Mahila SEWA Sahakari Bank to meet the credit needs of the workers, and from time to time trains members on the importance of financial literacy and management. It also offers members training in the latest innovations in their respective sectors or trades, including how to use the new technologies to improve their productivity and livelihoods. SEWA also helps members to market their products so that they can get appropriate prices for their work. In addition, SEWA offers its own social security provision through its VimoSEWA scheme, providing members with protection in times of ill health or other misfortune.

To summarize, then, the four pillars supporting all SEWA's work for its members are:

- organization;

- capacity building;

- credit linkage;

- market linkage.

Strong leadership with a vision, inclusiveness, hard work, dedication and teamwork are among the factors that have enabled SEWA to build solid and mutually trusting relationships with state and central governments, funding agencies, other trade unions and civil society organizations. In addition, by mobilizing its members, it can also help them to respond through their work to the challenge posed by climate change. The next section of the chapter will turn to SEWA's recent initiatives on green livelihoods, illustrated through a few case studies.

Reviewing SEWA's initiatives on green livelihoods: A note on methodology

The study of SEWA's green livelihood initiatives presented here drew on both primary and secondary data, including video material produced by SEWA. In addition, group discussions were organized with the informal women workers involved in both urban and rural contexts, and in four different areas of work, in order to arrive at a deeper understanding of the initiatives and to assess progress to date. The different areas and types of work covered are shown diagrammatically in figure 10.1.

Among the green livelihood initiatives studied here is that promoting the use of solar lamps and clean cooking stoves by rural saltpan workers, who were specifically chosen for this study because they need the solar lamps and clean cooking stoves most urgently for their daily chores. However, it has been decided that these two items should be distributed not just among saltpan workers but among all the members of SEWA living in rural areas. The clean stoves are now being tested experimentally in a pilot project.

Figure 10.1 Outline of study coverage showing types of location, activities and workers examined

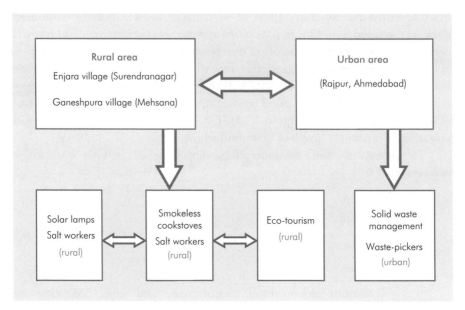

To address other green livelihood initiatives appropriate to rural areas, including tree plantation and horticulture, organic farming, composting using worms, water conservation and eco-tourism, a group discussion was conducted at Ganeshpura village in Mehsana district.

In the urban context, the study focused on waste-pickers organized by SEWA. Studies show that municipal waste contributes significantly to GHG formation; the informal waste-pickers, working on the principle of the "three Rs" (reduce, reuse and recycle), are contributing through their work to combat this process. To understand the work of this group, a focused group discussion was held with women working as informal waste-pickers in Ahmedabad.

In addition, discussions were held with a few SEWA management executives regarding the concept of green livelihood in general: an account of these is given in the next section of the chapter.

Group discussion 1: SEWA Gram Haat, Ahmedabad

In this discussion, at SEWA Gram Haat, Navarangpura, Ahmedabad, a group of SEWA executives recalled how the concept of green livelihood evolved from SEWA's livelihood initiatives spread across a number of trades that are basically eco-friendly, contributing positively to the health of the environment by reducing GHG emissions.

SEWA began campaigning long ago on the issues of "women, water, and forest", believing that gender has a large role to play in the move towards sustainable development. It is poor women who are the first victims of climate change: for example, if there is drought, they have to travel long distances in rural areas to collect water. Water shortages not only deny SEWA members' basic right to safe drinking water, but also hinder their efforts to achieve full employment and economic self-reliance, the central goals of all SEWA's activities (Verhagen, 2004). Similarly, if there is deforestation, women also have to walk long distances to collect fuelwood. Two-thirds of SEWA members live in rural areas and around 150,000 members depend on occupations related to water, forestry, agriculture and energy.

One of SEWA's major aims is to provide members with a professional identity and hence self-respect and dignity, creating an owner and manager in each worker. In order to do this, it provides education and training for members on technical, managerial and financial issues through collaboration with reputable technical and management institutions, thereby helping the workers to improve their skills in a variety of areas.

SEWA began its "green livelihoods" (*hariyali rojgar*) campaign in 2005, under the dual rubric of employment generation and protecting the environment. The issue of green livelihoods became even more important in 2007–08 and the following years because of the global economic recession. In these circumstances, over-production generates excess goods and services for which there is no market, while also damaging the environment. Through the green livelihoods initiative, which now occupies a central place in all SEWA trade committees, poor informal workers can both make a living and help to protect the environment. SEWA works to inform *behenes*[3] about the issues of climate change, especially global warming, and how they are going to affect the life of the poor in general and women in particular. Around 300 members from nine districts of Gujarat came together after the Copenhagen climate summit in 2009 to discuss the effects of climate change, their experience of it and how to tackle it, focusing on the central question: What are the alternatives available to generate income at the same time as protecting the environment? In 2010 SEWA organized a national seminar on green livelihoods at Ahmedabad Management Association to draw policy-makers' attention to the concept.

It was clear from the group discussion that members understood that climate change is happening, and that the effects will bear heavily on poor informal workers – but also that efforts to adapt to climate change can create employment opportunities and also improve the health of workers.

SEWA initiatives

SEWA found that each rural household spends 30 per cent of its income on fuelwood and kerosene oil. In order to supply fuelwood, forests are being cut down. The collection of fuelwood and the cooking of food are tasks done by the female members in Indian society, and both have negative effects not only on the environment but on their health. To collect the wood they have to walk long distances, cut the wood and then carry it back on their heads. The wood is then used in traditional cooking stoves known as *chulas*, which emit smoke. The women keep the stoves alight and hot by pumping air into them, using iron or bamboo pipes; this puts a lot of pressure on their lungs, especially in the rainy season when the wood is wet. Together, then, the collection, carrying and use of fuelwood has an enormous impact on women's health. Studies show that smoke from indoor biomass cooking is associated with a number of diseases, including acute respiratory illnesses and even cancer, with women and young children affected disproportionately. It is estimated that smoke from cooking fuels accounted for nearly 2 million deaths in 2009 (World Bank, 2011).

The use of traditional biomass stoves for household cooking, which is widespread in developing countries such as India, is linked to local environmental problems. Open fires and primitive stoves are inefficient at converting energy into heat for cooking; the amount of biomass cooking fuel required each year can reach up to 2 tonnes per family (World Bank, 2011). There is mounting evidence that biomass burned inefficiently contributes to climate change at both regional and global levels. In developing countries, about 730 million tonnes of biomass are burned each year, generating more than 1 billion tonnes of carbon dioxide emissions and other products of incomplete combustion that further exacerbate the problem.

SEWA's experiment with clean, smokeless cooking stoves known as *nirdhum chulas* goes back to 1986. Realizing the dangers associated with traditional cooking stoves, SEWA took up the challenge of finding clean alternatives for its members that would also help them to earn a livelihood, marketing the new cooking stoves among their fellow members. By this means they can contribute to a cleaner environment and better health for themselves and their fellow members as well as earning a few rupees in this process. SEWA aims to sell 200,000 stoves among its membership, all assembled, installed and repaired by the members.

Other SEWA initiatives covered in this discussion with SEWA executives relate to forestry, vermiculture (composting with worms), water harvesting, and the operation and maintenance of rural infrastructure. SEWA has invited experts in these fields to train women workers in skills including water testing technology, forestry, nursery, grafting of plants and seed production. Training in forestry and plant management enables members to contribute towards afforestation as well as to earn money from selling plants. Members can also earn good incomes from supplying vermicompost for organic farming to the 265,000 small and marginal farmers associated with SEWA. Water conservation through watershed development yields positive ecological and environmental benefits. SEWA has constructed 4,000 small water harvesting structures in the state of Gujarat which help members to save time in collecting drinking water. It has also launched a bio-gas project to stop the burning of cow-dung cakes, which is responsible for lung disease. SEWA's construction of

145 bio-gas plants in the Kutch district of Gujarat has reduced these damaging smoke emissions and brought down carbon dioxide emissions by nearly 3,000 tonnes every year.

In all, the green energy and green livelihood campaign has generated annual incomes amounting to 1,175 million rupees (INR) for 139,685 members in 2011/12. By 2015 SEWA aims to have launched 25,000 young green entrepreneurs who, it is estimated, could help to create 200,000 green jobs (SEWA, 2010).

In urban areas there is great scope for green employment in the waste-picking sector. SEWA has a long tradition of organizing the informal waste-collectors and has organized around 45,000 women waste-pickers in Gujarat alone. The World Bank has estimated that around 1 per cent of urban populations in the developing economies are engaged in waste collection (Medina, 2008). In India, waste collectors earn their livelihood by collecting paper, plastic, metal and glass scrap for sale to the recycling industry. In doing so, they not only supply recycling plants with their raw material but also keep the city clean, protecting the environment and reducing municipal costs. SEWA has started training the workers to reuse and recycle the collected waste themselves to produce stationery and other products that generate a livelihood.

Group discussion 2: Waste-pickers' cooperative, Rajpur, Gomtipur, Ahmedabad

In order to explore SEWA's green livelihood initiatives in urban areas, a group discussion was organized with the members of Geetanjali Mahila SEWA Audyogik Stationery Sahakari Mandali, Rajpur, Gomtipur. The objective of the discussion was to study the contribution of the waste-pickers towards reducing GHG emissions and generating employment out of waste.

It emerged from this discussion that even in cities such as Ahmedabad there is evidence of climate change. The intensity of rainfall has increased, and in 2009 and 2010 there were floods due to water logging. Also, temperatures are rising, reaching unbearable levels in summer.

There are around 50,000 workers in Ahmedabad who earn their living collecting waste, most of them living in the eastern part of the city. Most of the waste-pickers are poor and walk long distances, carrying the waste bags on their backs for at least five or six hours every day, starting early in the morning to go out and collect the various types of wastes, then coming back home to sort them out according to their usability and value, and finally taking the sorted waste to a scrap dealer (*pitha*) to sell them. On average, a waste-picker can earn around INR60–80 per day.

Members agreed that if waste were not collected regularly from the various parts of the city then the resulting pollution and stench would lead to environmental and health hazards. Piling up of solid waste would lead to the formation of GHGs, thus contributing further to the increase in temperature within the city already noticed by the workers. The participants in the discussion pointed out that mechanization of waste collection would not be helpful in reducing GHG emissions, because it would not necessarily separate the dry waste from the wet wastes that lead to GHG formation. The waste-pickers, however, do segregate the dry waste from the wet wastes and recycle the dry waste, thereby helping to reduce GHG emissions.

The owner of Jivraj Bidi (a local cigarette manufacturer) has provided a large hall at Gomtipur to accommodate the SEWA waste-pickers' activities. Members collect different types of waste such as mill broke, wood-free unprinted waste, wood-free printed waste, and mechanical and unsorted wastes from various offices,[4] and then clean and sort them. Out of the waste they produce notepads, office stationery, pens and pencils, jewellery and recyclable paper bags. SEWA has made arrangements with companies including Staples, Weconnect, Gift Link and Exchanger to train members in better techniques for recycling the waste. The Geetanjali Waste Collectors' Cooperative was founded in the year 1995; now it has 150 active members involved in recycling wastes. The cooperative faces many challenges in its work to bring more members into this area of green livelihood, notable among them:

• the need to change workers' attitudes to attract more into waste recycling;

• the need to improve the finished products in order to compete effectively in the market;

• the need to gain access to finance and markets.

Group discussion 3: Vanalaxmi tree growers' cooperative, Ganeshpura village, Mehsana district

The third discussion was organized with the executive members of Shree Vanalaxmi Ganeshpura Mahila SEWA Vruksh Utpadak Sahakari Mandali, a tree growers' cooperative. The objective of the discussion was to find out about the cooperative's initiatives in wasteland reclamation, watershed development and management, water conservation, planting and nursery work, organic farming, horticulture and eco-tourism.

Ganeshpura village is located 51 kilometres from Ahmedabad on the way to Mehsana, adjacent to Kadi and Kalol *taluka*, which is home to a large number of small and medium-sized enterprises. The participants in the discussion agreed that climate change as a result of industrialization has brought about an increase in the local temperature. As a result of the heat, even poor people are now drinking bottled water, which was never used 20 years ago. The village has 150 households, most of which belong to *dalits* (lower castes) and other less educated classes (*senema*). There is a substantial number of women workers in the village struggling in poor socio-economic conditions. When SEWA first arrived in the village, they saw women facing many problems, including:

- lack of sufficient and regular employment, leading to dependence on the landlords for survival and migration from the village in search of livelihood;

- long distances to be covered to collect fuelwood and fodder, and a decline in the numbers of livestock owing to lack of fodder, leading in turn to poor health and loss of employment;

- long distances to be covered in order to collect drinking water.

Realizing their plight, in 1981 SEWA approached the women, inviting them to become members, with the aim of introducing the smokeless cooking stove into the village. With the agreement of the village *panchayat* (local self-government), the SEWA leaders launched their project, and around 25 poor women agreed to use the new stove.

The land reclamation project

This success encouraged the SEWA leaders to make further efforts to improve the livelihoods of these poor women. They found out that there were 10 acres of waste land lying unused at the end of the village. The land was barren, growing natural grass only in the rainy season, when it was used by the shepherds of the village. There were no trees except the Israeli *ganda babool* (*acacia totilis*), used by most households for fuelwood.

In 1986 SEWA asked the *panchayat* for permission to take a 30-year lease on the waste land in an attempt to address the problems facing the women of the village. The idea was to use it in ways that would both conserve nature and benefit the women. By establishing a tree plantation, growing nursery plants, introducing water conservation and pursuing horticulture culture and organic farming, they would relieve the women of the need to spend their time collecting drinking water, fuelwood and fodder and would provide them with employment in the process. Furthermore, the project has taken advantage of the growing interest among the urban population in eco-tourism, attracting visitors to the reclaimed site and thereby generating additional income and employment.[5]

Participants in the discussion shared their experience of addressing the problems they have faced and the impacts of this project on their social and economic condition. When SEWA proposed the land reclamation scheme, both the *sarpanch* (village head) and officials of the district forestry department were sceptical about the capabilities of these women, most of whom were either illiterate or educated only at primary level. Nevertheless, in 1987, 55 women became the first members of the cooperative and it was registered as Shree Vanalaxmi Tree Growers Cooperative under the Cooperatives Act at the office of the registrar of cooperatives in Ahmedabad. At that time, each member engaged in the land reclamation work received INR13 per day from SEWA's own fund. Now the members are earning INR4,500 per month.

First the entire area was fenced using barbed wire by the women members themselves. The problem of water supply was first dealt with by constructing ponds on the cooperative's land to collect water for drinking and irrigation purposes; however, owing to the sandy soil, water could not be stored in these for long periods. To overcome this problem, members went to Indian Petrochemicals in Baroda for training in the construction of plastic ponds to prevent water loss; these have now been constructed at the Vanalaxmi Cooperative complex, which can now store up to 202,000 litres of water.[6] In addition, members have also learned to harvest rainwater in troughs for plantation and domestic use, and have been trained in *tapak sinchai* (sprinkler irrigation), which saves precious water. In 1989/90 the cooperative introduced the first bore well inside the complex. By these various means, the water requirements of the cooperative have been met, and members no longer need to travel long distances collecting household water.

After initial work on landscaping and water supply, the members started plotting the land and making decisions on what kinds of plants were to be planted. At the outset it was decided that non-fruit-bearing trees beneficial to the environment would be grown along with fruit-bearing trees in a ratio of 70:30. Seasonable vegetables would be grown inside the cooperative.

As work progressed, the cooperative received support for further development from various agencies and institutions. For example, some members undertook a training programme on topics including seed technology, greenhouse use and vermicompost with help from the faculty of Anand Agricultural University. At the outset, the members bought in seeds from outside suppliers, which cost them money. Later they decided to grow seeds on their own, and gained certification from the Department of Agriculture of the Government of Gujarat. In the first year they produced 20 kilograms of seed and are now supplying all the seed the cooperative requires. The members also successfully developed a cotton seed of their own.

Another eco-friendly project pursued by this cooperative is vermiculture. Members were trained in producing organic manures by Anand Agricultural University, and are now using the organic vermicompost instead of chemical fertilizer both inside the cooperative and on their own private land. Sales of this compost are also expected to be a good source of livelihood for the members.

On the fruit and vegetable plots the cooperative grows *amla* (*phyllanthus emblica*), mangoes, lemons, *chikoo* (*achrus sapodilla*), guava and other vegetables. The cultivation and proceeds are shared among the members through a system of drawing lots. Those who draw the winning lots each will "own" a plot and take care of its cultivation; they will then sell the products at the market, after which they will keep one-third of the total proceeds while two-thirds goes to the account of the cooperative. Any production surplus is processed, packed and sold through SEWA's own brand, Rudi.

In addition to these activities on the cooperative's reclaimed land, the members also use solar lamps and clean cooking stoves both within the cooperative and in their own homes, again contributing positively both to their livelihoods and to the environment.

It emerged from the discussion that the cooperative's members had been pursuing all these activities for years without knowing that what they were doing amounted to a green livelihood. However, over the past three years, owing to the large number of campaigns on green livelihood that have been conducted, they have come to realize that they are making a contribution to the environment as well as to employment generation, and have started to consider how the cooperative can promote more livelihood opportunities.

The area reclaimed and cultivated by the cooperative is now covered with a thick green canopy of mature trees that is home to many species of birds rarely or never seen in urban areas. Realizing the potential of this rich and peaceful environment, SEWA initiated an eco-tourism project. Facilities have been created allowing urban visitors to spend a relaxing day at the cooperative, with breakfast, lunch and tea provided, for a minimum price of INR150, including meals. During the three years since this initiative was launched, many visitors have come to Vanalaxmi to take advantage of these facilities, including bank officials, lawyers, schoolchildren, senior citizens, forestry officers and foreign tourists.

The impact of the project on the environment and on members' livelihoods

Participants in the discussion reported that in the past most of the cooperative's members lived in subordination to the male-dominated culture, wearing the veil and prohibited from talking to men. They were also victims of caste-based discrimination and exclusion. Since the cooperative was set up, they have gained in collective strength and are no longer subject to these severe social constraints. Migration has also been reduced, and as a result school dropout rates are lower and enrolment rates higher. Increased income has empowered the women, and 30 families now live on the proceeds of this cooperative. Through their association with the project, some members have had the opportunity to travel abroad to share their experience, visiting China, Italy, Sri Lanka, Thailand and the United States (New York), and receiving widespread acclamation.

In discussing their future plans for the cooperative, members spoke of expanding the range of plants grown and moving into floriculture. One idea is to grow the gerbera flower, for which there is a high market demand. At present there are 3,000 trees inside the cooperative, most of the babool trees having been replaced by amla plants. There are now plans to adopt a *suraksha chakra* (security cycle) cultivating cereals, vegetables and lentils in cycles, and also to start producing herbal medicines. In order to increase the visibility of the cooperative, members want to install a billboard on the Mehsana–Ahmedabad highway.

Group discussion 4: Saltpan workers' cooperative, Enjara village

The fourth group discussion, held with the members of Mahadev Mitha Mandali (a saltpan workers' cooperative) at Enjara village in Halvad *taluka* of Surendranagar district, focused on promoting green livelihoods through the use of solar lanterns and smokeless cooking stoves.

Enjara is 23 kilometres from Dhrangadhra, in a part of Gujarat famous for its production of salt and its traditional saltpan workers. Enjara and other villages lie on the edge of the desert area known as the Little Rann of Kutch (LRK), which spreads over an area of 5,000 square kilometres that crosses the borders of six districts of the state. There are 181 cooperatives of salt workers working within the LRK, which is famous for supplying 70 per cent of all the salt used in the Indian economy. Most of the saltpan workers are found in Halvad, Dhrangadhra and Patdi *talukas* of Surendranagar district, where around 30,000 women rural workers are organized by SEWA.

The salt workers draw water from underground with the help of diesel pumps that contain a chemical known as bromine necessary for salt production. These pumps run constantly in order to produce a good quality of bromine. Sizeable sums of money are spent on procuring diesel to operate the pumps; also, burning the diesel generates carbon dioxide, adding to the total output of GHGs. Salt is still produced here by traditional manual methods, and the salt workers and their families have to spend eight months of the year in the LRK to generate the final product. In recent years the workers have reported erratic rainfall in this region, including episodes of heavy rainfall that washed large amounts of salt away. Saltpan workers are particularly vulnerable to climate change and are likely to be affected if there is either an excess or a shortage of rainfall.

As well as diesel to run the pumps, salt workers need kerosene oil to light lamps after dark. This is because they work out in the desert, far from their original homes and without any facilities including electricity, and salt farming is a continuous process that requires bright light in the working area 24 hours a day. The wells where water is pumped from the ground are a long way from the huts where they live, and light is also needed to protect these isolated workers against threats from wild animals and storms. Another requirement is fuelwood for cooking food. The women here still use the traditional smoky *chulas* that cause health and environmental problems.

SEWA has calculated that the salt workers spend significant proportions of their hard-earned money on kerosene and fuelwood. Each family of salt workers needs between 10 and 60 kilograms of fuelwood every day for cooking food, and on top of the cost of this the women lose working time in collecting it. If they do have an electricity connection then they have to pay INR350 a month in electricity charges. In addition, each family consumes on average 8 litres of kerosene oil per month at INR14 per litre.

SEWA discussed these problems with the salt workers and decided to try introducing alternatives to the traditional lamps and cooking stoves. It made arrangements with 17 companies, including Philips and Environfits, to manufacture clean smokeless cooking stoves that consume less fuelwood and emit less smoke, and with Gautam Polymer to make solar lanterns, which have already been distributed among 6,000 members at a price of INR1,800 or 3,000, depending on the type of lantern. Godiben, an active SEWA member in Enjara village, has now been using the lamp for six years and reports that it is working with no problem.

The smokeless cooking stove is currently at the experimental stage; once its development is considered complete and successful, stoves will be distributed among the members. The following points were made about the smokeless stove:

- As well as emitting less smoke than the traditional stove, the smoke it does emit is grey rather than black, containing less carbon.

- The stove is small and easily portable; it is sufficiently large for a small family of four, but may not be appropriate for a larger household.

- There is a problem in using it to prepare *bajra no rotlo* (bread made of pearl millet), an important food item for people in rural Gujarat.

In discussions on the solar lantern, members made the following points:

- The lantern is light in weight and attractive in appearance, and can easily be carried and hung anywhere.

- No fuel is required, no smoke is emitted, and there is no threat of fire.

- Since the lantern uses an LED bulb, the lights are good for the eye.

- The lantern has a mobile charging port, so that workers out in the LRK can recharge the mobile battery without having to travel the 30 kilometres to a village with electricity.

- It can easily be assembled and repaired by the members themselves with a little training. This helps them to earn some income.

Conclusions and recommendations

In developing countries very high proportions of the population work in the informal sector: in India the proportion is over 93 per cent of the total workforce, and as economic reforms continue their numbers are likely to increase. Women's participation in the informal sector is likely to increase because more family members need to work to supplement the household income. Also, as noted above, climate change is likely to bear especially heavily on the poor, among them most informal workers and most women. Under such circumstances, SEWA's green livelihood strategy is definitely proving beneficial to informal workers, and should be more widely adopted and financially supported in its contribution to both employment and environmental protection.

This chapter has examined some of SEWA's initiatives with regard to green livelihoods. The following recommendations emerge from this exercise:

- **The price of solar lamps and smokeless stoves should be reduced.** The prices of solar lamps are currently rather high, putting them out of reach of most poor women. Efforts should be made to produce a lamp that would be affordable to large numbers of women. The same applies in the case of smokeless cooking stoves. Further innovations are needed to produce a stove that can cook food for more than four people.

- **The use of solar pumps should be promoted.** Pumps are used extensively by farmers as well as salt workers. It is estimated that, on average, each pump burns 1,500 litres of diesel over the course of a season, giving rise to substantial carbon dioxide emissions. The LRK receives very bright sunshine, with summer temperatures exceeding 50°C, making it highly appropriate for producing solar energy. The incorporation of solar pumps into the green livelihood model would improve the informal workers' livelihood considerably.

- **Small cooling systems should be developed.** Not only lighting and heating but cooling systems can simultaneously provide livelihoods and contribute positively to the environment and food security. Small and affordable refrigerators could help the workers to preserve food for longer times and so reduce the necessity of cooking that in turn requires fuelwood to be burnt.

- **Eco-tourism projects could be developed in the areas bordering the Little Rann of Kutch.** The Gujarat Government is encouraging tourism, including eco-tourism, in the state. Since SEWA has experience of eco-tourism at the Ganeshpura village, it could apply this near Dhrangadhra, Halvad and Patdi. Already some entrepreneurs have started eco-tourism projects adjacent to the LRK. This area has great scope for eco-tourism, which could provide livelihoods for many of the informal workers.

- **Carbon credits should be measured and compensated.** Policy-makers should develop a proper methodology to estimate the contribution of the informal workers to the reduction of GHG emissions, whether by the use of solar lighting, clean stoves, tree-planting or waste recycling, and should compensate them accordingly, either through financial means or some other form of recognition.

With the global population rising very fast, serious attention must be given to how all these people are to be provided with adequate employment and livelihood. It seems unlikely that such a huge workforce could all be accommodated in the formal sector, and even if this were done it may not be sustainable. Hence we must ensure that the mass of informal workers obtain employment that simultaneously protects the environment. To this end, more and more innovative forms of green livelihood must be explored in order to tackle the twin challenges of population growth and climate change.

Notes

[1] http://www.unep.org/roap/Home/tabid/roap/Activities/ResourceEfficiency/GreenEconomyInitiative/tabid/6825/Default.aspx [accessed 2 July 2012].

[2] http://www.sewa.org/Thirty_third_issue.asp [accessed 2 July 2012].

[3] *Behenes* is a Gujarati word meaning "sister", widely used among poor informal workers.

[4] On the ABCD analysis of waste, see http://rps.gn.apc.org/info3.htm#abcd [accessed 2 June 2012].

[5] For details, see http://www.sewaecotourism.org/index.htm [accessed 2 June 2012].

[6] Indian Petrochemicals also donated agricultural equipment, including a power tiller.

References

Chen, M.A.; Khurana, R.; Nidhi, M. 2004. *Towards economic freedom: The impact of SEWA* (Ahmedabad, Self Employed Women's Association (SEWA)).

Medina, M. 2008. "The informal recycling sector in developing countries: Organizing waste pickers to enhance their impact", *Gridlines* (Public–Private Infrastructure Advisory Facility), Note No. 44, Oct.

Nanavati, R. 2008. *Empowerment through mobilization of poor women on a large scale: A case study on Self Employed Women's Association (SEWA), India* (Ahmedabad, SEWA).

Self Employed Women's Association (SEWA). 2010. "SEWA and green livelihoods", in *We the self-employed*, SEWA electronic newsletter, Jan. Available at: http://www.sewa.org/Twenty_Fifth_Issue.asp [2 June 2012].

—. 2011. "SEWA unveils green livelihoods initiative", DNA Ahmedabad, 16 Jan.

United Nations Environment Programme (UNEP); International Labour Organization (ILO); International Organisation of Employers (IOE); International Trade Union Confederation (ITUC). 2008. *Green jobs: Towards decent work in a sustainable, low-carbon world* (Washington, DC, New York and Nairobi, Worldwatch Institute and Cornell University Global Labor Institute for UNEP).

Verhagen, J. 2004. *SEWA's water campaign*, paper presented to conference on "Attaining the MDGs in India: The role of public policy and service delivery", Delhi, 17–18 June. Available at: http://siteresources.worldbank.org/INTINDIA/Resources/swc.pdf [31 May 2012].

World Bank. 2011. *Household cookstoves, environment, health, and climate change: A new look at an old problem* (Washington, DC). Available at: http://climatechange.worldbank.org/sites/default/files/documents/Household%20Cookstoves-web.pdf [24 August 2012].

INDEX

Note: Page numbers in bold indicate references to tables; those in italics indicate figures. Because the entire work is about "labour" and "the global South" the use of these terms as entry points has been restricted.